The Impatient Muse

UNC | COLLEGE OF ARTS AND SCIENCES
Germanic and Slavic Languages and Literatures

From 1949 to 2004, UNC Press and the UNC Department of Germanic & Slavic Languages and Literatures published the UNC Studies in the Germanic Languages and Literatures series. Monographs, anthologies, and critical editions in the series covered an array of topics including medieval and modern literature, theater, linguistics, philology, onomastics, and the history of ideas. Through the generous support of the National Endowment for the Humanities and the Andrew W. Mellon Foundation, books in the series have been reissued in new paperback and open access digital editions. For a complete list of books visit www.uncpress.org.

The Impatient Muse

Germany and the Sturm und Drang

ALAN C. LEIDNER

UNC Studies in the Germanic Languages and Literatures
Number 115

Suggested citation: Leidner, Alan C. *The Impatient Muse: Germany and
the Sturm und Drang*. Chapel Hill: University of North Carolina Press,
1994. DOI: https://doi.org/10.5149/9781469656731_Leidner

Library of Congress Cataloging-in-Publication Data
Names: Leidner, Alan C.
Title: The impatient muse : Germany and the Sturm und Drang / by
    Alan C. Leidner.
Other titles: University of North Carolina Studies in the Germanic
    Languages and Literatures ; no. 115.
Description: Chapel Hill : University of North Carolina Press, [1994]
    Series: University of North Carolina Studies in the Germanic
    Languages and Literatures. | Includes bibliographical references and
    index.
Identifiers: LCCN 93036492 | ISBN 978-1-4696-5672-4 (pbk: alk. paper)
    | ISBN 978-1-4696-5673-1 (ebook)
Subjects: Sturm und Drang movement. | German literature — 18th
    century — History and criticism.
Classification: LCC PT317 .L45 1994 | DCC 830.9/006

"A Titan in Extenuating Circumstances: Sturm und Drang and the *Kraftmensch*"
was originally published in *Publications of the Modern Language Association* Vol. 104,
No. 2, 1989, and is reprinted here by permission of the present copyright holder, the
Modern Language Association.

For Lil

Contents

Acknowledgments

Chapter 4 of this study appeared as an article in the March, 1989 issue of *PMLA*, and an earlier version of chapter 6 was published in the 1986 *Goethe Yearbook*; I am grateful for permission to reprint this material. It is a pleasure to have the opportunity to thank Mark E. Blum, who helped me think through most of the arguments in this book as they developed, and who added something at every stage. As the idea for the book first took shape, I also had the benefit of several conversations with Benjamin McKulik. Friends and colleagues who gave me various kinds of assistance on individual chapters include Scott Abbott, Frank Baron, Benjamin Bennett, Dale B. Billingsley, Thomas B. Byers, Susan M. Griffin, Edward P. Harris, David Hershberg, Michael W. Jennings, Hans Petersen, Frank G. Ryder, Arthur J. Slavin, and the late Eric A. Blackall. I am also indebted to Lil Leidner, Les Essif, and Helga S. Madland, who looked over the manuscript in its final form, and to Professor Paul Roberge and the anonymous readers of the University of North Carolina Press. Dr. Martin Germann and Dr. Judith Steinmann of the Handschriftenabteilung of the Zentralbibliothek Zürich were helpful during my visit there in April 1988, and my work during two other research trips was made more pleasant by the hospitality of James and Bonnie Witkowski and Kurt and Verena Scheller-Krattiger.

This project had the generous support of the Graduate Research Council, the President's Research Initiative, and the College of Arts and Sciences of the University of Louisville.

1. Introduction: The Impatient Muse

Literary history has long cast Sturm und Drang in a supporting role. For the majority of nineteenth-century critics, the work of Lenz and the young Goethe, Schiller, and Klinger was simply a youthful preamble to Weimar Classicism. Hermann Hettner, for example, maintained in his six-volume *Literaturgeschichte des achtzehnten Jahrhunderts* (1856–70) that the tradition was a necessary—though muddled and "irrational"—proving ground for the mature work of Schiller and Goethe.[1] Perhaps owing to its simplicity, the view was taken up by generations of teachers and scholars, and despite Erich Schmidt's suggestion later in the century that Sturm und Drang be studied as a separate phenomenon, critics continued to see this literature as an ideological rival to the "rational" Enlightenment—and as the mulch out of which the more dignified art of the 1790s would grow.[2] Even Gustav Keckeis, a sensitive reader of Klinger and Lenz, attempted to defend Sturm und Drang in 1907 by maintaining that its texts were not "formlos," but simply "noch nicht geformt."[3]

Our own century has tried to correct this prejudice by looking at Sturm und Drang not as an irrational counterpoint to Enlightenment, but as an integral part of it. In his landmark study *Geist der Goethezeit* (1923), Hermann August Korff defended the tradition against the charge of irrationality by pointing out that the critique of society contained in Goethe's *Götz von Berlichingen* (1773) and Schiller's *Die Räuber* (1781) is an almost predictable continuation of the European Enlightenment.[4] But Korff, typical of his generation, still saw Sturm und Drang's progressive and violent aspects as separate threads of eighteenth-century history; thus he considered such factors as the proto-Kantian morality found at the end of *Die Räuber* to be atypical of Sturm und Drang. It was left to perhaps the most talented Marxist critic of the century to complete the critical revolution: Georg Lukács, writing in the 1930s, maintained that Sturm und Drang was an outright extension of *Aufklärung*. Lukács claimed that even those critics who noticed the influence of Enlightenment in these texts still did not recognize how vividly Sturm und Drang's depictions of explosive frustration reflected the class struggle.[5] Particularly after the appearance of Edith Braemer's *Goethes Prometheus und die Grundpositionen des Sturm und Drang* (1959), interpretations based on Lukács's Marxist approach emerged as the dominant school of Sturm und Drang criticism, with commentators

1

from Wolfdietrich Rasch to Heinz Stolpe pointing out that the tradition is a continuation of broad European trends: rationalism, empiricism, and the typically contradictory class consciousness of the European middle class.[6]

Yet where has this left us? Sturm und Drang is a cultural phenomenon unique to German-speaking Europe, but a great many critics, especially in Germany, have seized on the concept of an "enlightened" Sturm und Drang so fervently that one wonders if the hope of understanding this literature has been abandoned in favor of pointing out the ways that it reflects British empiricism and aesthetics, the new emphasis on individualism in Rousseau, and the class struggle. Can Lenz's scrambled plots, the abject superbia of Klinger's raging protagonists, or a play like Schiller's *Die Räuber*, which seems designed to make an audience side with a murderer, really be traced to relatively homogeneous currents of eighteenth-century European thought and sensibility? I do not think so. Like a growing number of critics working on this tradition, I have come to question whether claiming Sturm und Drang for the European Enlightenment has taken us very far. In this book, I suggest that many of the more puzzling features of these texts are the result of cultural work that writers were trying to do in an extremely unusual national context. The argument I set forth had its beginnings in a 1984 conference paper in which I suggested that Schiller's *Die Räuber* owed much of its success in the theater to Karl Moor's charismatic leadership of his robber band.[7] Spectators moved by that play fell under the sway of Karl, I argued, in much the same way as his followers did, and with his first drama Schiller offered his German public the opportunity to share feelings they sorely lacked as members of a terribly disunified nation. Of course, the notion that it might be possible for a play—or culture—to be carried forward by sheer strength of character is a recurrent idea of Sturm und Drang.[8] But few texts of the age depict leaders as engaging as Karl, and even to study the tradition more broadly as a matter of leadership and its legitimacy would be to address only one way that these writers deal with Germany's unusual national situation. Schiller's attempt to flatter and unify audiences with *Die Räuber* is just one author's reaction to a widespread impatience to enjoy the benefits of a unified Germany much sooner than was realistically possible.

I have been speaking of Germany and Germans, but that can be misleading. True, eighteenth-century German writers referred to the texts they wanted to create as "deutsche Literatur." Herder, in *Fragmente über die neuere deutsche Litteratur* (1766), and Gerstenberg, with the *Briefe über die Merkwürdigkeiten der Litteratur*, written the same year, continued Lessing's interest in fostering a German nation through a national literature. But the issue of Germany as eighteenth-century nation is more complicated than that. Just as one cannot hope to understand Sturm und Drang by looking outward to general European trends or forward to the literature of the 1790s, it is also misleading to view the literature of the 1770s as the product of a cohesive eighteenth-century state called Germany. Germany would not be a nation until almost a century after Lenz wrote *Der Hofmeister* (1774). And since, strictly speaking, there must be a nation before there can be national culture, *Der Hofmeister* is in a certain sense not a German text at all. Germany at the time of the Sturm und Drang was, as we know, a patchwork of some three hundred principalities, free cities, and bishoprics, many of which had been granted sovereign rights in the Treaty of Westphalia. Some "states" were Protestant, some Catholic, and most had their own currency, tariffs, and legal systems. This area of sprawling diversity and disunion was one in which commerce thrived only in a few cities. The legacy of the past benefited princes whose status depended in part on political fragmentation and conflict over religion, trade, and other issues. Without a common forum where such conflicts could be discussed, and with an almost total lack of natural boundaries, Germany as national state was more an aspiration than an actual achievement.

Yet despite these problems, it took little more than a generation after Lessing had admonished his countrymen to write a national culture into existence for Germany to experience a great flowering of literature, music, and philosophy. Figures like Kant, Beethoven, Goethe, and Hegel brought Germany permanently out of its provincialism. We might ask ourselves what contributed to the realization of Lessing's dream in such a brief span of time. Germans could not help feeling some measure of pride after Prussia's victory in the Seven Years' War (1756–1763). But although writers were encouraged by the serious attention paid throughout Western Europe to folk culture, there was no question that Germans faced serious obstacles to the formation of a truly national culture anything like that existing in France or England. Not only did writers lack a nation and the readership to go with it; they felt they had no older literary tradition on which to build. The German medieval literary heritage was practically unknown, and baroque literature was dismissed as inferior. Without a public steeped in a common tradition, how does an author give powerful resonance to the words and actions within a text? Who were the heroes whose triumphs might flatter audiences and whose fall might be felt as tragic? What were the norms from which the comic figure must deviate to make audiences laugh?[9] For German writers, these questions were difficult to answer. J. M. R.

Lenz, whose literary awakening occurred in Strasbourg when he experienced deep concerns about German language and culture, complained of having no "Standpunkt."[10] Friedrich Maximilian Klinger spoke of his search for "Festigkeit."[11] And Wild of Klinger's drama *Sturm und Drang* (1777), the play that gave the tradition its name, would tell Blasius and Le Feu: "Ich will mich über eine Trommel spannen lassen, um eine neue Ausdehnung zu kriegen. Mir ist so weh wieder. O könnte ich in dem Raum dieser Pistole existieren, bis mich eine Hand in die Luft knallte."[12]

Klinger's grotesque image reflects a feeling experienced not only by German authors of the age, but also by the educated middle class that would make up their first audiences: the desire to live a very different kind of life—right now and, as it sometimes seemed, at whatever the cost. There was good reason for Klinger to believe that this might be possible. Montesquieu in France, Vico in Italy, and Winckelmann and Herder in Germany were founding a new way to look at history by uncovering an unsuspected capacity for development in culture. At the same time, Rousseau and Diderot were considering the potential for societies to undergo revolutionary change, and with the American Revolution (the setting for Klinger's *Sturm und Drang*) the eighteenth century put these world-wrenching ideas into practice. If cultures were malleable, as the eighteenth century suggested they were, then Germans might not have to be satisfied with the disunity they had had for so long; the time might be ripe for progress by leaps and bounds. But the governments of Germany, whose petty aristocrats jealously guarded their privileges and rights, were not likely to be overthrown by a middle class that had never found a way to thrive outside a few northern cities. This was the state of affairs confronting writers and their scattered public in the 1770s: an educated German elite, anxious for a more powerful sense of itself, was impatient to experience feelings that it imagined were part of a national state with a developed society and common culture.

A sign of this impatience can be found in the German reception of the theory of genius, which begins in the 1760s with Gerstenberg and Herder.[13] With its total disregard for traditional rules of art, genius theory was the perfect weapon to use against French Neoclassicism. It gave the artist license to make a clean sweep of the past and discard every prior conception of art as irrelevant. Yet for German writers it represented an opportunity even greater than that promised by its rejection of French models. It meant that not just a work of art, but attitudes toward the world, perhaps even whole national communities, could be generated apart from the existence of a nation-state. Genius theory justified taking short-cuts to greatness: "What, for the most part," wrote Edward Young in *Conjectures on Original Composition* (1759), "do we mean by genius but the power of accomplishing great things without the means generally reputed necessary to that end?"[14] The writer of genius, anxious to help create a national literature, seemed not to have to wait for a German nation: the genius, Young promised, was "a magician that raises his structure by means invisible."[15] Eight years later, in 1767, Herder would write: "So bildet ein Genie sich selbst, und tritt auf einmal gebildet hervor, um die Bewunderung der Welt zu sein."[16] Still others would see a certain emptiness in the promise of genius. "Das Wort 'Genie,' wrote Goethe, "ward eine allgemeine Losung."[17] And Gerstenberg realized that an inspiring aesthetic could never create more than mere illusion: "Der geständige Ton der Inspiration, die Lebhaftigkeit der Bilder, Handlungen und Fictionen, die sich uns darstellen, als wären wir Zuschauer, und die wir mit bewunderndem Enthusiasmus dem gegenwärtigen Gotte zuschreiben: diese Hitze, diese Stärke, diese anhaltende Kraft, dieser überwältigende Strom der Begeisterung, der ein beständiges Blendwerk um uns hermacht, und uns wider unsern Willen zwingt, an allem gleichen Antheil zu nehmen—das ist die Wirkung des Genies!"[18] Nonetheless, despite the doubts of Goethe and Gerstenberg, genius theory appears to have helped inspire writers of the German 1770s to feel that, as artists, they had access to a powerful principle that promised to change their otherwise ineffective lives.

All this may seem to imply that Germany possessed no national tradition on which writers could build. What about the discovery of the rich cultural inheritance of the German *Volk*? In the 1750s and 1760s, Johann Georg Hamann, arguing that language was richer and more powerful prior to the "abstract" eighteenth century, praised the simple, "poetic" character of native German culture, and the birth of Sturm und Drang is often set in the winter of 1769–70, when Hamann's student Herder drew Goethe's attention to the culture of the lower classes as a promising source for the writer in search of Germany. Herder had in mind the discovery of a national collectivity that could commune with itself in an unmediated fashion, not according to principles laid down by some foreign authority. Yet it is interesting to note how few texts of Sturm und Drang find it possible to rely for their effects on the power and beauty of their German homeland. Throughout Sturm und Drang, one gets the impression that authors may have internalized a measure of Friedrich the Great's disdain for his own culture. There is, of course, obvious reverence for small-town German life in the "Abend" scene of Goethe's *Urfaust*, where Faust confronts the beautiful yet parochial world of Margarete. But even there, the force of small-town German life does not survive the intrusion of Faust, who, like so many other creations of the German 1770s, demands to sense his own power as quickly as possible, even if it means not only dealing with the devil but also leaving the values of his provincial homeland behind.

It is a fact that a few texts of the age, like Lessing's *Minna von Barnhelm* (1767), do find a way to draw upon the specific character of German culture. But native German culture never seems to be enough for Sturm und Drang, whose plays often have their settings transplanted elsewhere—to Italy, to North America, or to some other century. These are writers who clearly want more power than they think their native land is capable of providing. As it turns out, Sturm und Drang is the result of the appearance, side-by-side, of two promising sources of literary success that needed desperately to be reconciled with one another: on the one hand, the seemingly unconditioned world of the genius; on the other, the traditions of the German *Volk*. Out of this odd interplay of two rather elusive factors, the 1770s found a new way to be German by paying homage to the *Volk* while, at the same time, going beyond its limitations.[19] Constantly in Sturm und Drang the disappointing specifics of German life are played against, or traded for, something else: Werther neglects the Germany he has inherited as he dreams of eternity; Klinger's Wild and his companions, who often seem neither to know nor to care where they are, long for "das unendliche hohe Gefühl"; Robert Hot of Lenz's *Der Engländer* (1776) prefers, despite his intensity of feeling, to love from afar with the idealism of the Minnesänger.

If native culture is not enough to inspire writers of the German 1770s, it may be because eighteenth-century Germany does not promise to provide Germans what they need most of all: a sense of who they are that comes as second nature, and a sense that this self-identification makes them powerful. Virtually equating the genius with the powerful protagonist, the age coined a single term for both writer and hero: the *Kraftgenie, Kraftmann,* or *Kraftmensch.* Herder encouraged writers to depict "große Taten" and, following Breitinger, recommended the use of "Machtwörter," arguing that "Kraft ist das Wesen der Poesie."[20] It was their zeal to have what Germany did not yet offer them that led to their interest in character: Gerstenberg admired Shakespeare for his attention to it; Klinger would admire "Stärke des Charakters"; and Goethe's zeal to locate the German character led him to the erroneous conclusion that Gothic architecture originated in his homeland.[21] But can character burst on the scene all at once if there is no culture that can give it a foundation? Is character a phenomenon that grows spontaneously from within, and can we expect it to arise under any conditions? Or does it require a vital tradition on which to draw? Unquestionably, writers of Sturm und Drang tried to simulate a great deal in their texts: not only strength of character, but also spontaneity and a sense of personal effectiveness. This they attempted by depicting the violent actions and language of the *Kraftmensch*, by creating the melancholy Werther, and by crafting Wild's images of the drumskin and pistol shot.

But Sturm und Drang's hoped-for progress by leaps and bounds was unnaturally forced, and the literature it produced was often as grotesque as Wild's image. An appeal to instant nationhood is premature in a culture not yet ready to provide an inner store of possibilities that can be put into practice. In this book I argue that, as authors of Sturm und Drang shape their texts, they react to an impatience that tempts them to find ways to make a personal sense of power and effectiveness resonate despite difficult national circumstances. This impatience governs not only authors of Sturm und Drang and the characters they create; it involves German audiences and readerships ready to partake vicariously in feelings that they ordinarily cannot have. While the stage for this impatience was set by the wider European influence of the theory of the original genius who could create despite his or her background, Germany's special circumstances in the late eighteenth century, as a particularist land whose cultural practices were scattered and undervalued, turned the literature of the 1770s into a cultural phenomenon quite unlike anything in the rest of Europe. It is a literature created by writers who want a German nation at all cost, even when circumstances do not oblige.

My aim is not to treat every text or even every author of the tradition; for a comprehensive view, the best source is still Roy Pascal's *The German Storm and Stress* (1952). I want instead to present a reading of the Sturm und Drang with reference to the major texts of the tradition. Of course, Sturm und Drang is a variegated phenomenon: just as there was no one Germany in the 1770s, there is no one way to react to the situation in which writers found themselves. But one constant in this literature, as I argue, is its attempt to produce a substitute for Germany on paper—a surrogate, yet also an inspiration, for readers and audiences unwilling to wait for political cohesion and what they imagine to be its emotional benefits. I find I can show this best through an eclectic methodology. One of the strengths of Pascal's study is that it does not labor under the restraints of a single critical approach. I have come to believe that no single literary methodology, taken to the exclusion of the others—whether based on close reading, the history of ideas, or the political economy—can result in a satisfying view of the Sturm und Drang, or, for that matter, of any cultural movement. Here I agree with Horst Albert Glaser, who notes that literary methodologies are not like religions in that they demand the right belief; they can be used to greater profit collectively, for where one may not take you, another might.[22] Thus, while my general argument must rely heavily on literary sociology, chapter 4 applies the approach of intellectual history, chapter 5 employs the methods of textual criticism, and so forth.

In part so as to lay out my argument as chronologically as possible, I begin with the Swiss clergyman Johann Kaspar Lavater (1741–1801), a man whose role in Sturm und Drang is constantly acknowledged but never really explained. One of the most widely read exponents of early German Idealism and the patron saint of every pious *Schwärmer* of the late eighteenth century, Lavater had something that German writers of the 1770s wanted very badly: a way to get from the limited world of one's almost oppressively specific experience to another kind of world, one that promised a greater sense of personal effectiveness. My intention in devoting a chapter to Lavater so early on is also to help define the aims of the German Sturm und Drang by exploring its writers' well-known infatuation with this controversial figure. These writers are more interested in effectiveness than in truth, and this leads them to be more concerned with ritual than with mimesis.[23] When Lavater argues that the most reliable knowledge we can have derives from our immediate sense experience, it is easy to mistake him for an empiricist and child of the Enlightenment. But for him, sense experience is always a hieroglyph of God; everything we see in the mundane world points to an unconditioned, limitless realm he imagines beyond every specific human society. Lavater, although he distrusts symbol and metaphor, was engaged in an idiosyncratic version of the rhetoric that was already beginning to emerge in modern poetry, where words are used to provide experiences in language that do not exist in reality.[24] This man, called the Magus of the South, helped show Germans how to overcome parochialism as a charlatan would—how to "use God," as he put it, in order to reach out to audiences ready to flatter themselves for their ability to sense something great within their otherwise mundane lives. With his success in forging a language that inspired a sense of community and self-importance, he attracted German writers of the 1770s who also sought ways to lift themselves above the specifics of their particularist culture.[25]

Chapter 3 treats Goethe's *Die Leiden des jungen Werthers*, by far the most widely read text of the tradition. In this novel Goethe lays out two possible paths open to the sensitive, educated member of the middle class in the second half of the eighteenth century: either become engaged in the struggles that grow out of the given rules of the time and place one inherits, or live a life governed by the pure vocal incantation common to visionary poetry. It is easy to believe that Werther is an unspoiled character whose eventual suicide is a result of a foundering on his own purity and virtue. But in his aloofness toward his surroundings and his fellow human beings—which he finds too trivial to approach with compassion—he is a subtly arrogant figure. In part by considering the historical personality upon whom Werther is based, Karl-Wilhelm Jerusalem, I try to show that the book depicts what I call a cold strain of German *Empfindsamkeit*. Refusing to avail himself of the chief employment opportunity he inherits as a member of the middle class—service in the state government—he chooses instead to reach for the abstract realms he finds in poetry such as that of Klopstock, whose work inspires, as Eric A. Blackall puts it, "without recourse to the intermediary of actions or things."[26] In *Werther*, the love of symmetry and perfection fostered by a tradition of Idealism stretching from Meister Eckhart through the eighteenth century finally confronts limitations presented by social and political realities. I also suggest that Werther is, in subtle fashion, a descendant of the ministerials, a social class unique to Germany that engaged in an insidious denial of its allegiance to the class that gave it power. Behind Werther's repeated requests of Lotte for tasks to perform, even while he declares himself aloof from all authority, is the ambivalent, self-important yet subservient attitude of the ministerial class.

The balance of the book is devoted to the theater. Early in our own century, literary critics in the tradition of *Geistesgeschichte* would argue that the outstanding feature of Sturm und Drang was its unbridled individualism.[27] Yet one important lesson to be learned from studying Lavater and *Werther* is that when words inspire powerfully—as, let us say, the poetry of Klopstock does—that inspiration seems always to play on values that transcend all narrow cultural specificity. This is, of course, one of the paradoxes of the age: the originality desired by writers of the age had always to be compromised in some way or another if it were to be understood; theoretically, it is hard to see how true originality could enjoy a broad response. Precisely because of contradictions such as this, the concept of genius was scrutinized all through the 1770s, as a glance at the progress of Herder's thought shows: at the end of the 1760s, he glorified the autonomy and even the irrationality of the genius; yet by the mid-1770s he begins valuing the genius's modesty and sense of proportion. Perhaps understandably, then, writers of Sturm und Drang deal in Titanic individuals who, from the point of view of the text, are not individualistic at all. In chapter 4, in an attempt to understand the violent figures standing at the center of so many dramas of the 1770s, I draw parallels between the Sturm und Drang and the problem of moral accountability in Kant. If audiences delight in identifying with this tradition's violent protagonists, it is because the texts in which they are situated subtly exonerate them for their actions. With its culmination in Schiller's *Die Räuber*, the drama of the *Kraftmensch* gives German audiences license to burn every bridge connecting them with the insignificant and oppressive world in which they live—all the while luxuriating in the illusion that they possess a powerful sense of who they are.

Fragmented works are said to be typical of Sturm und Drang, and chapter 5 deals with the tradition's most fractured text: the first draft of Goethe's *Faust I* (1808), called the *Urfaust*. Korff called *Faust* "die tiefste aller dem Sturm-und-Drang-Geiste entsprungenen Dichtungen" because of its handling of rebellion not as social but as metaphysical.[28] But perhaps the focus of a play in progress should be the process itself, and in chapter 5 I explore the impulses of Sturm und Drang by analyzing the genesis of this drama that was never finished until long after the movement had played itself out. When *Faust* was completed in the next century, it would go on to be regarded as the greatest drama in the German tradition. But how did it happen that Goethe, who could write *Werther* in a few weeks, allowed *Faust* to remain for thirty years as a text split into two seemingly irreconcilable halves? The history of the play is a tale of impatience deferred and eventually forgotten, and the split in the *Urfaust* results from Goethe's neglect of the impatient muse that had so many writers of Sturm und Drang fabricating a German nation that did not yet exist. In 1775, Goethe was concerned less with writing a performable play than he was in slowing down and understanding himself; the question that appears to absorb him in this draft is whether there can be common ground between the clearly circumscribed culture of the *Volk* to which he is attracted and his own rather self-indulgent desire for power and unconditioned knowledge. When Goethe came back to his Faust play twenty years later, he returned with a considerably more practical attitude toward the text: his primary interest was in linking the two halves on the surface; the play's disturbing origins were far from his mind. Thus *Faust I* evolved into a drama very different from the draft he left behind. The *Urfaust* is not a reassuring text about striving and salvation, but a searching text about the free subject and its relation to the inevitably limited world Germans had inherited. If Goethe could not go beyond the draft in the 1770s, it was because he could not find a way to reconcile Faust's groping for absolutes with the parochial world of Margarete. But the draft, to its credit, records a thoughtful confrontation with a particularist Germany that Goethe seems later to forget.

Before Sturm und Drang drew to a close, one author would momentarily close the gap between the impatient muse and the German nation. Judging from a famous eyewitness account of *Die Räuber*'s first production in 1782, Schiller discovered a way to make the drama of the *Kraftmensch* a liberating ritual for German audiences ready to express their pent-up hostilities while temporarily enjoying the feelings of national community for which they longed. In *Die Räuber*, Schiller involves audiences in the same charismatic relationship that exists between Karl Moor and his band of robbers. For Karl, despite his violence, is a character designed not to topple community but to build it: spectators could feel as they identified with him that their frustrations with Germany were legitimate. Yet more than that, the play is a ritual of self-forgiveness in the theater. As audiences pardon Karl for his violence, they can also dream themselves momentarily, if only emotionally, into a functioning national community. The culmination of Sturm und Drang, more than any other text of the tradition, *Die Räuber* demonstrates that this literature is less concerned with mimesis than it is with ritual. Schiller could not have accomplished all this, I suggest, without harnessing the German religious past—without taking audiences back to the final, closed vocabulary of Lavater, where heaven and hell are the urgent extremes of life. Of course, fifteen years later, in the 1790s, the cult of the creative personality would be left behind to be replaced by the cult of the artwork, and with the idea of cultivating the best ideals of humanity. But with his great play of Sturm und Drang, Schiller gave in to the temptation to write a German nation into existence at any cost. And while critics have argued that it belongs outside the tradition, I argue that it is the crowning achievement of the literature of impatience.

I conclude with J. M. R. Lenz, a writer whose work appears at times to be written for our own century. Lenz writes theater in a different mold not only from the German theater envisioned by Lessing, and even Herder, but also from the rest of Sturm und Drang. For his texts recoil unequivocally in the face of the impatient muse and present Germany to the reader without the encouragement, the momentum, the artificial sense of power that Goethe, Klinger, and Schiller tried to build into their texts. Unlike *Götz von Berlichingen*—and unlike any other texts of the tradition—Lenz's creations refuse to press their author's rhetorical advantage into service. Despite his nationalistic writings, the Germany he sees is one too fragmented to overcome with words—thus he will not situate individualism in contexts that offer it a place to resonate. He would rather avoid creating a tragic hero altogether than to simulate one by creating inspiring resonances where his mimetic sense, unusual for the 1770s, tells him they do not belong. Despite what he maintains in his essay *Anmerkungen zum Theater* (1774) about the independent hero around whom tragedy should turn, Lenz's plays consistently exit the edifices of meaning that they begin to construct, and his honesty and patience produce ironic, self-interrupting forms. Lenz shows us not only how difficult it is to communicate with words; he shows us the power of language to thwart expression. As he turns words back on themselves, he creates a stage that begins to confront the almost irresistible power of the impatient muse.

2. What They Saw in Lavater

Against the violence and explosive frustration of Sturm und Drang, Johann Kaspar Lavater (1741–1801) seems at first to cut an odd figure. Neither German, nor primarily a literary man, Lavater first attracted attention in Germany through *Aussichten in die Ewigkeit* (1768–73), a book full of hope, not the pessimism for which Sturm und Drang is renowned. Yet it was precisely his optimism that made Lavater an object of admiration for Herder, Goethe, and Lenz, who beat a path to his Zürich church in the early 1770s, then corresponded with him for most of the decade. They were fascinated by this man who stressed forgiveness and the divine quality of humanity. "Die tiefe Sanftmut seines Blicks," wrote Goethe in *Dichtung und Wahrheit* (1811–14), "die bestimmte Lieblichkeit seiner Lippen, selbst der durch sein Hochdeutsch durchtönende treuherzige Schweizer-Dialekt, und wie manches andere was ihn auszeichnete, gab allen, zu denen er sprach, die angenehmste Sinnesberuhigung."[1] What Lavater stood for never went out of fashion in the German 1770s: the power to make alternatives to parochial culture seems tangible. A gifted orator, from childhood on he felt that it was his destiny to have a powerful effect, "mächtig zu wirken." In Zürich's Church of Saint Peter, Lavater applied ideas worked out in his devotional literature to grant vivid if fleeting illusions of a realm far from mundane specifics; and it was a place to which German authors also wanted access.[2] What I would like to show in this chapter is that there is more involved in the optimistic message of *Aussichten*, or in Lavater's inspiring oratory, than the mere invocation of God. His much-admired influence over others, and his skill in coaxing listeners to dream their way immediately into a more pleasant world, results from the outright assumption of divinity as part of a rhetorical method, a process he described as "das Gebrauch Gottes"—the use of God.[3]

A three-volume work of over a thousand pages, *Aussichten in die Ewigkeit* was written as a series of letters to Johann Georg Zimmermann (1728–95), the Swiss physician who corresponded extensively with Bodmer, Breitinger, Haller, Nicolai, and Wieland, and whose works include the treatises *Vom Nationalstolze* (1758) and *Betrachtungen über die Einsamkeit* (1756), expanded into a four-volume work in the 1780s. In the introduction to *Aussichten*, Lavater announces that his book is to lay the groundwork for a long didactic poem on the future, a poem he never wrote, but which he envisioned as a companion piece to Klopstock's *Der Messias* (1749). But the lineage of the *Aussichten* extends even further back, including the Pietistic chiliasm of Philip Jacob Spener (1635–1705) and Johann Albrecht Bengel (1687–1752), as well as fifteenth-century chiliastic movements that predicted a thousand-year reign of Christ on earth and helped bring about the Peasants' Rebellion of the sixteenth century.[4] The underlying goal of the *Aussichten* was also a central urge of Sturm und Drang: to provide the prospect of an entirely new relation to the world, one that seemed like a heaven on earth, a place where one had a sense of community impossible to achieve at the moment. Where does it say, asks Lavater, speaking of the joys of heaven, "daß nun alles *geistlich* verstanden werden müsse?" (2:lxxiv). Laying the groundwork for an ideal basic to his more famous *Physiognomische Fragmente* (1775–78)—the idea that humanity's bright future can be intuited now, and that it can be read even in the gestures and physical features of human beings—he contrasts two kinds of human communities: those of the here and now, "menschlichkeitleere Gesellschaften" (3:127) where people say only "was der andere bereits und besser noch weiß" (3:126), and that of the hereafter, a world that for now can be depicted only in our imagination. The power of the imagination is a factor as vital to Lavater's arguments as it was to genius theory: "Wie schnell alle unsere Erkenntnißkräfte empor fliegen, wie herrlich sich mit jedem Augenblicke vervollkommnen!" (3:30). With an apparently sincere desire to help free people from the dissatisfying world into which they were born, he encourages his readers to forget the present and believe instead in the prospect of having eternity right now. It is not hard to see what an uplifting effect his vivid portraits of a heaven on earth might have had on those who experienced a lack of community in their lives. Allow me to cite a rather long section of the *Aussichten* where Lavater paints such a portrait:

> O mit welchem heitern, klopfenden, freudenvollen Herzen, mit welchem sanften, von Menschlichkeit überfliessendem Auge, das den Himmel und den Herrn des Himmels mit der Ruhe und der Hoffnung eines *Kindes Gottes* ansehen kann, eilen wir in solche Gesellschaften!—Mit welchen Empfindungen von der Erhabenheit unserer Natur, welchem Bewußtsein, daß wir izt der Gottheit gefallen, und eine Stunde unsers fliehenden Lebens auf eine kluge und würdige Weise benutzen, wohnen wir einer solchen Gesellschaft bey! Wie sehr wird da das Beßte, was die Erde hat, das, was der Himmel so gern zu seinem Eigenthum haben mögte,—der *Mensch*, der *Mensch*—genossen!—Und, o welch ein Genuß—der

so wenig gesuchte, uns so nahe gelegte, so leicht mögliche, so unentbehrliche, so beseeligende *Menschengenuß*; Wenn eines Bruders, einer Schwester heller Verstand den meinigen erleuchtet, und von dem meinigen erleuchtet wird; wenn unsere Herzen einander erwärmen; unsere Liebe zum Beßten anwesender, abwesender, zukünftiger, noch nicht geborner Menschen zusammenflließt, und Eine grosse, weitleuchtende und erwärmende Flamme wird; Wenn jeden Augenblick unsere Seele andere Seelen genießt, und von andern genossen wird; Wenn jeder reicher an Erkenntniß und Weisheit, an Kraft und Liebe, jeder vollkommner, menschlicher, mehr existirend, lebendiger, wesenreicher, Gottähnlicher wieder nach Hause kehrt, als er ausgegangen war?—

O mein Freund—welche wahre, erhabne, würdige, dauerhafte Freuden gewähren uns solche Gesellschaften bey allen ihren Unvollkommenheiten schon in dem gegenwärtigen Leben!

O du wenig gekannte, du beßte aller Freuden,—*Menschen-Freude*! du Freude, du Seeligkeit Gottes—welche überirdische, mit unserer ganzen Natur und mit der ganzen Welt, und allen Offenbarungen und Stimmen der Gottheit und ewig harmonirende Freude bist du!—Wie wenig ist derjenige—*Mensch*, der die *Freude des Menschengenusses* nicht kennt, nicht zu schätzen und zu nutzen weiß!

Freundschaft—was ist sie anders, als *Menschen-Freude*? *Freund*, was anders, als ein *Erfreuender*?—Sie, Sie fühlen es, mein Theurer! mehr als tausende fühlen Sie es—was es ist, Menschen zu lieben, und von ihnen geliebt zu seyn? Menschen zu geniessen, und von ihnen geliebt zu sein? Menschen zu geniessen, und von ihnen genossen zu werden? (3:128–31)

The habit of explaining Lavater's relation to Sturm und Drang in terms of a shared pantheism avoids a much more essential shared concern. Here and in many other passages, Lavater is speaking to readers who have difficulty identifying with, enjoying, and communicating with other human beings. With his halting language he paints the paradise to which Werther aspires, and which Schiller's Karl Moor, seven years later, will miss in his world as well. Here on earth, Lavater maintains, the goal of turning "das ganze Menschengeschlecht zu Einer Familie" (3:92–93) will never be realized. It is, of course, a sentiment Karl Moor will formulate similarly in act 3, scene 2 of *Die Räuber*, where he exclaims: "Die ganze Welt *Eine* Familie und ein Vater dort oben—*Mein* Vater nicht—Ich allein der Verstoßene."[5]

According to the scheme Lavater develops in *Aussichten*, the beyond and the here and now involve two different kinds of knowledge: in eternity we will have true knowledge of events, while in the here and now we must be content with a mere image of those events. This Neoplatonic distinction governs Lavater's career as theologian, physiognomist, and orator. In the future that he thinks we can evoke if we try, we will go beyond the *Bilder* of the here and now, beyond the "entbehrlich" (3:24), "überflüßig" (3:25), and "willkürlich" (3:26). Truth is clearly not an empirical matter, not an issue dependent upon the particular political and social world we have inherited from the past. He appeals instead to a supposedly superior form of knowledge, one offering a "wahres Bild der Sache" and arrived at through "anschauende Erkenntnis." It is continually opposed to the inferior one, which he calls "symbolische Erkenntnis":

> daß die symbolische Erkenntniß—ungleich unvollkommener ist, als die anschauende, oder unmittelbare; daß die symbolische Erkenntniß an sich durchaus keinen inneren wahren Werth hat, sondern nur eine auf die gegenwärtige Eingeschränktheit unserer Wahrnehmungswerkzeuge relativen Werth; daß sie bloß eine Krücke für den Lahmen ist; daß sie, wie diese weggeworfen werden wird, wenn wir allein gehen, unmittelbar Vieles zugleich und deutlich wahrnehmen können. (3:17)

Unlike the "successive" world of the here and now, whose "symbolic knowledge" is always incomplete, heaven provides a knowledge that is "succeßiv und momentan zugleich" (3:106).

Lavater frames the issue largely as linguistic: to overcome the present, this "Geburtsort des Irrthums" (3:28), we must learn to speak together: "Wir müßten concertmäßig sprechen können" (3:107). But only the language of eternity, this "laute unmittelbare Sprache" (3:108), can supply the required point of view; this "blosse Veränderung des Gesichtspunkts" (3:302), he argues, can give our perceptions an entirely new turn—toward "sinnliche, anschauende Erkenntnis, Wahrnehmung, Erfahrung" (3:3). While in the here and now a "fataler Standpunkt unsers Geistes zu den Gegenständen" (3:29) offers us a view of the world governed by "willkürliche Zeichen" (3:15), in eternity we will have an "unmittelbarer Wahrnehmungspunkt" (3:26) that lets us dispense with such arbitrariness. There we will finally see clearly and speak what he calls a natural, universal language—resembling, he says, that of Christ—and avoid all the disagreements to which our limited languages are prone (3:104, 34). Almost like a person who lacks the patience necessary for gradual change, Lavater prefers to consider the prospect of an entirely new perspective on life. Because the steps between the particulars of our experience are always infinite in number—a rather pessimistic idea that he had been developing since the early "Abhandlung von der unausdenklichen Theilbarkeit des Raums und der Zeit" (1766)—there seemed to be only one solution to the debilitating limitedness of our arbitrary world: we must begin thinking about a God's-eye view of eternity.[6] And improvement in our "Gesichtspunkt" (3:5), he reasoned, would give us an eternal perspective through which we would see the universe from every possible angle, from angel to human being (3:297). Not surprisingly, he finds common ground between himself and Klopstock, who also glorified a transcendent world beyond every specific time and space: poets like Klopstock, he observes in the tenth letter of *Aussichten*, have the power to lift us "über unsere kurzsichtige Art zu denken."[7]

If the poem for which *Aussichten* was to lay the groundwork was never written, there is a good reason for this. In Lavater's view, truth resides beyond humanity's "merely" symbolic world. Thus metaphor, another realm of symbol, is automatically suspect, whether he realized it or not. His language in *Aussichten* is consistently more abstract than concrete, more analytic than metaphorical, and anyone who has read Lavater's poetry knows that he is not comfortable with figurative language. As it turns out, for Lavater poetry is not a matter of images of nature but something else: "sie [Poesie] ist mir nichts als Empfindung, Empfindung über Gott."[8] Poetry, by this reckoning, is not a matter of expressing feelings about human beings in specific cultures, each with its own sets of symbols. For as creatures made in God's image, we do not require a specific, limited, accountable human context; symbol and metaphor are therefore misleading points of reference. Lavater never gives human society credit for developing viable foundations of life, viable forms and signs, and even his patriotic *Schweizerlieder* (1767), like so many other patriotic poems, are designed to convince listeners to embrace eternal values.[9] Because he distrusts signs that mean different things to different cultures, Lavater deals instead in a kind of truth that does not apply to human relationships at all, and which discounts the inherited and unchosen values that make up the life of real communities. The *Physiognomische Fragmente* have us focus on the human body so closely, yet with such a supposedly universal scope, that all narrative, discourse, and symbol are shut out, and we end up with a register of physical characteristics shorn of every specific context.[10]

Yet Lavater claims that individuality can thrive alongside eternity and maintains that every individual is a species unto itself: "Bei Gott ist jedes Individuum eine Klasse" (3:39); "es giebt so viele Klassen der Wesen als Individua sind" (3:42–43). The direction Lavater looks to find the divinity is inward: "Wisse, mein Herz," he writes in the *Geheimes Tagebuch* (1771–73), "daß unter allen Freundschaften auf Erden keine weiser und segensreicher ist, als die Freundschaft und Vertraulichkeit eines menschlichen Herzens mit sich selber!"[11] In fact, what he wants to find within himself is not only God, but a feeling of power and self-sufficiency: "Ach, es fehlet mir noch eine lebendige Ueberzeugung, die mich immer leiten und beseelen sollte; eine Grundkraft, die die Seele einnimmt, *für sich selbst tätig* und gewissermaßen von äußerlichen Erweckungen unabhängig ist."[12] Of course, the value of personal autonomy, either viewed politically or from the point of view of sentiment, is simply a product of Enlightenment culture. But what is notable here is Lavater's concatenation of autonomy and eternity, and with it we come to a key principle of Sturm und Drang, one that stretches from the *Aussichten*, through the arrogance of Werther and the ambiguous violence of the *Kraftmensch*, to Karl Moor's self-righteousness. I am referring to the puzzling coexistence in Sturm und Drang of individuality with eternal values. Consider the first entry in Lavater's *Geheimes Tagebuch*, where in a 1769 entry he says that he considers virtue not to be a matter that can be verified by the rest of us because it is part of a specific tradition, but one that relies on a certain species of independence and self-sufficiency:

> Sollte nicht *Selbstständigkeit* der wesentlichste Charakter der Tugend seyn? Das Bewußtsein unter *allen* Umständen recht zu handeln; die *Sicherheit* in Ansehung seiner Selbst, sollte die nicht erst entscheidend für unsern Charaktern seyn?—Aber *Empfindungen* können die nicht aufrichtig, nicht moralisch seyn, wenn sie gleich bloß von zufälligen Umständen veranlaßt werden?—Schwere Aufgabe.—Doch ist so viel gewiß: Erst die Empfindungen, die ich durch wahre und große Gedanken *so oft* in mir erschaffen kann, als ich *will*, die mir unter *allen* Umständen möglich, natürlich und geläufig sind,—werde ich mit mir in die künftige Welt hinüber nehmen.[13]

This is not the virtue of the beautiful soul who does the universally correct thing spontaneously; it is, as Lavater explains it, a virtue driven by individuality. Feelings important for eternity, says Lavater, originate in "Selbstständigkeit"—autonomy. Lavater's positive, confidence-building Christianity taught his followers to give themselves a great deal of credit for their faith, and often it seems that he wants them to guide themselves in their belief by what makes them feel good about themselves. In his essay "Magnetismus und Christenthum" (1785), he would write: "Was Leben raubt, Leben hemmt, Leben kränkt, tödet—

ist, als solches, *böse*. . . . Alles was belebt, erfreut [ist], als solches, *gut*."[14]

Such is the overall style of Lavater's Christianity. As Janentzky points out, it was not one of quietism and contemplation, but of the intensive use of human and divine powers, of a community of strength, and it appears to have given up on more gradual solutions.[15] The oratory and the following that it produced for him provided an immediate and satisfying sense of effectiveness. Consider this remarkable passage from 1779 in which he speaks of his desire to have power over others:

> Ich war in meinen Gedanken immer Aufbauer, Erfinder und Bau- meister babylonischer Türme—, wie denn wirklich das immer noch in meiner Seele liegt und meinen Kindern und Freunden nicht verhehlt werden darf, daß es ein unaustilgbarer Grundzug meines Charakters ist—, gereich es nur zur Ehre oder Schande!— ungeheuer große Dinge zu sehen, zu bauen, in Gedanken wenig- stens zu veranstalten, und zwar ohne Rücksicht auf Ehre und Ruhm. Es ist Bedürfnis meiner individuellen Kraft und Natur— mächtig zu wirken. Alle meine frühesten und spätesten Unter- nehmungen haben in mir, in meinem Innwendigen wenigstens, dieß Gepräge. In meiner frühsten Jugend war mir jedes Gebäude zu klein, jeder Thurm zu niedrig, jedes Geschöpfe zu unausge- dehnt. Wenn ich einen hohen Thurm sahe, oder auch nur davon hörte, klopfte mir das Herz. Die entzückendste Freude war's mir, aller meiner leicht schwindelnden Furchtsamkeit ungeachtet, Thürme zu besteigen, u. von der Höhe herab alles klein, und nur das groß zu sehen, was mir nahe war.
>
> Wenn ich Fürst geworden wäre, meine Neigung zum Größt- möglichen, was gemacht werden kann, hätte mich zum Narren, und mein Land arm gemacht.[16]

What is needed if specific, limited culture is to be overcome is, quite simply, power—here, Lavater's own power over his congregations and readership. In the 1779 autobiography he goes so far as to call his religion a secret potion that he would gladly tell a friend about, but cannot: "Meine Religion war mir damals, in der zweyten Lateinischen Schule gerade das, was man ein *Arkanum* nennet. Ich besaß ein Ar- canum, das ich gerne einem Freunde vertraut hätte—keinem ver- trauen konnte—."[17]

How are Lavater's effects accomplished, and what bearing does his own tactic of persuasion have on the literature of the German Sturm und Drang? The stage, as Benjamin Bennett has reminded us, has always been a temple of artifice, and the craft of rhetoric is as important to drama as it is to homiletics.[18] This fact was well known to J. M. R. Lenz, who has his character Haudy in *Die Soldaten* (1777) go so far as to argue in act 1, scene 4 that a play has ten times the power of a sermon. To achieve the powerful effects he wants, Lavater needs first of all to be familiar with his listeners' beliefs, for persuasion rests not so much on facts as on what people believe to be true. Not surprisingly, Aristotle devotes much of his *Rhetoric* to the particular situations of human beings: to persuade, one must always take into account the beliefs of one's audience. There is no persuasion without entering the listener's point of view, and without employing some version of enthymeme, a word that in Greek means simply "thought" or "piece of reasoning." But enthymeme refers more specifically to a syllogism with an implied premise that the speaker hopes will be filled in automatically by listeners impatient to, as it were, flatter themselves that they have made some important connection by themselves. Essential to all rhetoric, enthymeme works in large part through making listeners feel that the convincing logic of the speaker is actually their own.[19] Lavater's erratic diction—with its apparently careless punctuation, and its repetition, parataxis, and dashes—allows readers and listeners to feel themselves skipping over steps in the reasoning process and, as if by magic, finding a way to close by themselves what he has deliberately left open. Consider this attempt to convince his readers that love begets love, all part of one of his breathless discussions of the Prodigal Son:

> Wer kann das alles, und noch mehr von dieser Art, lesen und hören, und muß nicht sehen, und muß nicht empfinden, daß wir immer sicherlich den Schluß machen dürfen; Wenn ich Mensch, wenn mein Herz dieß oder jenes schön, edel, löblich finden muß, wenn ich so liebreich handeln kann, so darf ich von dem Vater der Barmherzigkeit—von der Quelle aller Liebe noch viel mehr erwarten, ihm allemal viel mehr zutrauen, als ich meinem Herzen zutrauen darf. (3:273)

His seemingly inspired repetitiveness helps instill confidence through the reassuring reiteration of brief words and phrases: "Laß mich, Liebster Jesu heute," runs a typical passage, "immer also leben, also handeln, also reden, also gedenken."[20] As the drone of such language resounds, a congregation can find great confidence in what it is thinking and feeling, if only temporarily. But Lavater would come under attack for his rhetoric: as early as 1775, Leonhard Meister writes in *Ueber die Schwärmerei* (1775–77): "Ein wenig Chiromantie, Wahrsagungsgeist, Wunderkraft können durch einen Sprung noch einmal so weit fortrücken als hundert Syllogismen.''[21] The minds of those taken in by such rhetoric, writes Meister, are too sluggish to follow arguments step by step.[22] But such language still prods listeners and readers to believe in themselves as it coaxes them to move from premise to conclusion.

This loose employment of the enthymemic syllogism that is completed by the audience involves a rhetoric quite the opposite of that of Lenz, who, as we will see in chapter 7, employs not enthymeme but aposiopesis—the gap that can simply stand as a gap without encouragement to close it. But Lavater wants his audiences to skip over the premises on which his often unspoken conclusions rest. And it is not just in his treatises that Lavater's language is highly rhetorical and evocative: even in his correspondence, such as this letter to Goethe, with its jumpy, associative, periodic organization, he pens formulations reminiscent of some of the most urgent prose of the German Sturm und Drang: "Ich kann nur—zittern, glühen, schweigen—aber nicht aussprechen—wie sehr ich wünsche—mehr große Winke, ausgedachte *Ahndungen* meiner Seele—von Ihnen zu sehen—zu empfangen—und wie sehr ich insonderheit nach einem Christusideal von Ihrer Erfindung und Ihrer Hand—schmachte.''[23] Lavater is by no means counting on some direct mimetic effect on his listeners: he certainly does not want his audience to imitate his incoherent stammering; by deliberately failing to complete something, he coaxes them to complete it. Here we are in the realm not only of the leaps and tosses of language admired by Herder, but also of Christ's frightening apocalyptic language, especially the warnings he sounded in his last days.[24] Christ's character combined the balanced temper evident in the blessing of the children with jarring, sudden, and profoundly disturbing apocalyptic pronouncements—a heritage of the latter apocalyptic writers of the end of the Exile, such as in Daniel, a book of which Lavater was especially fond. Of all the writers associated with Sturm und Drang, no one was more ready to bend syntax and coin new words, to use inarticulate speech in order to inspire. It is strange how such broken syntax can help solidify an audience; it is a method that operates, in large part, by flattering listeners with their own capacity to make the synecdochic jump from the stammering pieces to the unshakable whole.

The overall rhythm of the *Aussichten* depends first on storming heaven with powerful reassurances of a complete and perfect hereafter, then exercising his audience in its confidence. Lavater asks listeners to consider their newly found strength, their ability to be invigorated rather than confused by his broken language, as God's presence in themselves. The effect is only temporary, but it is the basis of Lavater's powerful effect on his listeners, an effect that, if we believe his many admirers, also gave listeners a sense—or illusion—of spontaneity. It is this rhythm—from reassurance to spontaneity and back, from air-tight logic to fragments and back—that made Lavater seem like a God who could distribute divine grace to his listeners. Like other leaders, he taught his followers to be astonished at what they were capable of—to experience a certain "Bewunderung und tiefes Erstaunen" with themselves, even perhaps to conclude that their powers were akin to those of the genius.[25] His audiences were made to agree on the deepest matters spontaneously, to feel that they were determining their own destiny—a need shared by many Germans of the age. Lavater's language had the power to help congregations and readers feel like a spontaneous and powerful collectivity. Yet to show others how to find the unsuspected power of their own moral authority, he also needed to turn them away from their own specific cultural—and moral—background. And the chief danger involved in forgoing such specifics is that humankind rapidly becomes construed in a way dependent on rhetoric rather than actual conditions. All realism, which recognizes the authority of time and place, is avoided. So is the route of Weimar Classicism, with its Neohellenistic Idealism and its newly found respect—perhaps clearest in the final version of *Faust*—for the balanced infrastructure of the text. As Lavater gives God, not human culture, credit for the power his listeners are flattered into finding within themselves, he becomes a pipeline to the absolute for listeners ready to believe that they are among the chosen few who, insulated from the cultural contents of their time and place, see with God's eyes.

As a man who could provide congregations a fleeting sense of confidence, power, and spontaneity, Lavater was a distributor of grace. He gladly played this role; he possessed, as he wrote in 1779, "ein Durst nach Dingen, die ich nicht sah, ein Streben nach Kräften und Wirkungen, die ich nirgend erblickte."[26] What he claimed to offer his congregations and his readership was not only to know that eternity was a prospect to hope for, but to anticipate eternity and feel it: "Ach wie schmachtet meine ganze Seele, etwas von meiner künftigen Seinsart, von jenem göttlichen Leben im voraus zu empfinden."[27] "Der Mensch ist der Unsterblichkeit wert, weil er sie wünschen kann."[28] As he himself said, his intention was not edification ("Erbauung") per se, but a desire to have a vision of eternity as soon as possible, or at least insofar as it is possible here on earth. Grace in Lavater comes at the expense of accepting the unspecific promised land he offers; it also comes at the expense of giving up the specificity and limits of life, with its oc-

casional sense of mundaneness, and its continual demand for account-
ability. Yet it was a grace a number of Germans of the 1770s were eager
to have bestowed on them: Herder would write that Lavater, after
Klopstock, was "vielleicht das größte Genie in Deutschland."[29]

Enthralling audiences through balancing semiarticulate utterances
with visions of a utopian hereafter is a technical feat that few speakers
could accomplish. Lavater's bridging of heaven and earth is impres-
sive, demonstrating a paradoxical relation to his listeners: on the one
hand, he has them indulge their impatient urge to feel power that feels
self-directed; on the other, he makes them feel like a community. Both
these effects of his language were of interest to the Sturm und Drang,
and Lavater accomplished them in part by making his audiences feel
different from, and better than, other people. Lavater often claims that
what he says is personal and merely part of a private dialogue between
himself and the individual reader or listener. As he says in *Aussichten*,
his words are meant only for "die Auserwählten" (1:123). In the *Phy-
siognomische Fragmente*, which the preface warns is not for everyone,
he does much the same thing. Yet he also claims that in the future these
special people, these chosen few to whom he is speaking, will develop
special powers communally that are impossible to develop in solitude:
"Er wird in Verbindung mit andern ihm unentbehrlichen Wesen, Ver-
besserungen und Entwickelungen der Kräfte und Fähigkeiten anderer
zu Stande bringen, die er einzeln, die alle einzeln nicht würden zu
Stande bringen können" (3:94). People, he promises, will feel as if they
were "Ein Herz, Eine Seele, Ein Gebeth, Eine Empfindung, Eine Wahr-
heit, Eine Tugend" (3:133).

How did Lavater feel about his own sense of power? "Hier kommen
die grossen Dinge zur Welt," he once said as he tapped on the pulpit
while giving a visitor a tour.[30] Clergymen are used to taking on the role
of being a conduit to God, but Lavater's path to the pulpit appears to
have involved a conscious attempt to treat God not only as a goal, but
as a method. "*Gebrauch Gottes*," wrote Lavater in 1779, "ist eine der
ersten tiefsten Ideen und Grundgefühle meiner Jugend. 'Sie machen
ja keinen Gebrauch von Gott.' Ich suchte Gebrauch von Gott zu
machen."[31] Lavater's "use" of God is a rather arrogant use of flattery.
Rudolf Haym would call the author of *Aussichten* "ein warmherziger
aber in die feinsten Täuschungen der Eigenliebe verstrickter Mann."[32]
Lavater admits in 1779 that as a youth he prayed to God "um mich bey
Gott einzuschmeicheln."[33] "Herein, in diesem Schädel da, den ich mit
meinen beiden Händen halte," wrote Lavater in the *Geheimes Tagebuch*,
"wohnt etwas, das mehr wert war, als die ganze leblose Schöpfung."[34]
"Ein jeder Mensch, folglich auch ich, muß in den Augen Gottes unaus-

sprechlich viel wert sein. . . . kann ich meine Seele noch einen Augenblick geringschätzen?''[35]

As I have already begun to suggest, Lavater's effect both at the pulpit and in his writing depended on finding a way to flatter audiences into believing they shared with him inalienable values on which they could congratulate themselves as they absorbed his paratactic, impassioned, apparently spontaneous language. It is all part of a tactic to help audiences prove themselves worthy of the confidence that the speaker places—or pretends to place—in them. Such flattery resembles that operating in such figures as *Faust's* Wagner, who wants to possess power over others through the word, and *Die Räuber's* Karl Moor, who allows audiences to flatter themselves for seeing his virtuous side; Schiller knew how to turn an audience into a community by flattering it for the values it had in common. How unusual is Lavater's "Gebrauch Gottes"? If it were not for the sheer power of his rhetoric, one might simply answer: not very unusual at all. Shaftesbury wrote in 1711: *"No poet can do anything great in his own way without the imagination or supposition of a divine presence,* which may raise him to some degree of this passion we are speaking of."[36] And throughout the century, writers knew very well that a poet cannot evoke a sense of spontaneity without, paradoxically, employing the authority of God. In his methods, Lavater merely applies processes in which Europe was already engaged and takes them further. Still, he would come under attack for his methods in his own country, and Meister's critical *Ueber die Schwärmerei* provides just one example, criticizing the fanaticism of those who believe themselves "unmittelbar von Gott getrieben zu seyn."[37] How uplifting it must be, Meister suggests, for Lavater's listeners and readers to be able to imagine God beckoning from beyond, "vom andern Ufer die Hoffnung ihm winken."[38]

Lavater's unusually powerful evocation of God involves the outright rejection of abstractions, symbols—the specific narratives offered by specific societies—while arrogantly invoking the one society that he claims is beyond the "arbitrary" aspect of abstractions, symbols, and specific narratives because it is God's. Like the literature of Sturm und Drang that would follow in the 1770s, he deals with the task of building a bridge of words—sometimes threatening to collapse in incoherence, sometimes solid, but always suspect—between the impromptu and the absolute. Eventually Goethe, who had met Lavater in Frankfurt after his return from Wetzlar, would downplay his interest in and collaboration with Lavater, calling him merely a preacher. But his enthusiasm for Lavater was very much alive early in the decade: there is a great deal of Lavater in Goethe's Werther, a figure who himself "uses God" quite methodically. While critics have suggested that Goethe mentions Lavater twice in *Werther* to make up for his bad review of volume 3 of *Aussichten*, it is much more likely that Lavater's name (instead of that of Herder or Hamann, who go unmentioned in the novel) is there to mark the specific sensibility to which Werther succumbs.[39] For like Werther, Lavater deliberately cuts off access to specific and necessarily limited human communities. After all, Lavater did appear to see Werther's attitudes as worthy of emulation, writing to Marquise Maria Antoine von Branconi on June 8, 1779, that he considered Goethe's *Werther* absolutely harmless and the best and most instructive book Germany has ever produced.[40]

It is a timeless world that Lavater promises in the *Aussichten*, one "simultaneous," not "successive." This is not the world of ordinary people in their specific versions of civil society; it is one where eternity and the here and now will somehow merge without any of the discontents associated with the specific, the local, the parochial. This merging of eternity with the here and now in which the former takes on qualities of the latter is also the idea Lavater presents in the *Physiognomische Fragmente*, on whose first page stands the motto, "Gott schuf den Menschen sich zum Bilde." The *Aussichten* operates along much the same lines, continually stressing the power of Christ the human being, the concrete reality among us. Mankind's resemblance to Christ makes the faces of human beings "hieroglyphs"—not symbols—of God. Christ's face, thus man's face, is "ganz Natursprache," a place "wo alles Ausdruck ist" (3:108) and where nothing is dependent on "arbitrary" words. It is our resemblance to Christ, not our connection to a specific society, that lets us know the truth and gives us the ability to communicate with others as members of a community.[41] Just as Hamann had suggested that Adam was a typological figure of all mankind, the human body, says Lavater, is "hieroglyphisch" and can be read literally and without any system or symbolic presuppositions (3:LV). Lavater's promise to his followers is that they will experience a "simultaneous" confluence with the eternal unencumbered by the limitations of our hopelessly "symbolic" and limited lives.

Much of what Lavater accomplished from the pulpit comes under the category of a phenomenon that harnesses Lavater's principle of simultaneity: charisma. The word χάρισμα is a late Hellenistic equivalent of χάρις, which refers to the favor, or grace, that the divinity bestows on human beings. The Graces of Greek mythology are the personifications of χάρις, and those who did not inherently possess χάρις got it from them. The word is used in the New Testament, most famously by Saint Paul, to denote the "gift" of God's grace. In modern usage, the term has come to refer to an extraordinary, even divinely inspired, leadership ability. But as Max Weber has pointed out, it is a quality followers bestow on leaders: "darauf allein, wie sie tatsächlich von den charismatisch Beherrschten, den 'Anhängern,' bewertet wird, kommt es an."[42] Communities in difficulty, Weber argues, create leaders out of their own desperation. The insidious features of the phenomenon are obvious. One modern theorist of charisma, Irvine Schiffer, finds in the charismatic leader's followers an unacknowledged complicity in a scheme that invites them to look away from their shortcomings while the leader bolsters their damaged self-images. The charismatic figure, he writes, following Weber, is not engaged in "carving out his own public image from ingredients of his own personality, [but] is created by a mass of people evolving a process from within themselves, thence projecting it outward onto a suitable chosen object."[43] When we search for such a leader we are on a "quest for identity."[44] The leader's own confidence can bring about "a victory for our jeopardized self-esteem, an uplift from the depression and helplessness that would infiltrate our awareness, expose our limitations, and force us into a recognition of all those failures that we find most difficult to reconcile."[45] Caught up in an illusion we have created ourself, we find ourselves "adopting a posture of having already arrived at everything we wish to be."[46] Edward McInnes has pointed out that our identification with figures on the stage can also provide this function to a certain extent: Lenz and Klinger, he argues, were aware of "the coercive power of stage-illusion, which is dependent upon the urgent unacknowledged desire of the involved spectator to throw off the confinements of a habitual existence and the identity which this circumscribes, and to assume a persona in keeping with a hidden fantasy of himself."[47]

Social dynamics such as this depend most of all on the group's willingness to be deceived about itself and, at least temporarily, to forget its problems as it opens itself up to flattery. Once again classical rhetoric can help explain what Lavater is doing. In Pseudo-Longinus, the "cunning" formulator of persuasive writing and speaking (ὕψος) has a number of traits similar to the charismatic leader: he is "awe-inspiring," "godlike," and seems to rise to a "more than human level."[48] Most of all, ὕψος charms by false flattery: "Our soul is naturally uplifted by the truly great; we receive it as a joyous offering; we are filled with delight and pride as if we had ourselves created what we heard."[49] When the eighteenth century transformed Longinian ὕψος from a rhetorical to an aesthetic category, flattery remained an essential ingredient. Writing of the sublime in *A Philosophical Enquiry*

into the Origin of Our Ideas of the Sublime and Beautiful (1755), Edmund
Burke observes: "Now whatever either on good or upon bad grounds
tends to raise a man in his own opinion, produces a sort of swelling
and triumph that is extremely grateful to the human mind."[50] More
parallels between sublimity and charisma could be cited: the depen-
dence of both on striking but simple language, and their use of
violence, emotion, and individuality to inspire ideas that seem self-
evidently universal. Certainly there are also obvious differences:
charisma theory is concerned with historically and socially conditioned
group dynamics, whereas the aesthetic of sublimity grew to maturity
at the hands of predominantly ahistorical thinkers. Nevertheless, the
two concepts have so much in common—most of all, their dependence
on invigorating feelings of self-worth—that one is tempted to treat cha-
risma as an aesthetic category that might help explain not only the
appeal of Lavater's theology, but also Sturm und Drang's characteristic
impatience.

The issue of charismatic leadership will return again in chapter 6,
where I argue that the purpose of Karl Moor's charisma is less to unite
a robber band than it is to unite *Die Räuber*'s audience. But for now let
me just suggest, in taking leave of Lavater, that we could speak of La-
vater's effect on his congregations with a simple phrase that he used
himself, and which would soon provide the whole tradition with a
name as it passed from him to his follower Christoph Kaufmann (1753–
95), and then to Friedrich Maximilian Klinger: Lavater had the ability
to lead his congregations temporarily "aus Sturm und Gedränge hin-
aus"—out of Sturm und Drang.[51] Lavater flees "Sturm und Gedränge"
by swearing off all particulars, all narration, all symbolism—every-
thing that takes its meaning from a limited context. Not coincidentally,
the man called the Magus of the South would find an attentive audi-
ence among Germans unhappy with the limits of their own world. Just
as Lavater refuses to allow faces the status of particularity, Goethe's
Faust will find it impossible to live within one particular culture. The
highest thing on Karl Moor's mind will be vague "höhere Pläne" that
are continually a world away, while Werther's flight from particulars
will lead to suicide.[52] With few exceptions, writers of the German
Sturm und Drang insist on something more than particularity. As they
contemplate the land they have inherited, they find themselves vul-
nerable to postures of mind that offer a more powerful sense of who
they are.

3. Werther's Arrogance

In the first letter of Goethe's epistolary novel *Die Leiden des jungen Werthers*, Werther mentions an issue of inheritance that he has been asked to resolve. "Du bist so gut, meiner Mutter zu sagen" he tells Wilhelm, "daß ich ihr Geschäfte bestens betreiben, und ihr ehstens Nachricht davon geben werde."[1]

> Ich habe meine Tante gesprochen [he continues] und habe bey weiten das böse Weib nicht gefunden, das man bey uns aus ihr macht, sie ist eine muntere heftige Frau von dem besten Herzen. Ich erklärte ihr meiner Mutter Beschwerden über den zurückgehaltenen Erbschaftsantheil. Sie sagte mir ihre Gründe, Ursachen und die Bedingungen, unter welchen sie bereit wäre alles heraus zu geben, und mehr als wir verlangten—Kurz, ich mag jezo nichts davon schreiben, sag meiner Mutter, es werde alles gut gehen. Und ich habe, mein Lieber! wieder bey diesem kleinen Geschäfte gefunden: daß Mißverständnisse und Trägheit vielleicht mehr Irrungen in der Welt machen, als List und Bosheit nicht thun. Wenigstens sind die beyden leztern gewiß seltner. (4A)

The subject of his aunt's inheritance is dropped as quickly as it is brought up—exactly like several other matters of inheritance that come up later in the novel: on May 27, 1771, Werther encounters a young woman whose family is away fighting for an inheritance that she claims his relatives want to cheat him out of (15A); on July 11, 1771, Frau M. attempts to prepare her successor for the household debts she will inherit; and when Werther meets Lotte on June 16, 1771, the first information he receives about Albert, her fiancé, is that he is away settling an estate (20A).[2] The contested inheritance is far from unknown in the Sturm und Drang: it is a pivotal issue in Klinger's dramas *Sturm und Drang* and *Die Zwillinge* (1776), and in Schiller's *Die Räuber*. In *Werther*, the most widely read text of Sturm und Drang, issues of inheritance come up regularly, and each time Werther hears of a contested inheritance, he either ignores it or passes censure on it as a matter of no importance. Typical is his attitude toward his mother's request. "Es werde alles gut gehen," he says. But by the end of the novel there is no indication that he ever resolved the affair.

If Goethe begins his first novel with a problem of inheritance, it is because the question of what eighteenth-century Germans inherit as

Germans is very much on his mind in this book.[3] While throughout Western Europe the second half of the century saw a new attachment to one's native soil, German writers were of two minds about what they should value in their culture. The situation appears quite graphically in the *Urfaust*, the famous draft of *Faust I*, where the vast difference between Faust's values and those of Margarete, a simple young woman of the German *Volk*, effectively splits the play in half.[4] Germany was, in a sense, two different places at once: on the one hand, a fragmented social and political world made up of approximately 314 principalities, bishoprics, and free cities; on the other, the "Land der Dichter und Denker" that Madame de Staël discovered when she traveled to Germany at the end of the century. A tradition of abstracting away from their particularist world spans German literature from the medieval verse of Neidhart von Reuenthal to the odes of Klopstock, and Goethe's brief obsession with such abstraction brought him, as he tells us in *Dichtung und Wahrheit*, close to suicide. He wrote *Werther*, he said, to free himself from a "stormy element" that threatened to destroy him.[5] The book appears to have fulfilled its liberating function, for in 1775 he traded the sixteenth-century rebellion of *Götz von Berlichingen* and the more recent *Schwärmerei* of Werther for the stodgy life of the Weimar court. In choosing what one of those tiny principalities, limited as it might be, could offer him, he quickly put distance between himself and Sturm und Drang. But in his flight he gave expression to a particular arrogance that belongs to the German 1770s—a cold undercurrent of German *Empfindsamkeit*, which, as I will suggest, may have its roots in another, much older German tradition.

As *Werther* opens, we see a bright young member of the upper middle class turn away from the most promising inheritance that can come down to an educated but untitled German of the eighteenth century: employment in the state service. Werther claims the other German inheritance, one elusive, immaterial, and ultimately dangerous: the path laid out by the poets Albrecht von Haller and Friedrich von Klopstock. The path he chooses is not one that leads through what is possible in practice under current eighteenth-century German conditions, but rather through what is possible in the unconditioned world of the imagination. Goethe appears to have written *Werther* to demonstrate that despite the triviality of the society and politics of his time and place, the limited conditions Germany offered still made up an inheritance more dangerous to reject than to accept. Although Werther's story is presented through an essentially one-sided correspondence, through these letters to his stabler friend Wilhelm, the epistolary form still sets up a contrast, here between two very different ways to be

German in the eighteenth century. On the one hand, there is Wilhelm's commitment to inherited civil conditions, a commitment shared by Lotte's fiancé Albert. On the other, there is Werther's indulgence in the imagination, which lets him dream his way into a realm of unconditioned absolutes. It turns out that contrasting figures like Wilhelm and Werther are quite common in Sturm und Drang: Klinger, in *Sturm und Drang*, opposes Wild and Blasius. Friedrich Heinrich Jacobi's *Eduard Allwills Briefsammlung* (1775–76) gives us Allwill, a character combining the seeker after the conditioned and the seeker after the unconditioned within a single figure, who is urged by his friend Luzie to find a middle path.[6] These same two possibilities are, of course, open to Werther, after whom Jacobi patterned the character of Allwill: on the one hand, the choice to exercise his fantasy, live in the hereafter, and devote himself to something he cannot have; or, on the other hand, to choose the slower alternative—take the laws of his time and place seriously, avail himself of his mother's connections, and begin a career at the legal office.

Understanding how Goethe frames these two possibilities in *Werther* requires that we first look at how the idea for the book first took hold of Goethe's imagination. Soon after receiving his law degree in 1771, Goethe began a three-and-one-half-month apprenticeship at the Reichskammergericht, the supreme court of the Holy Roman Empire in Wetzlar. Working in the Reichskammergericht was a family tradition: Goethe's maternal great grandfather, Dr. Cornelius Lindheimer, was an attorney there from 1697 to 1722, as was his maternal grandfather Johann Wolfgang Textor and his father, who served from 1734 to 1738. When Goethe was there in the 1770s, the court employed about nine hundred attorneys, notaries, readers, chancellors, copyists, and envoys, and like every German administrative office of any size, the staff was a blend of aristocracy and middle class. Throughout Germany's decentralized bureaucracy, there were so many positions to be filled that, at least since the twelfth century, there had been no other choice but to hire officials from outside the nobility. The Reichskammergericht had had its seat in Wetzlar since 1693, when its former home in Speyer was destroyed by the French, and when it came there, this small, struggling town with a pronounced medieval flavor quickly turned into a thriving cosmopolitan community. For the sake of parity, the formerly Protestant town now had Catholic services, a cloister, and a Jesuit college. Unfortunately, however, there also developed a sharp social division between the approximately nine hundred employees of the Reichskammergericht and the rest of the town, whose population had grown to about four thousand by 1770. As the suppliers of goods and services, the original citizens of Wetzlar had begun to feel like employees of the court, while even middle-class members of the Reichskammergericht felt superior to ordinary citizens of Wetzlar. Only the Wetzlar upper-middle class socialized with those attached to the court, and of course within the Reichskammergericht itself, *Präsidenten* and *Assessoren* considered it below their dignity to associate with *Prokuranten* and *Advokaten*, to say nothing of lowly clerks and *Legationssekretäre*. These were factors that contributed to what Werther would describe on December 24, 1771, as "die fatalen bürgerlichen Verhältnisse" (75A).

But while Werther's problem is one of class, it is a rather complex class problem whose origins reach far into the German past. To understand the "awkward civil conditions" behind Werther's demise, one must first understand the ambiguous position of the middle-class bureaucrat who worked side by side with his aristocratic counterpart in the German bureaucracy. The middle-class *Beamter* was there, first of all, because employment in provincial and city governments was virtually the only way for a member of the middle class to advance himself, and the state offices of German absolutist government brought more security and prestige than being a mere advocate or notary.[7] A position in the chancellery also brought with it privileges that helped give the middle-class bureaucrat a special position between bourgeois and nobleman; even the lowest member of the chancellery was exempt from taxation and could be tried only by the chancellery, and not by the city according to its statutes.[8] Over several years it was possible to work one's way up to a higher position—Justus Möser (1720–94) did just that, eventually becoming *Kanzleidirektor* in Osnabrück. There were more applicants than positions even by the 1730s, and far more by the end of the 1760s. Appointments were much sought after—even Hamann, himself a critic of the German bureaucracy, entered the state bureaucracy in 1763 and again in 1767 in Königsberg.

Procuring such a position depended not only on one's academic qualifications and embracing the right religion, but also having the right connections. Applicants with family ties to the government had by far the best chances, and even Justus Möser was not above using his influence to give family members a better chance at government positions. The result was that the middle-class *Beamter* became virtually a class unto itself, "on the one hand without the opportunity to enter the nobility, on the other hand possessed of the highest possible positions for the middle class, officially representing the absolute state."[9] Whereas noblemen almost always had the highest positions, they were not always trained lawyers, even though for the same appointments, a middle-class applicant needed a law degree. Moreover, even officials at the lower levels of city, provincial, or imperial bureaucracies were usually better educated than those at the top. Middle-class bureaucrats, whose rigor and efficiency was their bond, took their conduct very seriously and were generally better informed and more competent than the noblemen working with them. It was an odd situation, and one duplicated nowhere else in Europe. Middle-class bureaucrats made many of the most important decisions themselves and, aware that they were an indispensable part of their increasingly complex German absolutist governments, they took pride in their work.[10] Nevertheless, the noblemen who depended on them made sure they were banned from aristocratic society—for example, as we know from the pages of *Werther*, the chancellery's official ceremonies were usually segregated.

While Goethe was in Wetzlar, the Reichskammergericht underwent an audit, which by all accounts was performed even more slowly and inefficiently than the court handled its cases. The delegation, which was in town from 1767 to 1776, consisted of twenty-four envoys (*Gesandte*, or *Subdelegierte*) and numerous clerks and legal secretaries (*Legationssekretäre*). One of these legal secretaries was Karl-Wilhelm Jerusalem (1747–72), whose suicide after a snub by aristocratic society at the home of Graf von Bassenheim was an important inspiration as Goethe set out to write the novel. Jerusalem, who arrived in 1771 and worked directly for one of the envoys, came, like Goethe, from a relatively wealthy and powerful family: he was the son of the well-known Braunschweig theologian Johann Friedrich Wilhelm Jerusalem (1709–89). The prince of Braunschweig was a family friend, and Justus Möser was a relative and frequent visitor. But like Werther, Jerusalem failed to take advantage of the social opportunities that Möser would exploit. Goethe had met Karl-Wilhelm Jerusalem seven years before in Leipzig and became quite interested in him but, like Jerusalem's other colleagues, never seems to have gotten very close to him. In *Dichtung und Wahrheit*, where Goethe describes, among other things, Jerusalem's blue frock coat and yellow vest, he also depicts the young lawyer in a seemingly contradictory way—as melancholy, yet also level-headed and well-meaning.[11]

Added to this seeming contradiction is an apparent insufficiency in Goethe's description of Jerusalem: there was, by all accounts, a *cold* side to the man that contrasts oddly to the melancholy side mentioned by Goethe. According to reports of his few close friends, Jerusalem considered himself a stoic and believed that individuals could be masters over their lives and deaths.[12] Lessing, who briefly corresponded with Jerusalem, called him "einen wahren, nachdenkenden, kalten Philosophen," while Kielmannsegge, apparently Jerusalem's best friend, called his friend's thinking "Starkgeisterei."[13] Yet in *Dichtung und Wahrheit*, Goethe looks away from this cold, arrogant, side of Jerusalem—the high-strung, brooding loner who resented his subordinate position at the Reichskammergericht and spoke more than once of suicide.[14] Jerusalem's letters to his father also speak to the cold aspect of his personality: they are full of mockery of the methods of the Reichskammergericht and its auditors.[15] At one point, in an effort to break Jerusalem's arrogance, the envoy to whom he was subordinate gave him archival duties for six hours a day and would not allow him to do the legal work for which he was trained.[16] For Jerusalem the end would come as he fell in love with Elisabeth Herd, the wife of another legal secretary. He declared his love for her on October 28, 1771, and on the next day, after being banned from the house by her and her husband Philipp, committed suicide after borrowing a pair of pistols from a fellow legal secretary, Johann Christian Kestner (1741–1800). The motives for Jerusalem's suicide are complex, including, of course, his attachment to Elisabeth Herd, which led to being banned from the house, and the matter of his attitude: an arrogant resistance to subordination, which led to punishment in the workplace and a reprimand after staying too long at Graf von Bassenheim's party.

What may have come across as arrogance in Karl-Wilhelm Jerusalem's manner was in one respect a symptom of eighteenth-century thought. For that century, more than any other before it, felt justified in replacing inherited rules with personal moral legislation: in 1712 Shaftesbury called the artist "a second *Maker*; a just Prometheus under Jove";[17] in 1759 Edward Young declared that humankind was "ignorant of [its] own powers" and spoke of taking "bold excursions of the human mind";[18] and Rousseau would open his autobiography by maintaining: "I may be no better, but at least I am different."[19] But not a few writers of the eighteenth century advised against the stoical attitude that imagines itself free of the demands of specific cultures: while Diderot, in his dialogue *Rameau's Nephew* (1823; written 1761–74?), warned of replacing moral conduct with sheer intellect, Hamann was equating reason and wit with dissimilation.[20] Vico warns in *The New Science* (1725) that we are being "made more inhuman by the barbarism of reflection."[21] Rousseau, writing his *Confessions* in the 1760s, tries to excuse the overly rational conduct of Madame de Warens as "a fault of nature."[22] And Hegel, summing up this trend in the *Phenomenology of Mind* (1807), maintains that so-called *reine Einsicht* was the great weakness of the Enlightenment.[23] Among the voluminous secondary literature on *Werther*, Eric A. Blackall approaches this aspect of Goethe's novel most closely, noting that the suffering of Werther alluded to in the title is the result of his inability to find a satisfying order of existence within himself. "Ultimately," writes Blackall, "the book is about the quest for order—order not in the sense of social or domestic order, but as the basic ontological necessity."[24] *Werther*'s subject is not only nature and freedom, but also the attempt "to construct an artificial world as a surrogate for reality."[25]

But I think we can go further than this, tying in the contradictory social status of the German middle-class bureaucrat with the historical Jerusalem and the fictitious Werther. Unfortunately, we have become accustomed to speaking of Werther's frustration at the legal office as a matter of the failed ambition of an oppressed middle class. Of course, this is the way the matter was approached during a conversation about the novel between Goethe and Napoleon in October 1808.[26] But if we take the parallels between Werther and Jerusalem seriously, which I think we should, it is hard not to conclude that a good portion of Werther's difficulty at the embassy was caused not by sheer ambition, but by a certain aloofness with a long social history. Werther is unwilling to take the prescribed route up the governmental ladder, a route that Jerusalem's family friend Justus Möser was willing to take. He insists, rather, on practically guaranteeing his own disappointment by assuming from the start that he must preserve a critical mass of authority; as high-strung as Jerusalem, he insists on having a world that corresponds with his dreams, which in his case are patterned after the unconditioned world celebrated in the poetry of Haller and Klopstock. Despite its abstractness, the world of poetry was, after all, a German inheritance much more attractive than the political legacy of particularism. Werther trusts words, thinking he can incant his way verbally to the absolutes, and to the ideal community he imagines they offer. Rejecting the most direct, viable, and promising route open to him, employment in the state service, he turns to the least viable: pure verbal incantation, which is demonstrated in probably the most famous scene of the novel, as Lotte, inspired by the storm on June 16, 1771, utters the name "Klopstock!" (28A):

> Wir traten an's Fenster, es donnerte abseitwärts und der herrliche Regen säuselte auf das Land, und der erquikkendste Wohlgeruch stieg in aller Fülle einer warmen Luft zu uns auf. Sie stand auf ihrem Ellenbogen gestützt und ihr Blik durchdrang die gegend, sie sah gen Himmel und auf mich, ich sah ihr Auge thränenvoll, sie legte ihre Hand auf die meinige und sagte—Klopstock!

Ich versank in dem Strome von Empfindungen, den sie in dieser
Loosung über mich ausgoß. Ich ertrugs nicht, neigte mich auf ihre
Hand und küßte sie unter den wonnevollesten Thränen. Und sah
nach ihrem Auge wieder—Edler! hättest du deine Vergötterung
in diesem Blikke gesehn, und möcht ich nun deinen so oft ent-
weihten Nahmen nie wieder nennen hören! (28A)

Later in the novel, Lotte will be carried away by Werther's reading of
his translation of *Ossian* in a manner comparable with that in which
the word "Klopstock" causes Werther to sink into a stream of feelings
beyond time, beyond the world of temporal succession. It has been
argued that such scenes point out that, with the rapid expansion of
the eighteenth-century book trade, a healthy community of readers is
beginning to develop in Germany—all leading to a literary culture in
which even a young country woman without literary schooling can
share.[27] But as a reader, Lotte is still part of a rather small community;
only few must have shared her literary tastes.

What does Werther think he finds when he meets Lotte on May 15?
He had said that he was searching for a society: "Ich hab allerley Be-
kanntschaft gemacht, Gesellschaft hab ich noch keine gefunden" (8A).
Can this one person, with whom he relates best when he dreams of
unconditioned realms, be the "Gesellschaft" he had been seeking? The
real point of the famous June 16 passage just quoted, the point I think
Goethe wants to get across, is that there is something precious, hollow,
and merely rhetorical about this language of the heart that Werther
glorifies, this language in which words are supposed to resonate with
perfect accuracy and have a powerful emotional effect. In the letter of
June 16 there is a sudden change of tone: Werther appears to have
found this "Gesellschaft" he was seeking, yet if this is true, then we
must conclude that what he was looking for never was a society in the
usual sense. There is something inherently silly and self-indulgent
about this scene in which a world unfolds in almost operatic fashion
with the utterance of Klopstock's name. Not only are the feelings
Werther and Lotte share in this scene childish; they are indulged in at
the expense of society at large. The issue here is less the richness of
this experience than its poverty. For all the praise given Klopstock by
the Sturm und Drang, the most widely read book of the tradition, *Die
Leiden des jungen Werthers*, condemns him as the unacceptable opposite
of the here and now and its specific inherited culture. We get a similar
view of Klopstock in Schiller's self-critique of Amalia of *Die Räuber*,
another virtual suicide; there he asserts that Amalia had, in his opin-
ion, "read too much Klopstock."[28] The famous Klopstock scene is

there, first and foremost, to show that the limited society it depicts is a dangerous model for human interaction.

In the 1770s, it was the "Göttinger Hain" that heaped the greatest praise on Klopstock. Founded in 1772 by students at the University of Göttingen, and with a focus on poetry, its members included Ludwig Christoph Hölty (1748–76), Friedrich Leopold Stolberg (1750–1819), Heinrich Christian Boie (1744–1806), Gottfried August Bürger (1747–94), Friedrich Wilhelm Gotter (1746–97), and Heinrich Johann Voss (1751–1826). Klopstock, they felt, was a poet of feeling as opposed to abstraction, an opinion shared by Herder in his *Abhandlung über den Ursprung der Sprache* (1771). Yet I think Blackall sees the true nature of Klopstock's poetry when he calls it a form of "abstract metonymy"—a literature less concerned with concreteness and metaphor than with abstractions and universals.[29] As Blackall suggests, German *Empfindsamkeit* is different from English Sensibility precisely because of the religious strain provided by writers like Haller and Klopstock[30] The language of Albrecht von Haller helped Klopstock create his own elevated, abstract style. Consider a strophe from Haller's "Über die Ewigkeit" (1736), in which Blackall notes "the strange, evocative power of resounding abstract rhetoric."[31]

> Furchtbares Meer der ernsten Ewigkeit!
> Uralter Quell von Welten und von Zeiten!
> Unendlichs Grab von Welten und von Zeit!
> Beständigs Reich der Gegenwärtigkeit!
> Die Asche der Vergangenheit.
> Ist dir ein Keim von Künftigkeiten.
> Unendlichkeit! wer misset dich?[32]

Klopstock continued Haller's striving after absolutes, deriving haunting—and essentially religious—effects by avoiding the concreteness of his hero Milton while inventing a verbal style that soared to abstract realms. And the style of Klopstock's whole corpus is at issue here, not just "Frühlingsfeier" (1759), the poem that Lotte and Werther think of at the same time after the storm. In the following four strophes of "Dem Allgegenwärtigen" (1758), an ode Klopstock wrote just a few months before "Frühlingsfeier," there occur not only formal elements that press toward abstraction, but also several thematic elements present in *Werther*:

> Wenige nur, ach wenige sind,
> Deren Aug' in der Schöpfung

Den Schöpfer sieht! wenige, deren Ohr
Ihn in dem mächtigen Rauschen des Sturmwinds hört,

Im Donner, der rollt, oder im lispelnden Bache,
Unerschafner! dich vernimt,
Weniger Herzen erfüllt, mit Ehrfurcht und Schauer,
Gottes Allgegenwart!

Laß mich im Heiligthume
Dich, Allgegenwärtiger,
Stets suchen, und finden! und ist
Er mir entflohn, dieser Gedanke der Ewigkeit;

Laß mich ihn tiefanbetend
Von den Chören der Seraphim,
Ihn, mit lauten Thränen der Freude,
Herunter rufen![33]

With its abstract language and its themes of exclusivity and the search for eternity, "Dem Allgegenwärtigen," which also contains a storm, fits as well with the events of the June 16, 1771, letter as "Frühlings-feier" does. In *Werther* Klopstock is more than just a "symbol of creativeness" or even of "unproductive inwardness";[34] it was Klopstock who, more than anyone else, demonstrated to Germans how to replace a responsibility to be accountable to others with abstract effusions about eternity: "Klopstock!" refers not just to one poem, or to a spontaneous union of two souls, but to a general threat posed to writers in late eighteenth-century Germany, and that threat is the spaceless and timeless realm that Germans have inherited as part of their culture.

It is hard to read of Werther's passionate yet impossible love of Lotte, especially the way that Klopstock's poetry helps reveal it, without thinking of the last great era of German poetry: the Minnesang. The distance separating the age of the courtly lyric and the Sturm und Drang is vast, but the medieval courtly ethos, especially as manifested in the hyperbolic tones of the Minnesang, is in many ways not foreign at all to the German 1770s. In a way quite parallel to *Werther*, both Guido of Johann Anton Leisewitz's *Julius von Tarent* (1776) and Guelfo of Klinger's *Die Zwillinge* pursue women (Bianka and Kamilla, respectively) based on models of courtship derived from the medieval love lyric. We think also of Lenz, who in his life and work was a specialist in the idealistic love that operates from a distance and without hope.[35] The tradition of the Minnesang, like the Sturm und Drang, dealt in a hyperbolic love which often, as in Neidhart von Reuenthal, was stretched to its limits. German courtly love lyric was somewhat of an aberration in Europe: whereas in French courtly literature the knight fought mainly for honor, lord, and homeland, worldly goals were not available in fragmented Germany. Thus the knight had to settle for the exaggerated praise of courtly women. Like his counterpart in German courtly love poetry, Werther falls in love with a woman who is already answered for. The fact that he cannot have her is a foregone conclusion accepted from the beginning.

Further resonances between *Werther* and German medieval courtly culture, especially when considered in the context of the contradictory social position of the eighteenth-century bureaucrat, are even more promising as avenues to an understanding of this novel—and the Sturm und Drang in general. Walter Bruford mentions the resemblance between the rise of the educated middle class in the eighteenth century and the rise of another class in the German Middle Ages: the ministerials, a German service class that fashioned itself into a new nobility with a special character of its own.[36] A closer look at the ministerials reveals that Bruford indeed pointed out a fascinating connection. The ministerial class, unique to Germany, was a large lower-service nobility that helped Germany on its way to particularism by removing every possibility of a centralized German feudal structure while helping foster attitudes toward authority that bear an uncanny resemblance to those Goethe deals with in *Werther*. The class originated as German nobles of the ninth and tenth centuries required the services of administrators—messengers, servants, soldiers—to expand. In the thirteenth century, when the first *Bürgermeister* came on the scene, they were ministerials. And the class also accounts for almost all of the Minnesänger. The French nobility had similar needs and did not see such service as demeaning. But for reasons that are still unclear, Germans saw such service as incompatible with their free status, and it led to the formation of a unique German class, one that took an oath of service, but not homage, to the prince. Like that of the eighteenth-century bureaucrat, the status of the ministerial was ambivalent, suspended somewhere between lordship and service: he was educated, punctilious, and possessed a great sense of self-importance. His bureaucratic zeal, with a basis less in status than in ability, infused German administration with "einen neuen Geist des Rechnens und Kalkulierens, der dem alten Feudaldenken fremd war."[37] Yet as the ministerial found a new scale of accomplishment in administration itself, he also found himself denying allegiance to the very aristocratic class that gave him power. In Germany, the Minnesänger's homage of his lord's wife (the basis of his pride) is traceable at least in part to his membership in the ministerial class. For the ministerial, as Arno Borst has argued, harbored deep ambiguity about his social status. He felt a great sense of importance but was not an aristocrat—and this problem found resolution in the Minnesang, which in its highly stylized formal ritual combines acknowledgment of the ministerial's actual status with his taste for realms above himself. Reinmar von Hagenau's highly stylized and exaggerated praise of courtly women is a "Produkt der Krise," Borst argues, that demands and dreams the eternal image of humankind in order to forget a servile past.[38] The ministerials devoted themselves to courtly ideology even more intensely than the nobility. Can it be that in courtly poetry, the ministerial class hid from itself its own aggressiveness by adopting the obedient pose of the Minnesänger while simultaneously seizing an opportunity to glorify itself? Perhaps, exactly like so many protagonists of Sturm und Drang who pass judgment on their own civil inheritance, the ministerials chose not to admit that a particular past—one they would like to overcome—had shaped them in ways that they could not avoid.

Historians have found it difficult to make generalizations about the ministerials: understanding a fragmented country like Germany may never be possible except on a regional basis; moreover, no one has been able to pin down any particular eighteenth-century class as the specific descendants of the ministerials. Their influence, more than likely, cuts across classes, and for this reason such parallels as I have been suggesting can only be considered affinities, and certainly not influences. Nevertheless, looking at Werther as if he shared the ministerial posture of mind—with its movement away from rule based on a purely feudal model—leads to interesting results. For one thing, it helps unify those two themes of the novel that critics have traditionally seen as separate, namely, Werther's love of Lotte and his failed ambitions at the embassy, which even Goethe acknowledged in his 1806 conversation with Napoleon. Yet both themes involve confronting the necessity of culturally specific morality, and thinking of them as related in this way leads to a deeper reason for Sturm und Drang's reluctance to claim its political past. Werther arrogantly assumes that his impulses should have the status of authority, yet at the same time his devotion to timeless ideals amounts to an abandonment of traditional ties to the past that could give any claim to authority. Seen from this point of view, what could complement Werther's rejection at court more appropriately than the flight to hyperbole that he makes as he launches back into his impossible courtship of Lotte at the beginning of part 2 of the novel? "Ja, liebe Lotte," he writes, sounding like a courtly lover in the Minnesang tradition, "ich will alles besorgen und bestellen; geben Sie nur mehr Aufträge, nur recht oft" (46B).

Here, then, is a pattern—almost a ritual—in which the Minne-sänger, the ministerial, and Werther, take part, one where the servile figure humbly asks for tasks to perform, yet continually declares his aloofness from all authority. On June 29, 1771, Werther calls the doctor a "dogmatische Dratpuppe" (32A). The envoy's way of conducting business is "lächerlich" (79A). The wife of the new parson is "Eine Frazze, die sich abgiebt gelehrt zu sein" (98A). The unnamed figure who interrupts him on July 29, 1772, while he writes to Lotte is "uner-träglich" (91A). He considers Albert's love for Lotte shallow compared to his own: "Weiß er sie zu achten wie sie es verdient?" (118B). For Albert has a "Mangel an Fühlbarkeit" (91A). Aren't the aristocrats who call him "übermütig" after he stays on at dinner with Graf von C. quite correct? Critics have always praised Werther for his warmth and sen-sitivity: in the 1790s, Wilhelm von Humboldt spoke of the harmless pleasures of his "hohe, feine Sentimentalität";[39] and in our own cen-tury, Herbert Schöffler wrote: "Werther geht zugrunde an den besten Kräften seines Wesens, an allem, was gut ist in ihm, daß er liebevoll und treu ist," adding that *Werther* is "die erste Tragödie ohne Schuld, ohne Prinzip des Bösen."[40] On the surface, it is easy to see Werther as a sensitive, unspoiled, visionary man.[41] But there is also a cold side to him, and it comes out in his refusal to come to face the culture he has inherited. Very unlike the sympathetic heroes recommended by Les-sing, Werther values principles that are not only foreign to his social and political milieu; they are unreliable as universal rules. He is more willing to be guided by personal moral legislation than by a sense of accountability to a community. Typical is his ridiculous attempt to de-fend the Peasant Boy despite all the evidence marshaled against him.[42] *Werther*, as Blackall suggests, is about constructing an artificial order, but more specifically it is about an ordering that rushes in too quickly and too arrogantly—a state of affairs unacceptable to a Goethe who is already rejecting his own youthful *Schwärmerei*.

Of course, Werther also has moments in which he sees that his in-tentions, in and of themselves, can never make the world move ac-cording to his will: "Ich habe mich so oft auf den Boden geworfen und Gott um Thränen gebeten, wie ein Akkersmann um Regen, wenn der Himmel ehern über ihm ist, und um ihn die Erde verdürstet. Aber, ach ich fühls! Gott giebt Regen und Sonnenschein nicht unserm un-gestümen Bitten . . ." (104A). Such scenes insure that the greatest sense in which *Werther* is a revolutionary novel is not in its depiction of the free spirit of Werther, but in its attempt to penetrate to the moral center of its audience by drawing the reader's attention to precisely what Werther lacks. In the 1770s, it seems, Germany was in a position to treat feelings about self-governance in a less practical and entirely different way than they were treated in the rest of Europe. Each in his own way, writers of Sturm und Drang addressed the problem of this arrogance that defies Germany's cultural inheritance from within. It is as if, in his first novel, Goethe implies that a satisfying German society is beyond the reach of mere intentions: *Werther* delivers a strict verdict on a "cold" aspect of German *Empfindsamkeit* that occurs when a "liberated" modern emotional life denies its accountability to the rest of the world. As Werther attempts to conduct his life according to his private sense of logic and completeness, we see intentions misfire, and as the book draws to a close, Werther's botched suicide (he suffers twelve hours before dying) reminds us one last time how easily intentions can go astray. In the episode of the Peasant Boy, Werther lays great stress on the fact that the boy's intentions were always pure, "daß seine Absichten gegen sie [his victim] immer redlich gewesen" (94B), yet as Goethe seems to know, intentions easily go astray when they are without a culture to give them a foundation. When the judge proclaims that the Peasant Boy is doomed, Albert takes up a position of authority as never before and commands Lotte to see to it that Werther visits less often.

Nevertheless, there is still one possible line of defense against the charge of arrogance I have leveled at Werther: that Werther is a helpless victim of Albert and Lotte, who help him commit suicide by encouraging his affection for Lotte and even lending him the pistol. It is, in fact, easy to arrive at this conclusion when reading the 1787 edition, which is the standard edition of the book and still the only version available in English. But the 1787 edition differs significantly from the original 1774 version, for in 1787 Goethe downplays the cold side of Werther. In the 1774 edition, Lotte allows herself to be flattered by Werther, encourages him to visit, enjoys his attention, and is willing to use his vision as a means to escape from her parochial surroundings. As Erika Nolan has pointed out, Albert, who is flattered by Werther's attention to his fiancée, clearly encourages him to get to know Lotte better.[43] He allows her to visit and even makes a birthday gift of the ribbon she wore when Werther and she met. Lotte takes frequent walks with Werther, gives him tasks to perform, and shares responsibility for putting the suicide weapon in his hands. Especially in the 1787 version it is clear that Goethe meant Albert and Lotte to be partly conscious of the implications of their actions. After the suicide, Lotte and Albert silently blame each other for tempting Werther into a hopeless situation, yet neither can admit to the other that they played a part in Werther's death. The 1787 additions also include the long section on

Lotte's unwillingness to share Werther with her girlfriends (135B) and the letter of September 12, 1772, concerning the canary that Albert brought back from his trip: "Einen neuen Freund, sagte sie und lockte ihn auf ihre Hand, er ist meinen Kleinen zugedacht. Er thut gar zu lieb! Sehen Sie ihn! Wenn ich ihm Brod gebe flattert er mit den Flügeln und pickt so artig. Er küßt mich auch, sehen Sie!" (97B). Coquettishly, Lotte kisses the canary, then has the canary kiss Werther. "Er ißt mir auch aus dem Munde, sagte sie" (97B). Werther's reaction: "Sie sollte es nicht thun!" (97B). It was especially this scene, from the 1787 edition, that evoked Thomas Mann's comment that Lotte displayed "in Unschuld gehüllte Koketterie."[44]

Reading *Werther* as a text of the Sturm und Drang requires that we deemphasize the 1778 version, which has become standard, and return to the early editions of 1774 and 1775. And there it is Werther, not Lotte or Albert, who must take most of the responsibility for the suicide. His manipulative powers over Lotte are so great that he not only enlists her help; he imbues her with guilt. Think, for instance, of his last letter: "Weyhnachtsabend hältst Du dieses Papier in Deiner Hand, zitterst und benezt es mit Deinen lieben Thränen" (134A). Werther obviously wants Lotte to view his suicide as an altruistic, well-intentioned act committed for the sake of another: "Es ist nicht Verzweiflung, es ist Gewißheit, daß ich ausgetragen habe, und daß ich mich opfere für Dich, ja Lotte, warum sollt ich's verschweigen: eins von uns dreyen muß hinweg, und das will ich seyn" (132A). When Werther writes such lines as "Sie sieht nicht, sie fühlt nicht, daß sie einen Gift bereitet, der mich und sie zu Grunde richten wird" (106A), it is easy to take the assertion at face value and sympathize with him. Yet Werther is anything but a magnanimous soul with good intentions.

He is a cold engineer of relationships who, during the *Ossian* reading, when he claims to ask for her forgiveness for losing control of himself, seems more interested in shifting the blame for his suicidal course on her: "O vergieb mir! vergieb mir! Gestern! Es hätte der lezte Augenblick meines Lebens seyn sollen" (147A). Generally we think of the sensibility depicted in *Werther* as part of the secularization of a new inwardness stemming from the Reformation. But how can this cold, stoical aspect of Werther fit into that tradition? One way to approach this problem is to recognize that the Reformation's emphasis on the inward route to the absolute brings with it a focus on inner consistency. As Ernst Troeltsch points out, Lutheranism involved trading sacramental grace for free grace, and making the problem of Christianity not how the institution of the church guarantees salvation but, rather, how one can gain personal assurance.[45] In classic Lutheranism,

Troeltsch suggests, Christian individualism quickly becomes purely subjective, with no legal claim on either society or the church: "so ist der christliche Individualismus des Luthertums rein in die Tiefen der Gesinnung versenkt, ohne rechtlichen Anspruch an die Gesellschaft und an die Kirche, ohne Fähigkeit der äußeren Geltendmachung und im Grunde wesentlich und begrifflich ohne Gemeinschaftsbedürfnis überhaupt, indem er nur aus Liebe sich unter die Bedingungen des Gemeinschaftslebens beugt."[46] Max Weber would go even further, arguing that the inwardness of Reformation thought promotes a quite unexpected impulse, one we do not normally associate with Preromanticism: methodical conduct.

> Das "methodische" Leben: die rationale Form der Askese, wird dadurch aus dem Kloster in die Welt übertragen. Die asketischen Mittel sind im Prinzip die gleichen: Ablehnung aller eitlen Selbst- oder anderen Kreaturvergötterung, der feudalen Hoffart, des unbefangenen Kunst- und Lebensgenusses, der "Leichtfertigkeit" und aller müßigen Geld- und Zeitvergeudung, der Pflege der Erotik oder irgendwelcher von der rationalen Orientiertheit auf Gottes Willen und Ruhm, und das heißt: auf die rationale Arbeit im privaten Beruf und in den gottverordneten sozialen Gemeinschaften, ablenkenden Beschäftigung. Die Beschneidung alles feudalen ostensiblen Prunkes und alles irrationalen Konsums überhaupt wirkt in der Richtung der Kapitalaufspeicherung und der immer erneuten Verwertung des Besitzes in werbender Form, die "innerweltliche Askese" in ihrer Gesamtheit aber in der Richtung der Züchtung und Glorifizierung des "Berufsmenschentums," wie es der Kapitalismus (und die Bürokratie) braucht. Die Lebensinhalte überhaupt werden nicht auf Personen, sondern auf "sachliche" rationale Zwecke ausgerichtet, die Caritas selbst ein sachlicher Armenpflegebetrieb zur Mehrung des Ruhmes Gottes.[47]

According to Weber, ascetic Protestantism takes the intense control and regulation of personal life that was once expected only of the monk and generalizes it. Thus life becomes focused not on persons, but on impersonal, rational goals, and is governed by a relatively rational ethics. Virtue is no longer defined by the feelings one has based on a body of inherited traditions, but according to the completeness and correctness of one's own thinking. No longer accountable to God or to one's fellow human beings, individuals conduct themselves according to internal criteria.[48]

If Troeltsch and Weber are correct, and if Protestantism is itself a source of methodical conduct, then understanding Preromantic currents of Enlightenment may require that we recognize a drive for the rational and the correct within at least some versions of *Empfindsamkeit*. Werther's conduct, despite all outward appearances of sensitivity and magnanimity, indicates that he may even sense his own harrowing rationality. When he shudders at his own marionette-like actions at the embassy ("Wie ausgetroknet meine Sinnen werden . . . [ich] fasse manchmal meinen Nachbar an der hölzernen Hand und schaudere zurük," 77A) it points up a fact that critics of this novel generally avoid: that the embassy and Werther have a great deal in common. Like Albert, but on a less conscious level, Werther operates on a closed and inflexible set of principles. As this novel demonstrates, it is possible to qualify as a lovable, even charismatic *Schwärmer*—as a high-spirited personality who pulls others into his orbit—while embracing an impersonal relation to others. The cold side of *Empfindsamkeit* I have described, an obverse aspect of early Romantic inwardness, is at the center of this book, which laments that the mind is inadvertently becoming a bureaucratically organized structure in the eighteenth century, a structure designed to carry out personal plans while looking away from the broader implications of its own decisions. Perhaps understandably, it would be Germans, with their bureaucratic heritage reaching into the late Middle Ages, who would write more eloquently than other Europeans of the horrors of the rational and bureaucratic way of life: Lenz would conceive of eighteenth-century life as one in which, as Lenz put it, "wir drehen uns eine Zeitlang in diesem Platz herum wie die andern Räder."[49] Schiller's Karl Moor would call his age a "schlappes Kastratenjahrhundert."[50] And, fittingly, Werther's body will be carried to the cemetery by "Handwerker" (157A).

Opposing a sensitive and inspiring Werther to the bureaucratically organized thought of Albert and the Ambassador greatly oversimplifies this novel. For Werther is not who he appears to be on the surface. The calm logic of his last few hours shows that his suicide stems not from excessive emotionalism per se but from overorganization. Ignace Feuerlicht observes: "Werther has never been more disciplined and logical than on the day before his death."[51] Having decided to kill himself, he seems to be in perfect harmony with himself and is able to perform the seemingly impossible feat of climbing the rocky hill in the dark. Before shooting himself he calmly sits down to bread and wine and declares: "Alles ist so still um mich her, und so ruhig meine Seele, ich danke dir Gott, der du diesen lezten Augenblikken diese Wärme, diese Kraft schenkest" (154A). Goethe's first novel, with its arrogant protagonist, is not a warning against emotionalism per se; it is a warning that *Empfindsamkeit* is becoming infiltrated with reason.[52]

As for the issue of inheritance with which I began this consideration of *Werther*, Goethe positions such matters so that they effectively refute Werther's preference for the unconditioned over the conditioned: his notion that Lotte would be happier with him than with Albert is immediately followed by the letter of August 4, 1772, where we learn that Hans, the child referred to on May 27, 1771, has died and that his father has returned from Switzerland without his inheritance (91A). Werther's hyperbolic praise of Lotte and *Ossian* on July 10, 1771, is immediately followed on July 11 by another death, this time of Frau M., who is herself concerned with the budget deficit that her successor will inherit (41A–42A). Goethe wants us to see Werther's flight from German specificity as an avoidance of the complications involved in committing oneself to the past. It is not a utopia that Werther finds among the common people, as some have argued.[53] The utopia exists only in Werther's mind: he ignores the conflicts and disagreements that are part of every community, and precisely the most unnatural and artificial scenes of the novel are those in which Werther tries to depict the life of the common people as harmonious. For him, Lotte means refuge from dealing with precisely these sorts of struggles in society, and the sanctuary she represents is suggested as he takes refuge from a storm on January 20, 1772, and says: "Ach muß ich Ihnen schreiben, liebe Lotte, hier in der Stube einer geringen Bauernherberge, in die ich mich vor einem schweren Wetter geflüchtet habe" (77A), then goes on to tell her that he is working with people who are entirely alien to his heart.

The only people who do not seem alien to Werther's heart are those whose lives are largely unspecific to any particular culture, like the heroes of *Ossian*, who Werther thinks derive their greatness merely from being themselves. Werther could have chosen the positive, culture-bound, compassionate features of the ancient society Macpherson depicts in *Ossian*, the side that leads to Wordsworth and Coleridge's *Lyrical Ballads*. But instead he culls out its self-thwarting, suicidal aspect. What Count von C. tells Werther on December 24, 1771, after Werther had been working at the legal office for two months, is quite relevant to Werther's problem: "Die Leute erschweren sich's und andern. Doch sagt er, man muß sich darein resigniren, wie ein Reisender, der über einen Berg muß. Freylich! wär der Berg nicht da, wäre der Weg viel bequemer und kürzer, er ist nun aber da! und es soll drüber!—" (73A). Still, Werther will not accept the fact that human interaction naturally involves a given state of affairs that one simply has to work with, like the inheritance issue that opens the novel. Werther obviously discussed the matter only superficially with his aunt, and then avoids taking care of the problem. He consistently glosses over such problems, acting as if they are not there: after Hans's mother relates to Werther her anguish over the inheritance out of which she claimed her relatives wanted to cheat her husband, Werther remarks, inexplicably, that the sight of the woman calmed his soul: "so linderts all den Tumult, der Anblik eines solchen Geschöpfs," for she lives "von einem Tag zum andern" and "die Blätter abfallen sieht, und nichts dabey denkt, als daß der Winter kömmt" (15A). His impatience with what he perceives as an unworkable eighteenth-century Germany leads him to sleepwalk through the demands of the here and now and to find value only in the unconditioned realm of an impossible love. And this attitude, as I hope I have shown, gives him more in common with the rational life he despises than even he suspects. Yet *Werther* presents just one way that Sturm und Drang tried to resolve Germany's parochial circumstances in a seemingly innocent way. The texts to which we now turn will try to excuse the explosive frustration born of the German past by blaming it on circumstances beyond the protagonist's control.

4. A Titan in Extenuating Circumstances: Sturm und Drang and the *Kraftmensch*

"Prometheus is, as it were, the type of the highest perfection of moral and intellectual nature, impelled by the purest and the truest motives to the best and noblest ends."[1] With these words from the preface of *Prometheus Unbound* (1820), Shelley defined the significance of his hero for the Romantics: Prometheus is the perfect rebel who, free of self-serving ambition, intercedes on behalf of humanity with the best intentions. "I wish," Prometheus declares, his principles still intact after three millennia in the Ravine of Icy Rocks, "no living thing to suffer pain."[2] For a long time we have called the German 1770s an age of Promethean rebellion, and with some justification: the "pure" rebellion typified by Prometheus was something that writers of the Sturm und Drang seemed constantly to have on their minds. Klinger's Guelfo fights for the resolution of inequities within the feudal system and the family; in act 2, scene 1, Schiller's Karl Moor speaks of his "größere Pläne";[3] and numerous figures call out for "Freiheit!" Yet most go on to disavow such ideals: Guelfo and Karl Moor are murderers, and even Goethe's Götz von Berlichingen, for all his virtue, unleashes a vicious attack on the bishop's troops and helps lead the bloody Peasants' Rebellion. The tradition simply did not produce many rebels with the unswerving sympathy for humanity that Promethean rebellion exemplified for the Romantics. With a reputation for intransigence rather than altruism, the typical protagonist of Sturm und Drang is driven not by "the truest motives" to "the best and noblest ends," but by ambition and revenge to acts of violence. Even Goethe's unfinished drama *Prometheus* (1773), the earliest Romantic version of Aeschylus's *Prometheus Bound*, suggests the tradition's uneasy relation to Promethean rebellion: although Goethe completed a short poem based on the fragment in 1785, he never brought the play to completion.[4] The rebellious impulses of Sturm und Drang are, finally, ambiguous, combining violence with spurious expressions of humanistic ideals.

The depth of this ambiguity has never been fully appreciated, however. In this chapter I proceed beyond the mere disparity between the humanism and the violence in these texts to consider how their authors attempt to reconcile impatient, Titanic self-assertion with principles an audience can share. Writers of the German 1770s were strongly attracted to the ethos of individualism contained in Preromantic currents of the British and French Enlightenment. Particularly inspired by refutations of authority delivered by Edward Young and Rousseau, they developed their own theory of the *Genie* whose originality would, it was hoped, help overcome the influence of French Neoclassicism while invigorating German culture. But this battle for autonomy and originality was based not only on poetics. In the mid-1770s, German dramatists found themselves creating the *Kraftmensch*, whose violence seems to sum up the essence of Sturm und Drang. Depicted most vividly by Friedrich Maximilian Klinger, the *Kraftmensch* expresses an impulsive individuality that appears to need no authority beyond itself. But depictions of the *Kraftmensch* derive much of their power and momentum from plots that systematically absolve the figure of all blame for its violence, and the impulsiveness expressed in Sturm und Drang is much less spontaneous, and more complicated, than is generally supposed. Recently, critics have tried to fit Sturm und Drang neatly into a homogeneous view of the European Enlightenment, tracing its trust in the senses to Locke and Hume, its violence to the class struggle, and its subjectivism to Shaftesbury's view of the artist as "a second Maker; a just Prometheus under Jove."[5] But such endeavors draw attention away from the tradition's singularity among eighteenth-century literary movements and especially from its relation to evolving German moral philosophy of the 1770s and early 1780s. My argument begins by suggesting a new way to look at Sturm und Drang's well-known propensity for "self-critique"; goes on to examine the textual exoneration of violence in three central dramas of the tradition—Goethe's *Götz von Berlichingen mit der eisernen Hand*, Klinger's *Die Zwillinge*, and Schiller's *Die Räuber*; and concludes with a discussion of Jakob Michael Reinhold Lenz, who by consistently bringing the issues of freedom and accountability to the surface writes drama whose exception helps "prove the rule" governing Sturm und Drang's exonerative texts.

The word *Kraftmensch* has a number of synonyms and near synonyms, most of them compounds with *Kraft* or *Macht*, such as *Kraftgenie* and *Machtmensch*. Grimms' dictionary defines *Kraftmensch* as "urkräftiger Mensch, Kraftnatur" and associates the term and its variations with *Genie* and "verstärktes Genie," while noting that the word has often been used derisively.[6] That *Kraftmensch* is now employed more often than its synonyms is probably due to the influence of H. A. Korff, who in *Geist der Goethezeit* applied the term to Götz, Karl Moor, Guelfo, and other figures of the age who, in situations usually sparked by an offended sense of justice, felt that they had the right—even the obligation—to violate the laws and standards of their communities, generally through violence toward the other members.[7] Quite unlike Werther, *Kraftmenschen* respond to frustration by bursting explosively into action, and underlying that action is a curious ambiguity: on the one hand, they exhibit righteous indignation, brutal honesty about their situation, and even a sense of allegiance to higher ideals; yet they also seem determined "to luxuriate in provocative irresponsibility."[8] It is an ambivalence figured also in the paradoxical attitude of Goethe's Prometheus, who claims, "Ich bin kein Gott," yet dares to assume the divine prerogative of creating human beings.[9]

Sturm und Drang's peculiar combination of the lawful and the arrogant did not go unnoticed by the authors themselves. In *Dichtung und Wahrheit*, Goethe claimed that the writing of *Werther* was a beneficial exercise in self-critique: "Ich hatte mich durch diese Composition mehr, als durch jede andere, aus einem stürmischen Elemente gerettet."[10] But the writer most aware of the self-defeating Titanism to which he gave expression was Klinger, who said that he used the violent tirades of his characters to pour out—"ausschütten"—emotions he found alarming.[11] In 1933 Kurt May noted a mixture of "Selbstentfaltung" and "Selbstmeisterung" in Klinger, arguing that his drama fights for a new way of life that leads outward toward society;[12] in the 1960s Christoph Hering detected in Klinger's early drama a blend of direct expression and inner distance, adding that Klinger "schreibt Tragödien, nicht vom Triumph, sondern Untergang des großen Kerls," who in Klinger's plays is "objektiviert und kritisch beurteilt";[13] and in 1970 Karl S. Guthke called Klinger's *Die Zwillinge* a simultaneous "Höhepunkt und Krise" of Sturm und Drang, noting that while Guelfo aspires to be a Titan, he comes across as childish.[14] Guthke argued that the play grew from Klinger's own desire for strength of character and (as Goethe had noted) Klinger's great respect for "Festigkeit und Beharrlichkeit."[15] In fact, a great many Sturm und Drang dramas end with compromises that seem to recant their rebellious impulses. The dramas of the Sturm und Drang, writes Jürgen Zenke, "steigern sich nicht zu revolutionärem Appell, sondern münden, sofern sie nicht tragisch enden, in notdürftiger Harmonie, Anpassungsversuchen, bestenfalls zweifelhaften Reformvorschlägen (Lenz)."[16] Ironically, even Klinger's drama *Sturm und Drang*, which gave the movement its name, ends peacefully when a family feud is resolved in act 5. Class critics have argued that such self-critique of volition reflects the German bourgeoisie's consciousness of self-defeat in a political situation they see as backward.[17] And Michael W. Jennings has studied the problem intertextually, pointing out two conflicting discourses of literary allusion in

Klinger—one reflecting rebellion, the other keeping rebellion in check: "Es führt lediglich dazu, diejenigen Menschen zu neutralisieren, die sonst einen progressiven gesellschaftlichen Einfluß hätten ausüben können."[18] At the very least, to speak only of Sturm und Drang's spontaneity and immediacy is to tell only half the story, for such expressions are retracted, resolved, and condemned in a variety of ways.

What are we to make of Sturm und Drang's ambiguous attitude toward its own impulses? The concept of an apogee and crisis of childish Titanism is certainly attractive in its simplicity. But its dependence on the idiosyncrasies of Klinger's personality and its charge of immaturity make it a dead end for any critic who takes the movement's deep interest in freedom and impulsiveness seriously. Let me suggest that we adopt a broader and more sympathetic approach to the problem of Sturm und Drang's internal self-critique by imagining the overall pattern of the tradition simply as a sharp ideological turn—a turn in which irresponsible impulsiveness finds itself in the process of correcting itself by an appeal to rules of conduct that can help make it accountable. A glance at Herder's changing concept of the *Genie* in 1774 and 1775, during the flourishing of Sturm und Drang drama, helps support this view. By the late 1760s, Herder's aesthetic was firmly grounded in a theory of the *Genie* that embraced Shaftesbury's notion of the artist as a "second creator under God," but not his concept of the creator as a "moral artist." More under the influence of Young than Shaftesbury or Addison, Herder downplayed the role of learning in favor of the entirely untutored genius who was educated, he wrote in 1767, by "Leidenschaft und Empfindung."[19] "So bildet ein Genie sich selbst," he wrote, "und tritt auf einmal gebildet hervor, um die Bewunderung der Welt zu sein."[20] It was clearly an "aristocratic" theory of genius: "Es gibt Ausnahmen höherer Gattung, und meist alles Merkwürdige der Welt geschieht durch diese Ausnahmen."[21] And it was tied to a distinctly mystical theory of individuality in which, even as late as 1774, the individual was conceived as "eine unaussprechliche Sache."[22]

But there soon came a change in Herder's concept of the genius. In the essay "Ursachen des gesunkenen Geschmacks" (1775), we find Herder tracing the decline of taste in various cultures precisely to the freely creating genius he had formerly praised—namely, the *Genie* that "wird sich von selbst bilden."[23] We now see him arguing that the artist's rejection of "langsame Bildung zum Geschmack" leads to "falschen Geschmack, eine verführende, negative Größe."[24] Referring to this sudden change in Herder's thinking, Herman Wolf noted, in 1925, "Statt der Verherrlichung des autonomen, gigantischen intuitiv-irrational schaffenden Genies wird die 'Bescheidenheit' des von der 'göttlichen,' 'königlichen' Vernunft geleitet, vom Geschmack geführten Genies gepriesen."[25] By the time of the early, 1774 version of his essay "Vom Erkennen und Empfinden der menschlichen Seele," but especially in its last two versions, in 1775 and 1778, the key terms in Herder's aesthetic—now firmly under the control of *Geschmack*—are *Vernunft, Ordnung, Ebenmaas,* and *Mitgefühl.*[26] The *Genie,* he says, should strive to become "den humanisierten Gott der Erde," and he declares, "Die beiden großen Triebfedern aller Menschenhandlungen sind Selbst- und Mitgefühl."[27] Herder's new view of the artist is neither one-sided nor aristocratic: capable of "allgemeines Mitgefühl," the *Genie* "hat Ausbreitung nötig, damit es unter einer Empfindung nicht erläge."[28]

In rejecting his own transcendental theory of the *Genie,* Herder fell in with other members of Sturm und Drang who were rapidly becoming aware of the need to build regulative principles into their conception of individuality. Yet even more fascinating than the widespread and systematic character of this process is its affinity to similar currents in the emerging critical philosophy of Kant. While Herder corrected his view of the genius, and while Goethe and Klinger wrote their dramatic versions of individualism, Kant was busy writing the *Critique of Pure Reason* (1781), where he began to work out his ideas on human freedom even before formulating the principle of autonomy in the *Groundwork of the Metaphysics of Morals* (1785). As Bernard Carnois, Henry E. Allison, and others have pointed out, Kant struggled, in the *Critique of Pure Reason,* to bring two aspects of freedom into equilibrium: transcendental freedom, derived subjectively from the nature of reason and therefore independent of everything empirical; and practical freedom, which is relevant to human actions. Kant's early work toward developing the concept of autonomy "appears faintly even in the First Critique."[29] There we see Kant deciding whether the pure spontaneity of transcendental freedom—"das Vermögen, einen Zustand von selbst anzufangen"[30]—is, as Norman Kemp Smith puts it, "a purely speculative question with which Reason in its practical employment is not in the least concerned,"[31] or whether such spontaneity might need to be preserved as a prerequisite of morality. "Der Kanon der reinen Vernunft," one of the oldest sections of the *Critique of Pure Reason,* contains a seemingly "precritical" version of freedom, for here Kant suggests that practical freedom has no need of spontaneous, transcendental freedom, since the latter appears to be "dem Naturgesetze, mithin aller möglichen Erfahrung, zuwider . . . "[32] But in his analysis of the third antinomy in the Transcendental Dialectic, he is obviously aware of what is lost if transcendental freedom is discarded: "so würd die Aufhebung der transzendentalen Freiheit zugleich alle praktische Freiheit vertilgen."[33]

From this early encounter with the problem of finding the correct relation between a spontaneous form of freedom and a form relevant to practical experience, Kant moved toward developing the principle of autonomy, which made transcendental freedom a postulate of practical freedom while claiming, at the same time, that we are free only through our consciousness of standing under a moral law. Although Kant, who criticized Sturm und Drang for its undisciplined *Schwärmerei*, was at first skeptical about the value of an entirely spontaneous form of freedom, he finally gave it an important role in human conduct, however gradually and cautiously he proceeded.[34] Thus it turns out that there is a certain symmetry between Kant's thought on freedom and the views of the Sturm und Drang. Kant, acknowledging the necessity of giving spontaneity a role in morality, merges transcendental freedom with the rule-bound world of practical freedom; writers of Sturm und Drang, acknowledging the necessity of giving morality a role in spontaneity, merge the rule-bound strategy of absolution with the apparently spontaneous world of the violent protagonist. Kant, at first wary of a form of freedom unmediated by experience, eventually makes spontaneity an unavoidable ingredient in human conduct, whereas Sturm und Drang finds itself "making a fetish of spontaneity" while at the same time producing texts that acknowledge the need for principles of accountability.[35]

Goethe's *Götz von Berlichingen* displays just such an ambiguous relation toward unregulated freedom. An anachronistic *Reichsritter* who has somehow remained in tune with older ways despite far-reaching political changes, Götz rebels against a culture that has all but lost its capacity to support inspiring, seemingly spontaneous individualism. In the new, more organized but less "human" feudal government to which he must submit, the mercenary is as important as the knight, and the distinctive individual no longer plays a key role. Nevertheless, Götz insists on the validity of the older, unbureaucratic, "natural" government of personality—which he thinks results in greater freedom for everyone—though his community of followers has been almost completely absorbed into the feudal system. Even his closest friend, Weislingen, has left him for the pleasures of courtly life. What Götz does not understand is that his instinctual drives are not politically valid principles, that his "God-sanctioned" freedom is not in harmony with his loyalty to the emperor. Götz, writes Frank Ryder, "has never seen any conflict between the two. Far from it. They exist as mutually supporting components of a vigorous, functioning ideal of freedom."[36]

And he attempts to sustain his rule of personality even in situations where his sense of justice leads to violence. After unleashing a second bloody attack on the bishop's troops in act 3, he feels he can still declare, "Ich bin kein Rebell."[37] He has no trouble sustaining a vision of a world where the individual and universal principles continually invigorate each other: "Das wäre ein Leben, Georg!" Götz declares after he, Elizabeth, and Georg toast freedom in act 3, "wenn man seine Haut für die allgemeine Glückseligkeit dran setzte."[38] Götz's quixotic capacity to act as if such a world actually existed may well be part of the reason that Goethe characterized him in *Dichtung und Wahrheit* as "der wohldenkende brave Mann."[39] But the 1773 drama also depicts an embarrassing gap between the inspirational power of Götz's rhetoric and the position in which Götz and his followers find themselves at that moment: at the end of Götz's long salute to the way things once were, Georg suddenly jumps up. "Wo willst du hin?" Götz asks, and Georg answers, "Ach ich vergaß, daß wir eingesperrt sind."[40]

Such dialogue helps point up the incongruity of Götz's individualism—an individualism that inspires, but also leads to violence and culpability. Goethe, however, finds a way to overcome this incongruity by placing Götz in a situation that allows him to follow his instincts and vent his frustrations, yet still appear innocent of any wrongdoing, for forces beyond his control assume the blame for his actions. The play's exonerative strategy begins immediately in act 1, scene 1, with the introduction of Sievers and Metzler, two leaders of the Peasants' Rebellion. They play a central role in the text's absolution of Götz because they ultimately force him, by threats, to be the titular leader of their cause and thus give it the right appearance. Sympathetic with Götz's desire to express himself, Goethe constructed a text that goes out of its way to see that events conspire against the protagonist at every level. The coming rebellion is portrayed as a matter over which no one has control. Allusions are made to a recent tornado, the sight of two fiery swords in the sky, and a comet[41]—omens that signal the revolt's inevitability but that have the more important goal of underscoring Götz's innocence. "Ich komme mir vor wie der böse Geist, den der Capuziner in einen Sack beschwur," Götz says in a moment of insight at the beginning of act 4. "Ich arbeite mich ab und fruchte mir nichts."[42] "Er ist unschuldig," cries Maria, "so strafbar er scheint."[43] Even Weislingen absolves Götz. Dying in act 5 after being poisoned by Adelheid and feeling remorseful about his intrigue against Götz, he blames fate for his own treachery: "Götz! Götz!—Wir Menschen führen uns nicht selbst; bösen Geistern ist Macht über uns gelassen, daß sie ihren höllischen Muthwillen an unserm Verderben üben."[44]

Adding further to the sense of a miscarriage of justice—and supplemented, of course, by the complex intrigue leading from the bishop, through Adelheid, to Weislingen—is Götz's sentencing by secret tribunal. "Schließt eure Herzen sorgfältiger als eure Thore," warns Götz before he expires, and Elizabeth adds: "Die Welt ist ein Gefängniß."[45] We have seen Götz on the attack in both his encounters with imperial troops. We have seen him as the leader of plundering rebels who have put innocent women and children on the run for their lives. But Götz is a Titan whose guilt is mitigated by the exceptional situation in which he finds himself. Goethe allows his protagonist to ventilate frustrations with a situation in which individualism does not seem to function as it should. The self-exonerative pattern of Götz's rebellion sets the tone for Sturm und Drang as a movement dealing in "safe" individualism, individualism with an excuse.[46]

In the drama of Klinger, the raging ego comes to the forefront while the special circumstances that forgive it recede into the background— a difference that separates Klinger's *Kraftmensch* from the more obviously sympathetic Götz. Guelfo of *Die Zwillinge* is provided with a number of excuses to convert his sense of injustice into revenge. First, there is the event that sparks Guelfo's rage: the suspicion that he has been deprived of the rights of the firstborn. When he tries to learn whether he or his twin brother, Ferdinando, came into the world first, he receives only vague answers from the physician who attended the birth. Adding to Guelfo's suspicions (as well as our own), his father seems truly to dislike him. Finally, unable to accept his parents' assurances that Ferdinando is the rightful heir and convinced that his own combative character would make him the better ruler, Guelfo murders his brother on what was to have been Ferdinando's wedding day. But as Hering has noted, it is Grimaldi who plays the key role in inciting Guelfo to revenge, chiefly by pretending to be in awe of him: "Dieser Blick! dieses Wesen! diese sich ausbreitende menschenbeugende Gluth im schwarze, grossen, rollenden Auge!—Guelfo! Du bist für ein Königreich geboren. Eine weissagende Gottheit, mein Genius sagt mirs. Guelfo! Du bist Ferdinandos Bruder nicht."[47] This praise for Guelfo has a selfish motive: Grimaldi wants to avenge himself on Ferdinando for preventing his marriage to Juliette, who, he says, had chosen to die of grief rather than accept a marriage forced on her.[48] Grimaldi would commit the murder himself, but by his odd reckoning the crime would prevent his eventual reunion with Juliette in the beyond, whereas convincing Guelfo to murder Ferdinando would not. Borrowing the tactic Iago uses with Othello, Grimaldi tries to keep himself above suspicion by pretending to want to calm Guelfo: "Du wirst zu ernsthaft";[49] "Lieber Guelfo, nicht so!"[50] Guelfo is marginally aware of Grimaldi's deceit: "Du machst mich rasend mit Deiner Zweydeutigkeit. . . . Du sagst zu viel und zu wenig."[51] Still, Guelfo succumbs to Grimaldi's flattery and commits the crime—providing Grimaldi with revenge and providing Klinger with a protagonist who can indulge in impulsiveness while making only a minimal effort to abide by the community's rules of conduct. The specious reasoning behind Grimaldi's desire for revenge is an improbable aspect of the plot, but Klinger is willing to sacrifice verisimilitude to make the blame for Guelfo's murder of his brother come from without. *Die Zwillinge* also contains a dramatic "rhetoric" of predetermination similar to that found in *Götz von Berlichingen*—here, instead of a comet and swords in the sky, the ringing of nocturnal church bells and the destruction of Ferdinando's favorite tree are the supernatural portents that help justify the violence. Klinger goes to great lengths to disperse blame for the crime, and as Edward P. Harris points out, Guelfo's motivation remains one of Klinger's concerns in every subsequent revision of the play.[52]

Klinger is Sturm und Drang's expert in creating plots that shift the blame for the protagonist's recklessness onto others: in *Die neue Arria* (1776), Solina is blamed for inciting Julio in his revolt against a corrupt court; in *Sturm und Drang*, the hostility between the Berkleys and the Bushys is attributed at least in part to an unnamed third party who has set the families against each other for his or her own advantage. Still, Klinger is not alone. In *Golo und Genoveva* (1775/1781), Friedrich Müller adopts a similar strategy: inflamed by his passion for Genoveva, Golo commits murder, but remains above reproach because he falls under the pernicious influence of Mathilde, who refers to herself as a deus ex machina—and who even forgives him later when he mortally wounds her. Each of these dramas depicts aggressive impulses while excusing them. Guthke is right: there is a childish side to figures like Guelfo, for they seem to run blindly into their problems, as if giving little thought to the consequences of their decisions. But it is important to note the carefully wrought background of this behavior, for the intention of these dramatists is to pave the way for expressions of subjectivity in a world that still recognizes the need for rule-bound behavior. Unwilling—and perhaps unable—to depict a form of autonomy that merges naturally with shared principles, writers of Sturm und Drang permitted protagonists to rage with impunity while settling accounts with the community artificially. And in displaying the promise of individualism, they found themselves producing a devious sort of drama—one in which figures rebel violently even as all Titanism is retracted elsewhere in the text. Behind Götz's elegiac lament for the loss of charismatic leadership, and behind Grimaldi's use of insincere flattery as a weapon to persuade Guelfo that he has the right to kill, is an acknowledgment, however makeshift, that our autonomy depends on the very collectivity that we would like to believe we can rise above.

"The individual," wrote Howard Mumford Jones, speaking of the early Romantic rebel, "existed at a crossroad where his private impulses met his publicly avowed relations."[53] German writers, in particular, lacking a stable society to depict and feeling suspicious of a prescriptive Neoclassical tradition, were strongly attracted to the seemingly viable alternative that Rousseau's individualism offered to the polite society of the French. But the promise of individualism led them also to the difficult, perhaps unsolvable, problem of reconciling freedom and responsibility—a problem that they, like Kant, would solve on their own terms. The *Kraftmensch* takes individualism to the extreme, seeming at times not to believe that a crossroads, a middle ground, of public and private realms is possible. By assuming the correctness of either the individual or the law, but not both, the *Kraftmensch* polarizes the world into the irreconcilable opposites of inner impulse and outer authority. The result is a self-destructive antinomy that logically opposes the socializing aims out of which, at least to some extent, the figure rose in the first place. Fighting for "das Große und Unbedingte" can easily end in preventing a satisfying reciprocal relation between individualism and the rules within which it must operate.[54]

If I am right in characterizing Sturm und Drang as a tradition operating along a sharp ideological turn toward accountability, where it tries also to preserve a critical mass of unregulated individualism—and if this attempt to reconcile spontaneity and accountability is an inelegant version of Kant's own reconciliation of freedom and law in the principle of autonomy—then there may be another way to look at the famous predilection, in Sturm und Drang drama, for the repetition of words and phrases. Repetition is nothing new in drama, but critics have often felt that Sturm und Drang uses the device with new urgency.[55] Certainly many of its characters seem to feel that they have no way to make themselves understood other than through incessant reiteration: "O, diese Nacht! diese Nacht! und der morgende Tag! Ich seh dich wieder! und dein Bild, das bey mir bleibt, das mich hinüber führt—ich seh dich wieder. (*starr zum Himmel.*) Ich seh sie wieder! seh dich wieder, wie jetzt!"[56] Such repetition, insofar as it can depict individuality's urge for expression by emphasizing its own search for a rule of conduct, may simply express these writers' inherent awareness that only through the repeated actions of individuals does the practical world ever have a chance to become coherent. For impersonating the whole by the part, the original by the mimetic, was a talent in which eighteenth-century Germans seemed especially deficient. Germans of the age tried, but seemed unable, to play at being individuals while engaging simultaneously in rule-bound experience. "Es ist traurig an einem Ort zu leben," Goethe wrote to Salzmann while working on *Götz* in November 1771, "wo unsre ganze Wirksamkeit in sich selbst summen muß."[57] Although inspired by the promise of individualism, authors discovered that even individuality cannot exist without a fund of readily repeatable rules. It may be that the largest role played by *Götz* in the development of Sturm und Drang was to show Goethe's contemporaries that individuality had lost its ability to resonate within the collectivity and still reflect flatteringly on itself. Feeling as poor in gifts as Guelfo, for whom a gratifying sense of having a vital role in society could be produced only artificially, writers found themselves dealing with the problem of autonomy by legitimating individual expression in ever more complex and devious ways.

There is an enormous difference between the impromptu (Sturm und Drang Titanism's immediate impression) and the planned (the exonerative strategies of these texts). Yet the most famous Titan of all was himself a conscious "planner": Sturm und Drang contains an unmistakable measure of the cunning, the "forethought" of Prometheus, who in Hesiod stole fire for humankind and tricked Zeus into choosing the less desirable parts of animals to be sacrificed. In quite similar fashion, creators of the *Kraftmensch* also offer the insubstantial in the guise of the substantial. According to Nietzsche, human beings invented this devious half-God for the express purpose of allowing themselves to enjoy forbidden, Dionysian fire (originally the exclusive possession of God) without having to shoulder the blame for its theft,

> daß aber der Mensch frei über das Feuer waltet und es nicht nur durch ein Geschenk vom Himmel, als zündenden Blitzstrahl oder wärmenden Sonnenbrand, empfängt, erschien jenen beschaulichen Ur-Menschen als ein Frevel, als ein Raub an der göttlichen Natur. Und so stellt gleich das erste philosophische Problem einen peinlichen unlösbaren Widerspruch zwischen Mensch und Gott hin und rückt ihn wie einen Felsblock an die Pforte jeder Kultur.[58]

Titans of the German 1770s, tortured as much by their inescapable need for the affirmation of the group as by their desire to lose themselves in "Dionysian" individualism, refuse to occupy the no-man's-land of absolute subjectivity—thus the tradition's strategy of absolution, which amounts to an acknowledgment of the ethical responsibility that persists even when impulsiveness is allowed expression. It was chiefly as the rebellious benefactor of humanity that Prometheus captured the imagination of the Romantics, not as the thief who stole fire from heaven and deceived Zeus. Yet Sturm und Drang, when it gave Promethean rebellion its first Romantic treatment, drew heavily on these more devious features of the legend.

The split in Sturm und Drang's conceptualization of Titanism belongs to the well-known paradox of the "original genius," from whom eighteenth-century aesthetics demanded two mutually exclusive qualities: first, spontaneity and originality; and second, the ability to make such spontaneity and originality fit in with the experience of others. But the contradictory need to plan the unprompted was, of course, not the exclusive property of the eighteenth century—or, for that matter, of aesthetics. Western culture has been required to plan the unplannable whenever it has faced the difficult task of making individuality comprehensible enough to be appreciated. The doctrine of Christian grace, for example, emphasizes the value of the unique human soul while offering the promise of eventual entry to the universal order of God. The ὕψος recommended by Longinus promises an individualistic effect by flattering listeners for qualities they already have in common with one another. And Winckelmann, anticipating Hegel's idea of the concrete universal, speaks of the "inimitable" ancient Greek sculpture whose imitation can help unify society. Each of these represents a way to put a high value on individuality while arguing—as Kant would— that autonomy relies on shared conditions.

Safe, exonerated individualism was responsible for a stunning theatrical effect in 1781, when Schiller discovered how to use an absolved Titan to convince spectators that they could appreciate violent individualism on the basis of shared principles. "He is innocent," Maria had said of Götz, "no matter how blameworthy he seems." Not until this attitude could be fully embraced by an audience could the violent yet inspiring individuality sought by Sturm und Drang find full expression. With *Die Räuber*, Schiller managed to simulate precisely those principles that *Götz von Berlichingen* saw in decline: direct personal activity, oaths of allegiance, and charismatic leadership. The belief that the pious are often branded as heretics and that the real church is found among the persecuted (not in official ceremonies) stands behind Schiller's transformation of the *Kraftmensch*, in *Die Räuber*, from a destructive to a unifying figure. Schiller did as much as Goethe and Klinger to give the hero a valid excuse to rage: Karl's real enemy is his brother Franz, who has deceived Karl into believing that his father has rejected him. Here, as in Goethe and Klinger, the antagonist's deceit not only triggers the protagonist's rage; it works to the advantage of the protagonist, for it lets him pull out all the emotional stops and yet still have an excuse for any moral transgression. Schiller, however, goes one important step further: he takes the same surreptitious flattery with which Grimaldi boosted Guelfo's image of himself and uses it to provide the audience—not just a character in his play—with invigorating feelings of self-worth.

Die Räuber persuades spectators to flatter themselves with the belief that they can see the "greater plans" that stand behind this man who would repel the ordinary person. "Man wird," Schiller wrote in his original preface to the play, "meinen Mordbrenner bewundern, ja fast sogar lieben."[59] Schiller's exonerative text worked in the theater like no other play of Sturm und Drang—and revealed at last that the *Kraftmensch* was never an antisocial being but, rather, a figure struggling to unite spontaneous individualism with shared principles. Imitated and adapted more than any other drama of its age, *Die Räuber* made spectators forgive Karl for his crimes while convincing them to measure their moral depth by their capacity to sympathize with his frustration. Just before the play reaches its peak in act 5, even Karl seems to be infected by this audience worked up to a frenzy of forgiveness, for he virtually forgives himself, falling on his knees to thank God for making him captain of a robber band because it allows him to avenge his father. "Heute hat eine unsichtbare Macht unser Handwerk geadelt."[60] Schiller's first play, which hit a responsive chord with a public ready to flatter itself for its shared understanding of a character's otherwise horrible crimes, brings Sturm und Drang's interest in expressing absolved lawlessness into focus as does no other drama of the tradition.[61]

Thus lawlessness in *Die Räuber*, as in *Götz* and *Die Zwillinge*, finds itself absolved through a network of casuistry undergirding—and artificially legitimating—its expressions of impulsiveness. The texts considered here reveal an acute awareness of the transgression of the *Kraftmensch* precisely through their ambitious attempts to mitigate it. If we look for precedents to Sturm und Drang's tactic of shifting blame away from the protagonist, we find a similar gesture in Genesis 3.12–14, where God accuses Adam of eating the apple. Adam immediately responds not by turning to God and expressing sorrow for offending his benefactor, but by pointing to Eve as the real culprit, who in turn accuses the serpent. But no ontological ladder of blame mars the triumph of the *Kraftmensch*. In the exonerative texts of Goethe, Klinger, and Schiller, all is sacrificed to the urge for a greater sense of self-confidence; the transgressor need not shrink away from God in fear.

And the result is judgment and salvation in a different key, where the shifting of blame receives new credibility at the hands of the dramatist. The difficult issue of freedom versus law is reduced simply to crafting the right kind of plot.

Among dramatists of Sturm und Drang, only J. M. R. Lenz resists the temptation to design texts that justify every transgression. Lenz brings matters of responsibility to the surface, frequently depicting characters going overboard to accept responsibility for their acts. After impregnating his employers' daughter and having been told that she has committed suicide out of despair, Läuffer of *Der Hofmeister* emasculates himself. Fritz von Berg, her absent and inattentive boyfriend, also rushes to take the blame for the attempted suicide: "Meine Schuld! (*Steht auf.*) Meine Schuld einzig und allein—"[62] In the world Lenz depicts, our fates are so closely interwoven that it is hard to evade responsibility to others. Characters who sidestep the demands of accountability are immediately exposed and made to face the implications of their refusal to be responsible for their decisions. As Marie, in *Die Soldaten*, sets her sights on the aristocrat Desportes, she reconsiders the promises she had made to her fiancé Stolzius: "Gott was hab ich denn Böses getan?—Stolzius—ich lieb dich ja noch—aber wenn ich nun mein Glück besser machen kann—und Pappa selber mir den Rat gibt. . . ."[63] Before long, however, she is miserable. In act 3, Gräfin de la Roche tries to comfort her by proclaiming that her bad reputation is not really her fault but merely a fact deriving from her innocence regarding class differences—and from her reading of Richardson's *Pamela*. Lenz, however, will not let Marie off so easily. For as we know already from the opening scenes of the play, Marie understands class differences so well that she can even adapt her own speech along class lines when it is to her advantage. And if Marie's liability is not yet clear, her response to la Roche's attempt to shift the blame to *Pamela* removes all doubt. Marie's reply is, simply, "Ich kenne das Buch ganz und gar nicht."[64]

Preferring to deal in a style of volition more honest than that of other writers of the tradition, Lenz bans the *Kraftmensch* from his drama, using forceful language only when needed to characterize figures— the students in *Der Hofmeister*, the soldiers in *Die Soldaten*—or to achieve verisimilitude. Once, when accused of creating an excessively explosive figure in Donna Diana of *Der neue Menoza* (1774), Lenz was quick to deny the charge: "Ich kann also dafür nicht, wenn Donna Diana gewissen Herren zu rasen scheint, die die menschliche Natur nur immer im Schnürleib der Etikette zu sehen gewohnt sind, und daß es solche Empfindungen gebe, können die, die in ähnlichen Umständen gewesen sind, doch nicht in Abrede sein."[65] Having sworn off the *Kraftmensch,* Lenz is free of the obligation to construct texts that justify—and retract spontaneity from—every impulse. And because his texts are free of such underlying architecture, he can, even with his mundane plots, depict individuality with more spontaneity than Goethe, Klinger, or Schiller could. In *Der neue Menoza,* Wilhelmine's initial refusal to marry Prinz Tandi is more true-to-life precisely because it does not follow from her earlier behavior—because, in other words, it seems entirely unmotivated. The same is true in *Der Hofmeister,* where Pätus engages in friendly banter with Frau Blitzer, then suddenly, with the provocation of only a mild insult, throws her coffeepot out the window.

In Lenz, it is clear that ideas are not always sovereign over actions: what we get is the spontaneous act deprived of every surrounding element that could undo its disturbingly unexpected character. When thought processes do take over, as they do in many of Lenz's final scenes, the spontaneous idea becomes an object of parody. *Die Soldaten* ends with the ridiculous suggestion (which Lenz seems never to have taken seriously) that prostitutes be provided for soldiers, who threatened to corrupt young middle-class women; and in the last scene of *Der Hofmeister,* Gustchen's illegitimate child is cited as one of the "advantages" of private tutelage, while Läuffer finds a wife—a young woman who pops out of nowhere and declares her indifference to his physical impairment. While the dramas of Lenz are already well known for their patient observation of behavioral and linguistic patterns, these texts do much more than merely draw our attention to specific social contexts and their rules—or to the determinism in our lives. They deal with the difference between two forms of freedom, spontaneity, and responsibility—one with, the other without, the support of the text.

Yet Lenz is the exception to the rule; most often it is the impatient muse that these dramatists hear, and the theater of the *Kraftmensch* dominates the tradition. The *Kraftmensch* displays a style of Titanism quite different from that expressed in the tradition of Promethean rebellion stretching from Shaftesbury to Shelley and Byron: its spontaneity is far less authentic, its concern for humanity far less "pure." Writers of the German 1770s, with an urge to depict characters challenging God with confidence, also share Kant's doubts about spontaneous freedom. And like Kant, they find a way to allow unregulated freedom to flourish while remaining conscious of the need for shared rules of conduct. Their own solution to the problem does not possess the elegant simplicity of Kant's concept of autonomy; instead, it preserves tensions inherent in the question from the start. Instead of expressing unbroken sympathy for humanity, literature depicting the *Kraftmensch* develops another, more devious side of the Prometheus legend. The result is still a Titan, but a Titan in extenuating circumstances. Sturm und Drang bequeaths its unusual form of individualism to Weimar Classicism, whose most famous text, Goethe's *Faust*, rose from a sympathy for the Renaissance magician already widespread among German writers of the age. Pardoned for every moral infraction committed during his long quest for knowledge and creativity, Faust would become the greatest imperfect rebel, the greatest forgiven Titan of them all—and a figure more than worthy of the strophe of Goethe's early "Prometheus" ode that reads:

> Wähntest du etwa,
> Ich sollte das Leben hassen,
> In Wüsten fliehen,
> Weil nicht alle
> Blüthenträume reiften?[66]

But that is the *Faust* of 1808; its early draft, the subject of the next chapter, is a very different sort of text.

5. The Forgotten Drama:
Goethe's Early Draft of *Faust*

We know very little about the early history of the most famous drama in the German language. It appears that Goethe conceived *Faust I* sometime between 1769 and 1771, yet it is not until 1774, after he completed both *Götz von Berlichingen* and *Werther*, that we receive news of the play.[1] The first reports come from his Frankfurt visitors: in October 1774, Heinrich Christian Boie (1744–1806) writes of reading sections of Goethe's "Doktor Faust"; in December, Karl Ludwig von Knebel (1744–1834) tells us that he saw several "herrliche Szenen" from Goethe's play in progress; and in January, Johann Georg Zimmerman reports that Goethe read him part of his new drama.[2] Goethe himself does not mention the play until the following September, and then only briefly in a letter to Auguste Luise Stolberg (1753–1835): "Ich machte eine Szene an meinem *Faust*."[3] And so it is that while the genesis of *Faust II* is richly documented, for *Faust I* we are thrown back entirely upon the early draft—"Goethe's gift to philologists," R. M. Browning called it—for answers to basic questions. Why, in the early draft, does Faust's character change so abruptly when he meets Margarete? Were the scholar's tragedy and the Gretchen tragedy meant to be two separate plays? And if not, why was Goethe unable—or unwilling—to mold the scenes into a unified composition already in the 1770s? "Die Erforschung des *Urfaust*," writes Valters Nollendorfs in the most complete study of the early draft of *Faust*, "ist eine der verwickeltsten Aufgaben der Literaturwissenschaft, besonders, weil man hier so wenig auf Tatsachen, so viel auf Deutungen und Gedankengebäude angewiesen ist. Deshalb besitzt auch das Urfaustproblem eine anhaltende Anziehungskraft und führt immer wieder zu neuen Auseinandersetzungen."[4]

Given the title *Urfaust* by Erich Schmidt in 1887, the earliest known draft of *Faust I* was found among the papers of Luise von Göchhausen (1752–1807), who transcribed it in her literary diary during Goethe's first years in Weimar.[5] About half the length of *Faust I*, the *Urfaust* lacks a "Zueignung," a "Vorspiel auf dem Theater," and a "Prolog im Himmel." It begins with the "Nacht" scene, which, shortly after the entry of Wagner, breaks off, beginning what critics have come to call "die große Lücke." Here *Faust I* will contain more dialogue with Wagner, followed by the suicide monologue, the Easter chorus, "Vor dem Tor," and the first "Studierzimmer" scene. But the draft does not continue again until approximately two-thirds of the way through what would become *Faust I*'s second study scene, where Mephistopheles interviews the prospective student.[6] After "Auerbachs Keller" there is no "Hexenküche," although from "Strase" to "Kerker" the *Urfaust*'s Gretchen tragedy proceeds rather coherently. While there is no "Wald und Höhle" scene, the last twenty-eight lines of the *Urfaust*'s very brief "Nacht. Vor Gretgens Haus" show up near the end of *Faust I*'s "Wald und Höhle." In the *Urfaust*, "Dom" appears before, not after, "Nacht. Vor Gretgens Haus." And finally, the *Urfaust* contains neither a "Walpurgisnacht" nor a "Walpurgisnachtstraum." The scene called "Trüber Tag" in *Faust I* is unnamed, while "Kerker," one of the scenes most changed, appears in the *Urfaust* in prose and does not conclude with a saving voice from above. Few texts have undergone such a long and complex process of editing and rewriting as *Faust*, whose second part Goethe finished just five days before he died. The drama remained unfinished so long that it appeared in the 1790 edition of Goethe's works as a fragment.[7]

By contrast, *Werther* was composed in a few weeks. How do we explain the slow process of *Faust*'s creation? The central problem with the writing of the play, of course, was that Goethe was confronted with the difficult task of pressing diverse material together into one text: the scholar's tragedy with which the *Urfaust* begins had to be reconciled with the middle-class "Gretchen tragedy." The task was parallel to others undertaken by writers of Sturm und Drang, with their impatience to reconcile their urge for power and completeness with the misgivings of German *Kleinstaaterei*. And it is a task Goethe had faced, and solved, once before, when he let the "iron hand" of the rebellious Götz find itself in accord with apparently unstoppable historical and supernatural forces. But the *Urfaust* is different. What is the source of the stubborn lack of harmony here, in Sturm und Drang's most famous fragment, between Germany and what its writers wanted it to be? Unlike *Werther*, where Goethe shows readers the uncanny power of the German inner life and the spoken word, the *Urfaust* shows us what the inner life and the spoken word *cannot* do. Refusing to engage in a casuistry that denies the rift between what Germans want and what they have, Goethe writes a play that lacks a unifying principle until, at the turn of the century, he invents his famous Romantic mythology of a God who rewards striving. But what does Goethe leave behind— what does he forget—when he completes his *Faust*? The play's early draft is one of the genuinely honest texts of the tradition; its open texture reveals at the same time something about Germany and about the temptations writers faced to create texts that were merely surrogates for a missing sense of community. In what follows I would like to show how the *Urfaust* moves from the vocal, performance-based sensibility of Werther, Lavater, and the drama of the *Kraftmensch*, toward a very different kind of literary work. I also hope to suggest, on the example of *Faust*'s genesis, that Sturm und Drang is in one sense just the opposite of a preface to the literature of the 1790s, and that Weimar Classicism involved a forgetting of some of the central issues with which writers grappled in the 1770s.

If Sturm und Drang means fragmentation, then the *Urfaust* is the eye of the storm. But there is something in this fragmented draft that we have not seen in texts we have looked at up until now: patience, a desire to slow down, and a pronounced honesty about Germany that we will see again only in the work of J. M. R. Lenz. Goethe tells us in *Dichtung und Wahrheit* that he began *Faust* at about the same time he began *Werther*. Yet "Nacht," the first scene of the *Urfaust*, already brings significant progress beyond Goethe's 1774 novel. When Faust succeeds in incanting his way to one sort of absolute—with black magic, not the rhetoric of Lavater or the literary tastes of Werther—the first thing he discovers is that the approach is a dead end. For in the "Nacht" of the *Urfaust*, altered very little in *Faust I*, the Earth Spirit rebukes Faust:

> Du gleichst dem Geist den du begreiffst,
> Nicht mir!

The rebuke, which Faust answers with the lame

> Nicht dir!
> Wem denn?

> (24)

alerts us to the fact that Faust's powers are not as effective as he would like them to be. This will be a drama about a form of self-realization that goes beyond mere incantation—verbal, magical, or otherwise. "The fundamental aim of magic," wrote E. M. Butler, "is to impose the human will on nature, on man, or on the supersensual world in order to master them."[8] But Goethe's version of the Faust legend moves away from the conception of Faust as a magician: very early in the play Faust condemns the magic of words. Immediately after the Earth Spirit's departure, Wagner comes on the scene with the question:

> Verzeiht! ich hört euch deklamiren!
> Ihr last gewiß ein griechisch Trauerspiel

In dieser Kunst mögt ich was profitiren
Denn heutzutage würkt das viel.

(24)

The conversation that ensues revolves around the feebleness, not the power, of rhetoric, which Faust calls a mere "Puppenspiel" (25). Here, where the scholar's tragedy ends and the Gretchen tragedy begins, precisely at the split between the two plays that make it up, we get a condemnation of rhetoric, a refusal to participate in traditional linguistic rituals that join speakers with audiences. Since the monologue in "Nacht," there can be no doubt that Faust wants desperately to find a new way to reconcile himself with absolutes. But neither he nor Goethe has found it.

Very possibly, Goethe was attracted to the Faust story precisely because it dealt with the same incantatory language to which Werther fell prey. As Frank Baron points out, the opposition of word and substance runs through Goethe's *Faust* already in the first version like a leitmotif.[9] The rebuke of the Earth Spirit inspires Faust to take a slower and more honest path to the absolute; it sparks his recoil away from incantatory words, words that are little more than solipsistic, flattering self-images. To a great extent, the rebuke prepares him for the pact with the devil, where his dreams, propelled formerly by speech, are now forced to make compromises with a real, empirical world, with limits and conditions. Yet even without the invention of the Earth Spirit, it would be hard to imagine a plot better suited to dealing in the sober acceptance of responsibility than the Faust legend, for a pact signed in blood makes the implications of one's actions in the world as clear as possible. When Faust the idealist joins the cynical Mephistopheles, it means that the untouchable heights of Lavater's *Aussichten*, Werther's eternity—even the irreproachable *Kraftmensch*—are suddenly tempered by considerations of realism. Far less confident in purely verbal solutions, Goethe was creating a plot significantly different from that of most Sturm und Drang plays.

In other dramas of the tradition—for example, Leisewitz's *Julius von Tarent*, Klinger's *Die Zwillinge,* and Schiller's *Die Räuber*—idealists like Faust are contrasted sharply with cynics like the devil. Very often the contrast is set up by creating two very different brothers: an intellectual, honest, or sensitive brother, who seems designed to appeal to audiences ready to identify with high ideals (Klinger's Ferdinando, Leisewitz's Julius, Schiller's Karl); and a dishonest, manipulative brother (Klinger's Guelfo, Leisewitz's Guido, Schiller's Franz), who can even provide an excuse for the first brother to become violent. But in the *Urfaust*, this scheme is altered as Faust and Mephisto are depicted not only as brothers, but also as business partners. Faust's dislike of the establishment notwithstanding, they drink together in "Auerbachs Keller" as brothers, and the partnership soon has the idealist Faust—his libido worked up into a frenzy over Margarete—command the realist Mephistopheles: "Hör du must mir die Dirne schaffen" (133). Thus Goethe defuses a common rhetorical formula of the Sturm und Drang, a formula that succeeds in uniting audiences behind the idealist. Quite in keeping with this change, when we measure the *Urfaust* against the other great play of the 1770s dealing with child murder, Wagner's *Die Kindermörderin* (1776), we see that Goethe is much more ready to allow the honest "brother" to open himself up to the sins of the dishonest one. Evchen Humbrecht declares in act 2 of *Die Kindermörderin*, "Welch ein Schatz ist doch ein gutes Gewissen!" But the *Urfaust* finds a way to be more comfortable with yielding to urges; at the end of "Am Brunnen," Margarete will declare "Gott! war so gut! ach war so lieb!" (190). And later in the play, Faust may consider his responsibility to Margarete, but he still prepares to flee.[10]

Goethe's plan, in other words, to deal in a pact between an idealist and a devil is one of the reasons for *Faust*'s long genesis. Successful dramas of the Sturm und Drang, like Schiller's *Die Räuber*, have forms determined by considerations of rhetoric and the group dynamics of the theater. But in this play Goethe wants the protagonist to find a compromise between two moral positions, not play them off against each other for a powerful effect. The result is that even in *Faust I*'s early stages, as the draft reveals, the text is not designed to be a success, and certainly not as a performance. Both in the *Urfaust*'s scene-by-scene progress from "Nacht" to "Kerker," and in its progress from the *Urfaust* draft to *Faust I*, we see Goethe reject the dominant rhetorical formulas of Sturm und Drang. The message sent by the almost hopelessly split draft is that Faust and Margarete will never be the same person, and that the older oral, rhetorical, and communally oriented tradition of the *Volk* lauded by Herder and taken up enthusiastically by the Sturm und Drang will never be rational, enlightened, and cosmopolitan. For the play moves deliberately away from the language of *Götz*'s oaths of allegiance, away from the rhetorical evocation of shared sensibilities and mutual reassurance that we saw in Lavater. With *Faust*, Goethe did not want to deal in performances in which God could be imagined as speaking through a human oracle, whether in the form of Lavater's enthymeme or Lotte's "Klopstock!" At the beginning of the Gretchen tragedy, Margarete does begin to provide a similar oracle for Faust: at the end of "Abend," where Faust is so caught up in the beautiful simplicity of her room that Mephistopheles has to call him away before he is discovered, she sings a *Volkslied* ("Der König in Thule") and even verbalizes the vast difference between herself, in the "oral" tradition of the *Volkslied,* and Faust, the educated, "literate" man. But the scene also shows that Faust will never be satisfied with a life based on specific traditions. Moreover, it may also be that Goethe's deliberate retraction of Margarete's social and institutional support is an attempt to explore the weak position of human beings without the rituals to give life coherence.

Margarete is, of course, Goethe's own addition to the Faust legend. Aside from Helen of Troy, who appears in *Faust II,* other young women who appeared in earlier versions of the legend from Spieß's anonymous chapbook on were always minor characters. But Margarete is a major character in Goethe's *Faust.* As Ernst Beutler discovered in the 1930s, she is the namesake of Susanna Margarete Brandt, who was publicly executed in Frankfurt on January 14, 1772, for murdering a child she bore out of wedlock.[11] When Goethe arrived in Frankfurt from Strasbourg on August 14, 1771, he found his relatives caught up in the Brandt case: his uncle was the public prosecutor, his grandfather the judge, and his brother-in-law signed the death certificate. The *Urfaust*—as opposed to some *Ururfaust* that may have been created before the Brandt experience—appears to have taken shape just as the trial unfolded in late 1771. Goethe added the story of the child murderess to the *Faust* play already developing in his mind, and he retained it in every successive version of the play, despite the effort required to make it fit in with a seemingly different theme: a scholar's restless striving to learn the first causes of the universe.[12] The addition of Margarete is sometimes explained by reference to Goethe's personal life: before returning to Frankfurt in August 1771, he had just put an end to his affair with Friederike Brion of Sesenheim, and it is even possible that the Brandt case shocked him into serious thoughts about his own potential to have caused Friederike a similar misfortune.[13]

But of course Margarete means much more than this to the play. Her entry in the "Strase" scene brings a change in the character of Faust—from the seeker after the absolute who performs magic in "Auerbachs Keller" and shows deference to Mephistopheles to something else: a lover who no longer has magic powers and who dares to speak brashly to Mephistopheles. A change occurs in Faust's language as well: the rough, simple, seemingly improvised style of "Nacht" is replaced, in "Abend," with a more eloquent, expansive tone.[14] Prior to "Abend," "Auerbachs Keller" and Mephistopheles' interview with the student had instead emphasized detail, character, and immediacy, and the same is true of the opening lines of the play. The tone in these early scenes is that of Hans Sachs, whose work Goethe studied in 1772 and 1773:

> Hab nun ach die Philosophey
> Medizin und Juristerey,
> Und leider auch die Theologie
> Durchaus studirt mit heisser Müh.
> Da steh ich nun ich armer Tohr
> Und bin so klug als wie zuvor.

(18)

Yet suddenly, in "Abend" and "Garten," the tone changes from that of the *Budenspiel* to that of Klopstock. Compare the naïve, informative and expositional tone of the lines just quoted to Faust's words on seeing Margarete's room:

> Willkommen süsser Dämmerschein
> Der du dies Heiligthum durchwebst
> Ergreif mein Herz du süse Liebespein
> Die du vom Tau der Hoffnung schmachtend lebest.
> Wie athmet rings Gefühl der Stille,
> Der Ordnung, der Zufriedenheit,
> In dieser Armuth welche Fülle!
> In diesem Kerker welche Seeligkeit!

(137–38)

Vittorio Santoli sums up the contrast between these two styles of language in the following way:

What a difference when we cross over from the dialogue of Faust with Wagner to the soliloquy of Faust in the chamber of his loved one to his sentimental effusion in opposition to Mephistopheles, to the first and second conversation with Margarete! It is like crossing over from Sachs, and from the medieval forces to *Emile* and *La Nouvelle Héloïse*; from Bruegel and the sketches of the youthful Rembrandt, full of "the characteristic," to the style of Greuze. First the satyr, the plebeian caricature, and medieval morality; then the Pietistic air of *Empfindsamkeit* and Rousseau's sensibility. The squalid university halls, the tavern, the drunkards and adventurers and the female panderers have disappeared. In their place we find the rapture of the heart, the consolation of the solitude where the soul is alone with itself, the celebration of nature, of simplicity and innocence, the sentimental mysticism that despises words be-

cause of their inadequacy, and which praises itself for its own im-
mediacy. That crude and often plebeian language of late medieval
realism was in its own element in the mainly illustrative story of
Dr. Faustus. But this new language of the heart could be employed
only in a drama of sentiment.[15]

Thus on the level of the tone of Faust's language, the *Urfaust* contrasts
the primitive and the sentimental: contractive apostrophes are dropped,
and there is much less punctuation in general. Few plays in the Ger-
man tradition provide this range of voice within one character; Goethe
seemed to feel free to work with every style available to him, from
sixteenth-century *Knüttelvers* to *Empfindsamkeit*. And the main reason
for this experimentation is, I suggest, that Germany was straining to-
ward the right tone for a national theater. He was aware that the issue
was one of combining two traditions, and he was working out the prob-
lem in part on a linguistic level. Thus what we get in the *Urfaust* is two
styles available to his age, styles representing extreme opposites. The
first is the rough, simple honesty of Hans Sachs; the second, the world
of eighteenth-century *Empfindsamkeit* and the rhetoric of the heart. We
are speaking, once again, of that difference we see in *Werther* between
Homer and *Ossian*. The former represents the style of *before*, the other
after Klopstock demonstrated how writers could leap beyond the
simple honesty of the *Budenspiel* to sentimentality, self-conscious in-
wardness, and the flattery that unites audiences into an inspired
community.

I have been speaking of the *Urfaust* as if there were no question that
it was originally composed as a single play. There have been a few
critics who doubt this. Barker Fairley, for example, argues that the play
gives the impression of being "not planned or shaped."[16] And Hans M.
Wolff ventures that the beginning scenes must have belonged to an-
other play.[17] The most famous argument put forward on this topic is
Gustav Roethe's 1932 "Fetzentheorie," in which he argues that the *Ur-
faust* is two different plays pasted together and not originally conceived
as one.[18] But in a letter to Schiller of March 1, 1788, Goethe speaks of
the yellowed manuscript of *Faust* to which he was then returning: "Die
Lagen waren nie geheftet."[19] Goethe is telling Schiller that the quires
of his *Faust* manuscript were never stitched. The fact that they were
quires, and something more than just separate sheets of paper, makes
it especially difficult to understand the influence of any scrap theory
of the play. Nollendorfs has quite reasonably suggested that it may still
be possible to find a satisfying explanation for this obvious character
transformation that does not require that we consider the two halves

of the play as fundamentally separate.[20] The *Urfaust*, he suggests, grew out of a relatively constant conception in which the Gretchen tragedy was bound with the demonic element: "Die Begründung der Verknüpfung scheint in der Gestalt des Teufels zu liegen, die dem Teufelsbündner Faust unentbehrlich ist und die ebenfalls eine Rolle in den Zeugnissen der Brandt spielte."[21] But Martin Schütze takes a slightly different point of view, judging the *Urfaust* superior to *Faust I* while, at the same time, still calling the two halves "irreconcilable and mutually exclusive."[22] I believe that this very difference between the two plays within the play is germane to Goethe's confrontation with the Germany of his time: Goethe finds very early on that he cannot produce the effect of sincerity, honesty, and spontaneity (the tone of Faust's language as the play opens) without giving in to the devlish rhetoric that Wagner and Faust's fellow scholars are so eager to learn.

In a brief essay that went practically unnoticed when it appeared in 1959, Eric A. Blackall discusses the *Urfaust*'s linguistic heterogeneity within the context of the whole Sturm und Drang, arguing that many of these texts depend for their characteristic tone on a successful blend of two powerful but opposite styles of language, one extremely articulate, the other extremely inarticulate. On the "articulate" side is Sturm und Drang's use of the expansive style of Klopstock as it aims for what Blackall calls a *stronger* feeling than normal prose; Klopstock's rhetoric, which we find everywhere from Herder to Lavater to the *Urfaust*, is "highly indirect, and in its desire to achieve strong expression it cannot hope to attain closer, direct expression of emotion."[23] "Klopstocks Manier," writes Herder, "so ausmahlend, so vortreflich, Empfindungen ganz ausströmen, und wie sie Wellen schlagen, sich legen und wiederkommen, auch die Worte, die Sprachfügungen ergießen zu lassen."[24] Then there is the other side, the "inarticulate" language, especially in Sturm und Drang's use of rougher folk language, which allows the tradition to attain a *closer* expression of feeling than normal prose. In *Götz*, we get the language of people of "action": their words are clipped into monosyllables, word order is looser, and much freer use is made of ellipses, inversions, interjections, and imperative verbs. Blackall points out that this less sophisticated tradition, with roots in the sixteenth century, does have a link with the tradition of rhetoric, for example, in its use of repetition. Nevertheless, the former style is consciously less fashioned, the latter more fashioned. Goethe's famous draft moves from rough, understated, and apparently unfashioned language to more evidently rhetorical applications of the word reminiscent of Haller, Klopstock, and Lavater. The first slows thought processes down; the other tends toward recklessness. The first avoids self-flattery; the other indulges in it. The first is patient, the second impatient. And these two approaches to Germany stand side by side. The "Abend" scene is one of the most powerful in this play because it contains both these approaches, and one place this is evident is in the song with which it ends, "Der König in Thule," which Margarete sings as she gets ready for bed. While Margarete speaks mostly in *Knüttelvers* in the *Urfaust*, her speech is also under the influence of a language derived from the *Volkslied*. Here and in "Meine Ruh ist hin," where she sits at the spinning wheel after "Ein Gartenhäusgen" (and a gap where *Faust I* has "Wald und Höhle"), these tones break through dramatically. "Der König in Thule" is still considered one of Goethe's greatest achievements and, as Heinz Politzer argues, it was built from the ground up for inclusion in the play.[25] In it we see the same unrelenting rhythm from the unrhetorical to the rhetorical—or, better, from one kind of rhetoric to another—that we see in the whole draft. When Goethe told Schiller in a letter of June 22, 1797, of his renewed desire to return to *Faust*—he asked if Schiller would be so kind as to think the matter over during some sleepless night—he wrote: "Unser Balladenstudium hat mich wieder auf diesen Dunst- und Nebelweg gebracht, und die Umstände raten mir in mehr als in Einem Sinne, eine Zeitlang darauf herum zu irren."[26] Goethe does not explain the connection between his interest in the ballad and his decision to turn again to the play, but in every version of *Faust*, Margarete sings *Volkslieder*. Where do the ballads of the *Urfaust* fit into Goethe's plan? The Sturm und Drang, as we know, was deeply interested in the ballad and the *Volkslied*. Herder spoke repeatedly of the genre, although he provided no single clear definition of it, and definitions of *Volk* and *Volkslied* are notoriously difficult to cull from his writings. He did, however, maintain in *Von deutscher Art und Kunst* (1773) that *Volkslieder*, which he thought one needed to study to become a great poet, were "Lieder eines *ungebildeten, sinnlichen* Volks."[27] It was the character of the folk, their society and their religion, according to Herder, that made them a community.[28] Lugowski points out that Herder considered the *Volkslied* nothing less than "eine Trägerschaft von deutschen Menschen als Ziel seiner Sehnsucht."[29]

Herder also thought that Klopstock's odes, with their expansive and articulate rhetoric, also fell under the category of the *Volkslied*. What is most interesting about this blurring of the distinction between Klopstock and the *Volkslied* is that Herder seems to recognize that, as rooted in the folk as it may be, the *Volkslied* has a rhetorical orientation; it is not as simple and direct as we might think. For this reason, if Goethe had wanted to deal with the potential dishonesty lurking in the pur-

portedly honest and natural elements of his culture, he could hardly
have chosen a better subject than the *Volkslied*. The genre combines the
two kinds of language of which we have been speaking: on the one
hand, apparent naturalness and immediacy; on the other, a powerful
rhetoric. And this contradiction is symbolic for the forces that cause
the Gretchen tragedy. Margarete's flight to the world of the *Volkslied* is
another version of Werther's absorption in the principle of accord
evoked by "Klopstock!" What Goethe deals with in the *Urfaust* is the
question of whether the search for Germanness that Herder equates
with the *Volkslied* is as honest and straightforward as the sixteenth-
century language of Hans Sachs, or whether it is as dishonest and
insidious as the rhetoric Wagner would like to learn. It is in great part
an issue of honesty: is Werther the subject or the object of manipula-
tion? Is Götz self-consistent, or does he betray his own principles by
accepting the leadership of the Peasants' Rebellion? Does Protestant-
ism mean autonomy, or does it amount merely to the substitution of
an internalized and more self-consistent form of control for real social
responsibility?

Such questions lie at the basis of this play. If Margarete's role pro-
vides a quality that prior treatments of the legend lacked, it is chiefly
because she is a link between Faust's longing for the infinite and that
other side of what he has inherited: the limited world of particularized
and parochial Germany. Like Karl's (and Kosinsky's) Amalia in Schiller's
Die Räuber, Margarete is first and foremost a German and a member
of the *Volk*, and what interests Faust—and Goethe—in the limited life
suggested by the lyrical interlude contained in "Abend" is the infinite
realm that can spring from it. "Der König in Thule" pulls the ethos of
Margarete into proximity with that of Werther, for its theme is not only
true love, *Sehnsucht*, and loneliness, but also the *unconditionality* of love:
"True love, the love one finds in such purity only in ballads, Mar-
garete's ideal of love, a love that reaches beyond the grave."[30] Painting
a world where the values of the *Volk* are virtually equated with dreams
of an unconditioned life, "Der König in Thule" depicts a king who
leaves everything to his heirs but the cup that symbolizes eternal love:

> Und als er kam zu sterben,
> Zählt' er seine Städt' im Reich,
> Gönnt' alles seinem Erben,
> Den Becher nicht zugleich.

(141)

The cup was indispensable to him: after tossing it to the waves, he
never drank another drop. Fidelity such as that of this king, the song

says, is possible only beyond all obligations and reservations of the specific world in which human beings live.[31] Such fables, as Browning notes, are simply not part of the provincial life where Margarete lives.[32] But as one of the centerpieces of the play, the song reflects the split in the German tradition with which Goethe wants to deal. There seems no doubt that writers of Sturm und Drang began, quite simply, to see the *Volkslied* as a literature with the potential to lull Germans into dreams of the unconditioned. In Lenz's *Die Soldaten*, Marie is seduced at the end of act 2 as her grandmother sings a song that begins: "Ein Mädele jung ein Würfel ist." And in both the *Urfaust* and *Faust I*, the *Volkslied* provides Goethe an opportunity to consider just how insidiously the apparently natural and the clearly rhetorical can be interwoven.

When Goethe returned to the play in the late 1780s, he was evidently thinking less about how his Faust play helped pull him away from the rhetorical sensibility of Sturm und Drang and more about how he could bridge the gap between its two halves. In 1786 he wrote the scene that would link the scholar and the lover—"Hexenküche"—in which the witch makes Faust younger and gives him a love potion. Yet "Hexenküche" provides only a superficial link between the two halves of the play. The real problem here, which no scene could ever bridge, is between two entirely different styles of language and postures of mind— one immediate, thisworldly, and honest, the other lyrical, otherworldly, and artificial. It was these two realms and their difference that interested Goethe in the *Urfaust*, but the issue is forgotten in *Faust I*. Commentators who try to explain the split in the play by taking the "Hexenküche" scene as their departure misjudge the original split as a minor technical problem to be ironed out at the level of the surface plot—this, despite the fact that Schiller, on June 16, 1797, pointed out to Goethe that to complete *Faust*, his greatest challenge would be successfully to unite the love story with the philosophical part.[33]

One way to look at the problem of *Faust*'s long genesis is to see it as a difficulty in knowing what kind of text to write. The spoken language was of utmost importance for the Sturm und Drang; it was an undeniable feature of *Volk* culture. But the long path to *Faust I*, then to *Faust II*, led Goethe away from the spoken language and toward a kind of writing that would find its truths entirely within the text, a text that had to be written, rewritten, edited, and rearranged. This latter realm of the text is what Walter J. Ong calls "literacy," as opposed to "orality," and which requires "order, structure, inwardly structured sequential relationships," the world that recognizes the written word as "isolated from the fuller context in which spoken words come into being."[34] The progress made by Goethe in *Faust* away from Sturm und Drang might also be considered a move away from what Edward Said has called "affiliation," or the dependence of a text on a specific social environment, with its traditions and rituals and toward "filiation," or purely textual coherence.[35] Goethe's goal became to create a play that would demand an audience totally unlike the one Sturm und Drang was striving to create. He wanted a more "classical" product, a text that could stand as much as possible by itself. It is no accident that the audience Goethe would eventually achieve for his *Faust* was a reading audience: *Faust I,* and especially *Faust II,* would become "closet" drama, more read than performed in the theater. But the heart of the play was left behind in the draft. The *Urfaust* distinguishes itself from the communally resonant texts that most Sturm und Drang authors wanted to create.[36]

With this archaeology of the play in mind, it is easy to see why *Faust I* proceeds from the folkish and sentimental tone of "Der König in Thule" and "Meine Ruh ist hin" to the literate, chiseled quality of "Walpurgisnacht." The trip to the Brocken on Saint Walpurga's Night is certainly there, as Fairley has suggested, to strengthen the supernatural "Faustean" framework with which the play began and thus restore some balance to the play after it had remained so long with the Gretchen tragedy.[37] Yet there is another reason. The direction of the play from "Nacht" on was, already in the 1770s, away from the "natural" traditions of the *Volk* that fascinated writers of Sturm und Drang and toward the more "artificial," self-contained world of the *Volk*—and of the Romantic text. Fairley notes that "Walpurgisnacht" comes across "at first sight like an erratic block" into which the text "goes blindly or subconsciously" along with the "Walpurgisnachtstraum"—a scene Fairley calls "an undigested portion of it."[38] The "Walpurgisnacht" of *Faust I,* Fairley notes, "is not enacted at the level of the scenes that precede and follow it, but elsewhere, on some Brocken of the mind higher, or lower, than 'Marthens Garten.' "[39] Fairley attributes the "different planes of consciousness" represented by "Walpurgisnacht" and "Walpurgisnachtstraum" on the one hand, and much of the rest of the play on the other, to "Goethe's fluctuating temperament"—to the fanciful changes of mood that we find throughout Goethe's work.[40] But the blind, unconscious movement that Fairley notices is, I suggest, precisely this movement in the text of which we have been speaking—the one that ranges from an orally based text geared to the rhetorical needs of a theater audience to a literate-based text trying to find itself entirely apart from any audience. From its first scene, the *Urfaust* depicts a flight from drama that must include rhetoric for a specific audience, to a text made to stand on its own. The crowning touch of the "textual" aim of Goethe's *Faust* project is the "Vorspiel auf dem Theater," where we find the shuffling and correcting that goes on as the play is produced, augmented by the interactions of the actor, the writer, and the theater manager. Appropriately, while "Der König in Thule" was, as Politzer has shown, written exclusively for the play, the "Walpurgisnachtstraum" was inserted in *Faust I* only after Goethe sent it to Schiller with the thought of having it published in the *Musenalmanach* as a self-sufficient piece.

The issue of the rhetorical versus the more purely textual also bears on the question of whether Goethe intended Faust to find religious salvation already in the *Urfaust*. According to Blanckenburg, Lessing was going to save his own Faust at the end just as the devil was about to grab Faust's soul, but we have no such clue as to what Goethe had in mind for his Faust. Nollendorfs argues that the fact that Faust seems to be in control in much of his dialogue with Mephistopheles may indicate that Faust is to be saved, but concludes that we have no proof either way.[41] Adolf Metz argues that the question should not even be asked, since the *Urfaust* is not about good versus evil, but greatness ("Größe"). But it may be that the pact—and the rationale behind Faust's salvation—is missing in the 1770s only because Goethe had not yet come up with a deal whereby Faust could strive for the unconditioned and still give the text a unity centered in itself, not its audience. The audience's beliefs, harnessed so well by Lavater, have already been eliminated from the start in the *Urfaust*: if Faust is eventually to be saved, he requires a new kind of God, one concerned less with one's prospects of eternity and more with life in the here and now. In the *Urfaust* an upper, institutional layer—in this case, Germany—was missing at the outset. Did Goethe forget that this was at the center of his concerns in the early 1770s? In 1808, the "Prolog im Himmel" will find a way to give divine legitimation to Faust by bringing a new ethos into the center of his life, one under development in the *Urfaust* but by no means canonized: that of striving. God will call Faust, as errant as he seems, "mein Knecht" and declare:

> Ein guter Mensch, in seinem dunklen Drange,
> Ist sich des rechten Weges wohl bewußt.

(15)

The principle of striving lets Goethe avoid the problem of the split between the scholar's tragedy and the Gretchen tragedy by rising above it: with the principle of pure vocal incantation thoroughly refuted and behind him, Goethe has cleared the ground for the entry of a new principle—not pure vocal incantation, but pure striving.

That no saving voice from heaven speaks at the end of the draft speaks well of Goethe: he resisted the impatient muse that led so many writers of the 1770s to gloss over Germany's problems with rhetorical solutions. No doubt Goethe could have readily allied his fascination with absolutes to his instinctive sympathy for Margarete and the German *Volk*, fusing the whole into a play with a rousing theatrical effect. Still, when he went on to finish *Faust*, he forgot concerns inherent to the draft and let a universal register of human activity—forgivable striving—take the place of the problem with the German nation he struggled with in his youth. Georg Gottfried Gervinus was probably right when he argued that the cosmopolitan thrust of Weimar Classicism was at least a partial abandonment of the search for a German national identity.[42] In the 1790s, Goethe and Schiller would avoid the problems they had been ready to face twenty years earlier. They would find a less nationally specific foundation for German literature, and the Germany of Goethe's original *Faust* drama—born of the gap between limiting particularism and the dream of a coherent nation-state—would be forgotten.

6. A Fleeting Sense of Germany: Schiller's *Die Räuber*

For more than a hundred years following its first performance in 1782, Friedrich Schiller's *Die Räuber* was regarded as the quintessential drama of Sturm und Drang. But beginning with literary *Geistesgeschichte* early in our century, its seemingly unshakable position in the canon of Sturm und Drang began to come under attack: critics maintained that the play lay outside the tradition, or at least did not fit very comfortably into it. H. A. Korff argued in the 1920s that *Die Räuber*'s critique of religion gives it an "enlightened" aspect atypical of Sturm und Drang;[1] Roy Pascal, along similar lines, suggested in 1952 that in the play Schiller adopted "the basic concepts of Kant," thereby "opposing the rest of Sturm und Drang";[2] and in 1972 Manfred Wacker tried to show that *Die Räuber*'s closed, "architectonic" structure made it less a play of Sturm und Drang than of Weimar Classicism, and when he assembled sixteen essays for the Wissenschaftliche Buchgesellschaft's volume on Sturm und Drang (1985), *Die Räuber* went untreated.[3]

Adding to the sense that there is something different about this play, a well-known eyewitness account of its premiere performance strongly suggests that it enjoyed a reception quite unlike any other drama of the tradition: "Das Theater glich einem Irrenhause: rollende Augen, geballte Fäuste, stampfende Füße, heisere Aufschreie im Zuschauerraum! Fremde Menschen fielen einander schluchzend in die Arme, Frauen wankten, einer Ohnmacht nahe, zur Türe. Es war eine allgemeine Auflösung im Chaos, aus dessen Nebeln eine neue Schöpfung hervorbricht."[4] After a decade of raging *Kraftmenschen* who repelled as many audiences as they attracted, Schiller's Mannheim audience clearly understood and appreciated a violent protagonist. The immediate hostility of some critics, including Goethe, notwithstanding, and despite technical weaknesses and stylistic inconsistencies pointed out by Schiller himself, the play filled theaters like no other drama of the 1770s, Goethe's *Götz von Berlichingen* included, and inspired numerous imitations and adaptations.

From the beginning, critics were eager to explain the phenomenon: what was this devilry that enabled Schiller's robbers to murder and rape their way into audiences' hearts? At first, the success of *Die Räuber* was ascribed to the superior acting of Iffland (in the role of Franz) and Böck (Karl): "Schwerlich hat je ein Stück in Deutschland mehr Wirkung auf dem Theater gemacht . . . aber es ist auch noch kein Schauspiel in Mannheim so gut gegeben worden als dieses."[5] When the response to its next two productions, in Hamburg and Leipzig, immediately discredited this notion, its popularity was then attributed to other, equally superficial qualities, such as the sheer entertainment value of the plot, or the contemporary appeal of a tale about highwaymen.[6] These and other similarly inadequate explanations of the play's reception reflect a fundamental puzzlement surrounding its spectacular popularity. Even P. Klein, among the harshest of *Die Räuber's* early detractors, was confounded that "so viel Unedles, Ungereimtes, Scheußliches" could have been so effective, and, while conjuring up a comparison to the world of painting, inadvertently paid Schiller a compliment: "Die schwelgerische Einbildungskraft eines Malers schuf einst ein Bild, vor dem eine halbe Nation staunte."[7] Klein's review appeared in 1783, yet today we are still no closer to explaining why Schiller's first play, if we take the above eyewitness account seriously, seems to have had such an inspiring and even psychologically liberating effect on its audience. In chapter 4, where I considered *Die Räuber* as a drama of the *Kraftmensch*, I argued that the play allowed audiences to empathize with a violent figure. Here I would like to suggest that nineteenth-century critics, much closer than we are to the problems out of which the theater of the German 1770s rose, were right about *Die Räuber*: it is quintessential Sturm und Drang. If this play is unlike the drama of Klinger and Lenz, it is not because it is already a text of early Weimar Classicism; it is because it offers German audiences the sense of power, character, and spontaneity that Sturm und Drang had sought all along.

Like so many writers concerned with the issue of German nationality in the 1770s, Schiller knew that the lack of a settled, closely knit society was not just an intellectual, but also an emotional burden, and that the problem required an emotional, not a merely intellectual, answer. The inspiration for *Die Räuber* seems to have been a story idea formulated in very rough outline by Christian Friedrich Daniel Schubart (1739–91), a man who just might have attended the Mannheim premiere of Schiller's first play if he had not been serving a ten-year prison sentence for subversion imposed by the same man who kept Schiller from the performance: Duke Karl Eugen of Württemberg. In his essay "Zur Geschichte des menschlichen Herzens" (1774), Schubart outlined the story of a young prodigal son named Karl whose mail is intercepted by his brother—a plot going back to Fielding's *Tom Jones* (1749), and even further to Shakespeare's *King Lear*, where an honorable brother is thrown out of the house by the intrigue of a dishonorable one.[8] Schubart, who changed the scene to Germany and seemed to suggest that his story idea was based on an actual event, asked: "Wann wird einmal der Philosoph auftreten, der sich in die Tiefen des menschlichen Herzens hinabläßt, jeder Handlung bis zur Empfängnis nachspürt, jeden Winkelzug bemerkt und alsdann eine Geschichte des menschlichen Herzens schreibt, worin er das trügerische Inkarnat vom Antlitz des Heuchlers hinwegwischt, und gegen ihn die Rechte des offenen Herzens behauptet?"[9]

Schiller took Schubart's estimate of what Germans needed very seriously. His preface to *Die Räuber* begins by explaining that while his text happens to be a drama, it is a drama almost accidentally; he is simply using the stage as a way to have access to what Schubart called "die Tiefen des menschlichen Herzens": "Man nehme dieses Schauspiel für nichts anderes als eine dramatische Geschichte, die die Vorteile der dramatischen Methode, die Seele gleichsam bei ihren geheimsten Operationen zu ertappen, benutzt."[10] Schiller goes on to say that if his portrayals of violence are offensive, he needs to stage such horror, so he says, in order ultimately to avenge the offended moral order: "Wer sich den Zweck vorgezeichnet hat, das Laster zu stürzen und Religion, Moral und bürgerliche Gesetze an ihren Feinden zu rächen, ein solcher muß das Laster in seiner kolossalischen Größe vor das Auge der Menschheit stellen—er selbst muß augenblicklich seine nächtlichen Labyrinthe durchwandern—er muß sich in Empfindungen hineinzuzwingen wissen, unter deren Widernatürlichkeit sich seine Seele sträubt" (1:484–85). If Schiller's interests are not spelled out as specifically national, it is at least clear that his essays from this period see the stage as a route to a more well-defined nation. In "Die Schaubühne als moralische Anstalt betrachtet" (1784), he gave the theater a central role in forging the nation that Germany lacked: drama, he wrote, can have a healing role in awakening healthy emotions that our everyday public lives have dammed up, but which, when released, contain the potential to "give us ourselves": "Wenn Gram am dem Herzen nagt, wenn trübe Laune unsere einsamen Stunden vergiftet, wenn uns Welt und Geschäfte anekeln, wenn tausend Lasten unsre Seele drücken und unsre Reizbarkeit unter Arbeiten des Berufs zu ersticken droht, so empfängt uns die Bühne—in dieser künstlichen Welt träumen wir die wirkliche hinweg, wir werden uns selbst wiedergegeben, unsre Empfindungen erwacht, heilsame Leidenschaften erschüttern unsre schlummernde Natur und treiben das Blut in frischeren

Wallungen" (5:831). The stage he envisions, this theater that will "give us ourselves," is the kind common to healthier societies, such as ancient Greece or, more realistically, France, where the writer was a flatterer who invigorated his public by idealizing its sensibilities and values.

True, the theater of the *Kraftmensch* already took a step in this direction by providing texts that paved the way for violent self-realization. But prior to Schiller the *Kraftmensch* was still not a figure with whom audiences could readily identify: dramas from *Götz von Berlichingen* to Wagner's *Die Kindermörderin* to Klinger's *Die Zwillinge* (banned in Vienna) tended to overwhelm spectators rather than inspire them. As Kindermann notes of Schröder's production of *Die Zwillinge*: "Nun setzte Schröder alle Hoffnungen auf Klingers *Zwillinge*; mußte nicht dieses alle Elemente der Erde und des Himmels beschwörende Werk, das versuchte, den Sturm der Herzen und die Schauder des Abgründigen sichtbar zu machen, zum erstrebten Ziel führen? Aber die Hochspannung von Klingers revolutionärem Werk ging über das Fassungsvermögen der Hamburger, besonders der Frauenwelt, weit hinaus. So wurde trotz hervorragender Aufführung auch diese Premiere kein Erfolg."[11] Why was this the case? First of all, prior to Karl Moor, the violent figures of Sturm und Drang fought for limited, even outright personal causes: Götz fought for his own small class of aristocrats, the free knights; Wild fought for Caroline, or at most for harmony between just two families; Guelfo fought for his right to succeed his father. Perhaps more important, before 1781 Sturm und Drang heroes tended to suffer from serious problems of self-identity themselves. Think of Guelfo's frantic search for the facts of his birthright, or his pathetic acceptance of Grimaldi's flattery even when he suspects he is being manipulated. His sickly self-concern, his compulsive mirror-gazing, and his pathetic need for self-assurance probably reminded audiences of their own paucity of self-confidence and self-identity as Germans. Klinger had created a theater of power, but not a powerful theater; Sturm und Drang had not yet plunged, as Schubart put it, "into the depths of the human heart." But *Die Räuber* changed all this, bringing Sturm und Drang to its final, most powerful—and most manipulative—stage. In 1781, Schiller managed to depict rebellious individualism bursting the bonds of its frustration while, at the same time, drawing on an established moral tradition that already had its own centuries-long momentum. Yet it is not a play that goes beyond Sturm und Drang; quite the contrary, it provides the culmination of the tradition's main concerns: building a bridge from the absolute to the spontaneous, from the planned to the unplanned, from the divine to the arrogant, that the tradition had been building from the beginning.

Schiller's chief intellectual predecessor in the 1770s was a man of God—Lavater, who understood that the right kind of leader could flatter a group into believing that they were a worthwhile and vital community. For writing this play meant returning to the note struck in *Aussichten in die Ewigkeit*, which outlined a way to inspire readers with visions of eternity. In his first appearance in the play, in act 1, scene 2, Karl decries his own age by comparing it with the possibilities suggested by more heroic ages: "Das Gesetz hat zum Schneckengang verdorben, was Adlerflug geworden wäre" (1:504). By chance employing the same word—*Adlerflug*—Lavater spoke of the heights he claimed could be reached by artists in the hereafter.[12] In his 1779 autobiography, Lavater spoke of youthful fantasies in which there seems, paradoxically, to be a place for a violent individualism strikingly similar to that of Karl Moor:

> Bey dieser Gelegenheit soll ich einen andern Grundzug meines Herzens nicht verhehlen—der mir wenig Ehre macht, aber schlechterdings nicht verhehlt werden darf. Mein unermüdter Erfindungsgeist beschäftigte sich sehr oft mit zwo seltsamen Phantasieen— mit Plänen zu *undurchdringlichen Gefangenschaften*, ja sogar *Martern und Torturen,*—und hinwiederum—gefiel ich mir in der *Idee—* *Chef einer Diebsbande* zu sein; wohlverstanden, in diese letztere Idee mischte sich nicht die mindeste Grausamkeit; nicht ein Hauch von Gewaltthätigkeit. Ich wollte niemand weder tödten, noch plagen, noch erschrecken; davor zitterte mein blödes und mein gutes Herz. Aber mit *List* was hier zu nehmen, mit List dort das Gestohlene einem andern zu geben, und nur so viel davon zu behalten, als zu meinem Unterhalte nöthig wäre—kurz, nicht zu kränken, sondern seltsame Veränderungen hervorzubringen, *ungesehn*—große sichtbare Wirkungen zu bewirken—nicht meinen *Namen* groß zu machen; sondern den unsichtbar wirkenden zu spielen, war eine meiner tiefsten Lieblingsideen, mit deren ich mich oft Stunden lang auf die lächerlichste Weise beschäfftigte.[13]

Of course, it was also a theater of inspiring violence that Schiller had in mind when he wrote *Die Räuber* and its famous preface, in which he defends violent and immoral characters precisely for their ability to inspire great things, against great odds and as if by some invisible power.

Dalberg, the director of the Mannheim National Theater, was aware of the dangers involved in producing a play like *Die Räuber,* and to keep the audience in the dark as much as possible about the effects Schiller was trying to achieve, he struck a number of sections from Schiller's notes on the program printed for the premiere, sentences such as: "Der Zuschauer weine vor unserer Bühne—und schaudere—und lerne seine Leidenschaften unter die Gesetze der Religion und des Verstandes beugen" (1:489–90). But passages such as the following remained: "Jeder, auch dem Lasterhaftesten ist gewissermaßen der Stempel des göttlichen Ebenbilds aufgedrückt, und vielleicht hat der große Bösewicht keinen so weiten Weg zum großen Rechtschaffenen, als der kleine; denn die Moralität hält gleichen Gang mit den Kräften, und je weiter die Fähigkeit, desto weiter und ungeheurer ihre Verirrung, desto imputabler ihre Verfälschung" (1:482–83). Still, by the time Schiller wrote this, the idea that cruelty on the stage could be attractive had already been established. At the beginning of the century, Shaftesbury had written: "the completely virtuous and perfect character is unpoetical and false," for "Cruel spectacles and barbarities are also found to please, and, in some tempers, to please beyond all other subjects," adding: "But is this pleasure's right?"[14] Even Nicolas Boileau-Despréaux knew that art could make the monstrous appealing: the third canto of *L'Art Poétique* (1674) begins with "There is no serpent, no odious monster that, when imitated by art, cannot delight the eye; the artifice of a delicate brush turns the most frightful object into a pleasing one."[15] Thus it was perhaps not so bold a step after all to claim, as Schiller does at the end of the Preface, "Ich darf meiner Schrift, zufolge ihrer merkwürdigen Katastrophe, mit Recht einen Platz unter den moralischen Büchern versprechen" (1:488).

This brings us to the play itself, and to the question of how, just five years after *Die Zwillinge,* Schiller succeeded in transforming a theme very much like Klinger's—essentially, a bruised ego and the violence it engenders—into an uplifting theatrical experience that seemed to hold the promise of building social solidarity and self-confidence in the process. During the long reign of Neoclassicism, French culture was supported by a virtual army of writers who flattered their public while idealizing its values and sensibilities. At the heart of such dramatic rituals was an appeal to audiences to act as members of a community whose members not only shared the same culture, but saw their culture as the domain of a distinctive group. In his own early critique of *Die Räuber,* Schiller speculates that those who appreciate his play will flatter themselves into thinking that they belong to a small minority who can understand Karl's point of view: "Wir lieben das Ausschließende," he continues, "in der Liebe und überall" (1:623). Nineteenth-century critics faulted Schiller's understanding of human psychology, but here he seems to recognize how a dramatist can apply the principle of flattery in the theater. Of utmost importance to this ingroup dynamics is the exclusionary aspect, the shared feeling that "our" group is special, that "we" can see something singularly noble in certain things of which the ordinary, uninitiated nonmember would be indifferent, or even fearful.[16] Schiller knew that Germany lacked a society well developed enough for such unifying dramatic rituals to flourish, at least in the way that they flourished in France—through mimesis of action in the established social and political sphere of the French aristocracy. Consequently, he was forced to look for other means of making an audience discover itself as a community, for another kind of exclusive group membership for which a public could be flattered.

He found it in the same place Lavater found it: in religion. Korff, citing Schiller's critique of religion as evidence that the play owes a great deal to the Enlightenment, points out that Schiller lets two clergymen speak at length in *Die Räuber*—the priest in act 2 and Pastor Moser in act 5.[17] Yet we must not lose sight of the fact that in both those scenes the contemporary church may come under criticism for its hypocrisy, but religion itself, aside from how some clergymen have misused it, is treated with great respect. No character in this play is more disappointed with the broken moral order of the world than Karl Moor, and it is Karl's traditional ideals that make the play work. What are the "größere Pläne" of which he speaks as the priest leaves at the end of act 2 if not his hopes to be part of the harmonious family of believers— a group he fears, at the end of the play, he will never join. Like Lavater, Schiller knew that religion could be pressed into service to build the sense of a cohesive community, if only momentarily: "Religion," Schiller wrote in his essay on "Die Schaubühne als moralische Anstalt," "bindet streng und ewig" (5:822). And he continues:

> Welche Verstärkung für Religion und Gesetze, wenn sie mit der Schaubühne in Bund treten, wo Anschauung und lebendige Gegenwart ist, wo Laster und Tugend, Glückseligkeit und Elend, Torheit und Weisheit in tausend Gemälden faßlich und wahr an dem Menschen vorübergehen, wo die Vorsehung ihre Rätsel auflöst, ihren Knoten vor seinen Augen entwickelt, wo das menschliche Herz auf den Foltern der Leidenschaft seine leisesten Regungen beichtet, alle Larven fallen, alle Schminke verfliegt und die Wahrheit unbestechlich wie Rhadamanthus Gericht hält. (5:822)

Such a theater, with its foundation in religion—this "festeste Säule" of any state (5:822)—can make possible a dramatic experience in which people from all walks of life, "herausgerissen aus jedem Drange des Schicksals, durch eine allwebende Sympathie verbrüdert, in ein Geschlecht wieder aufgelöst, ihrer selbst und der Welt vergessen und ihren himmlischen Ursprung sich nähern" (5:831). The task Schiller sets for drama in this essay is one he accomplished two years before with the premiere of *Die Räuber*: to offer his public a means by which it can take advantage of its own strong suit: not a taste for the socially refined, but for the morally refined. Germany's forte was not its social and political life, but its inner life; despite three centuries of religious conflict, a German's most common ground with his countrymen was a deeply felt Christian heritage. In his 1781 play he acts on this knowledge through creating an ingroup in the theater, by encouraging audiences to glorify an admittedly "invisible" capacity it possessed, and by making a group that felt insignificant within the "visible" sphere of society and politics suddenly feel powerful.

Creating a community in the theater meant producing a denominational hybrid, and *Die Räuber*'s mixture of "Protestant" and "Catholic" features has already been alluded to in several essays dealing with the play's religious aspect. Von Wiese argues that the play's central theme is the "gestörte Vaterordnung" sensed by Karl theologically, socially, and in his own family, and he points to the influence of the baroque[18]—as do Kurt May[19] and Ernst Müller.[20] Yet as Blackall notes, the language of Protestantism can deal in the same extremes as God and the human soul strive toward unity.[21] And Ernst Müller writes: "Karl Moor ist ein religiöser Typus im ursprünglichen Sinne des Wortes, seine Empörung stammt aus dem lutherischen Protestantismus, er ist Sinnbild nicht eines antiken oder freigeistlerischen, sondern eines bedeutsam christlichen Empörertums."[22] Where did Schiller learn his baroque antithetics? There is reason to believe that he received little or no training in Catholic theology at the Hohe Karlsschule in Stuttgart, where the powerful Württemberg Landschaft demanded that "kein anders als das evangelisch-lutherische Religions-Exercitium —es sei unter welchem Vorwand es immer wolle—gestattet oder eingeführt werden dürfe."[23] In 1775, under pressure, Karl Eugen even promised to allow no more Catholic cadets into the academy. But *Die Räuber*'s debt to both the Reformation and the Counter-Reformation can be at least partly explained by reference to the peculiar tradition of Pietism to which Schiller was exposed as a child and especially in 1776 and 1777, just as he was beginning to find a way to put his feelings into dramatic form. One of Schiller's teachers at the Hohe Karlsschule was Georg Friedrich Gaus (1747–77), whose Pietism was charged with the irreconcilable extremes that we usually associate with the world-view of seventeenth-century Catholicism.[24] The religious profile of Schiller's first play, with its theme of the sinner who can never turn back, its dialectic of salvation and damnation, "Himmel und Hölle," is indeed a heritage of the seventeenth century, but as transmitted by Swabian Pietism, which in its theological treatises and prayers commonly invoked the urgent antithetics of worldly vanity and mystical unity with God. With his natural sense for drama, Schiller must have felt the possibilities for powerful ingroup dynamics in a theatrical experience that would create an emotionally charged, aesthetically rich ritual for all Germans, a ritual that melded the provocative tones of his own Protestant background with the apocalyptic resonances of the baroque.

Still, despite the promise of a religious approach, there was no discounting the difficulty of the challenge: to create a dramatic ritual that would make its participants feel like countrymen—and make Germany feel like a nation, despite the undeniable fact that it was not. For by itself, the baroque heritage only partly explains Schiller's success in forging a unified audience. This play, with its "good" robber, employs a social tactic of even greater power. The model for Karl that Schiller himself cites is the robber Roque Guinart of Cervantes' *Don Quixote*, but Karl's attractions far transcend the Catalan wit and inventiveness of Cervantes' robber captain: Karl is charismatic.[25] Schiller cannot provide his German public with an actual leader, but he can create a protagonist who offers relief for those willing to be manipulated for the sake of the temporary comfort it affords. "Man wird," he boasted in the play's first preface, "meinen Mordbrenner bewundern, ja sogar fast lieben" (1:483). Karl Moor, *Die Räuber*'s noble criminal, transforms crime, usually an antisocial phenomenon, into a facilitator of social unity, inviting spectators to revitalize their self-images by forgiving—even adopting the point of view of—the violent protagonist, all the while enjoying the shared feeling that they are special in being able to appreciate Karl's hidden, positive qualities, his deeply injured sense of what is right, and his vague "greater plans." Made privy to Karl's misunderstanding of his father's intentions, spectators sympathize and even identify with him—all leading, I suggest, to an unconscious agreement on the part of spectators to accept ordinarily contradictory terms, flattered, as they are, into measuring the depth of their own moral rigor by the horror of Karl's actions. If the famous report of the premiere audience's reaction I quoted at the beginning of this chapter is an accurate indication, *Die Räuber* was a success. But, as in all charisma, socially unifying flattery was purchased at the expense of self-deception. The drama functions the way it is supposed to—and provides its burst of communal feeling—when spectators accept Karl Moor as a leader rather than simply dismissing him as a murderer.

The first description of Karl's charisma comes from Franz, who refers in act 1, scene 1, with jealousy to his brother's "kindischer Ehrgeiz," "unüberwindlicher Starrsinn," and "diese Offenheit, die seine Seele auf dem Auge spiegelt" (1:495). Whereas Franz was always considered "der trockne Alltagsmensch, der kalte hölzerne Franz," Karl was "der feurige Geist" (1:496). Franz, whose Machiavellian nature is short on both conscience and ideals, is anything but charismatic: "Gewissen— O ja freilich! ein tüchtiger Lumpenmann, Sperlinge von Kirschbäumen wegzuschröcken!" (1:500–501). Karl, however, is moral even in his immorality—a difficult state of affairs to depict, but one upon which the play depends. Karl's idealism is never completely eclipsed by his cynicism, and he continues to react to the crimes committed by members of his own band with the same horror he displays in act 2, when he expels Schufterle for his sadistic account of Roller's rescue in act 3. Spiegelberg, with his own ridiculous yet unabashed claims to be a leader, helps bring Karl's very different qualities even further into relief. Spiegelberg is not charismatic for a very simple reason: in contrast to Karl, his innate self-love is unveiled, effectively eliminating the possibility that an audience could ever identify with him while remaining unaware of its own narcissism. It is hard to be attracted to a figure who speaks self-servingly of "wer ich bin, wer ich werden muß" and boasts that he is a "Universal-Genie" (1:507). Spiegelberg's honesty short-circuits charisma's creative self-alienation. This man, whom the audience can conveniently blame for luring the men into their criminal enterprise in the first place, is everything that Karl is not: he is constantly characterized as a person incapable of championing ideals over all else; and he is a coward: "Du bist ein Meister-Redner, Spiegelberg," says Roller, "wenns drauf ankommt, aus einem ehrlichen Mann einen Hollunken zu machen" (1:511). Spiegelberg remains sadistic, selfish, and trivial until the end, when he is killed by Schweizer after suggesting mutiny. "Ja," mocks Schweizer, "du bist mir der rechte Held, Frösche mit Steinen breit zu schmeißen" (1:587). For the audience, it is Spiegelberg's stubborn refusal to deal in charismatic dissimulation that makes his behavior unforgivable. Without Karl's "größere Pläne," Spiegelberg murders without reluctance, without subtlety, and without a well-focused, incorruptible sense of morality that shines through despite outward appearances.

Karl, on the other hand, is a murderer meant to be forgiven. Ironically, he is accepted by the audience as readily as he is by the robber band, whose intense interest in his special abilities confirms the corrupt nature of all charisma. Karl is recruited on the strength of his extraordinary leadership ability, which the men of the band, Spiegelberg excepted, feel will help turn them into an effective group with a positive self-image. By giving convincing expression to their righteous indignation, Karl will make the actions of misfits poignantly appropriate, make outsiders feel like insiders, make crime seem divinely inspired. "Ohne Moor," Roller exclaims, "sind wir Leib ohne Seele" (1:514). Schweizer, given the honor of committing a murder that will avenge Karl's father, cites his newly found pride when he exclaims: "Großer Hauptmann! Heut hast du mich zum erstenmal stolz gemacht" (1:597). Schweizer's statement is, again, one that might also reflect the mood of Schiller's audience. Both the robbers and the audience respond to the same finesse by which Karl masks an attractive contradiction: through this "good" robber, the audience will live a role denied to it by religious traditions that tended to answer the demands of morality by condemning the vainglorious affairs of worldly life. The audience is supposed to have ambivalent feelings about these robbers, who sing in act 4, scene 5, of their future in hell. But the play coaxes its audience to "suspend disbelief" in their crimes and accept the notion that, at least for Karl, a taste for violence can also be an index of one's moral perfection. As the demonic power of Schiller's ritual reaches its peak in act 5, Karl, as if himself infected by spectators whose hearts are already worked up to a frenzy of forgiveness, even forgives himself, falling on his knees to thank God for making him captain of a robber band, because it allowed him to avenge his father! "Weggeblasen sind alle Bedenken und Zweifel an der Rechtmäßigkeit der illegalen Handlungsweise, die Geister aller von ihm erwürgten rufen ihm ein Ja zu, im Auftrag Gottes darf er jetzt die Frevel des Bruders rächen und als irdischer Vollstrecker der höheren, beleidigten sittlichen Weltordnung sein Amt zu einem krönenden Abschluß führen."[26] The play gave audiences impatient with the limiting nature of German culture the opportunity to avert their eyes from those limits and dream themselves momentarily into a Germany where problems of community and character do not exist.

My suggestion that *Die Räuber* is the culmination of the tradition implies that Sturm und Drang is less a literature of mimesis than it is a literature of ritual. Von Wiese called this play a catalyst for the emotions, and, in fact, the anonymous eyewitness account that has come down to us suggests that *Die Räuber*'s liberating rite of identity was cathartic for its audience.[27] Catharsis (κάθαρσις), in the medical/homeopathic interpretation made famous by Freud's brother-in-law Bernays, is a beneficial release of tension that had been dammed up due to some inability to make an adequate response to a difficult situation. Often the process involves relief of the kind that seems to have been experienced by Schiller's January 1782 Mannheim audience. If a text like *Die Räuber* or the sermons of Lavater can refract the confused desires of an audience in such a way that their emotions appear both more focused and more expressible, then such a text might make people feel less helpless. I do not, of course, mean to imply that every eighteenth-century German, or every eighteenth-century German writer, needed the help of ritualistic texts like *Die Räuber*. Goethe, for example, who disliked the play, seems to have had little difficulty organizing and simplifying his life. But he may have been the exception. For the most part Schiller's first play was a sensation, and I think we have to ask ourselves why his respectable middle-class audience found itself luxuriating, for the most part, in acceptance of Karl's violence. In giving his public an opportunity for vicarious violence, Schiller gave Germans license to discharge frustration with a society that had let deeply felt needs—especially the need to locate and find corroboration for beliefs they had in common—go unanswered. His play allowed audiences to remember a rigorous inner standard on which they could find agreement. Just as Schiller made Karl's glaring moral contradictions go unnoticed, and even seem to be a source of virtue, he also invited eighteenth-century Germans to flatter themselves with the depth of their inner life while looking away from the infelicitous facts of German particularism.

Rather than a catalyst for political change, what we get in *Die Räuber* is a catalyst for the reawakening of inherited moral ideas. The play is designed not for Schiller and Goethe's elite 1790s audiences, but for that larger German audience for which Lenz wanted to write—the one for whom political solutions are out of reach and for whom the restraint of Weimar Classicism would be too subtle. Through the success of this play Schiller shows that his mind is on solutions that come not from cataclysmic social and political change, but from our ability to conspire to compliment ourselves for what we have in common. His ritual of self-elevation flatters audiences with the same spaceless and timeless inheritance that attracted Werther. Among dramas of the 1770s, Klinger's *Die Zwillinge* dealt with essentially the same national problem, but Klinger merely brought Germany's all too familiar frustrations into focus. Guelfo's awareness of his horrifying separation from the social group results in despair: "Mord! Mord! und wenn ichs denke, stehn mir die Haare nicht. Grimaldi! rette mich vor meinem Geist! Rette, rette mich!" (1:288). And he, too, had to discharge his frustration through action: "Grimaldi! Grimaldi! laß mich was tun! Ich will

eine Pistole losschießen—ich muß so was hören! Mein Herz heischts!''
(1:265). Guelfo launched an unequivocal attack on society, and the text
forgives him, but he was not yet the protagonist to flatter us for great,
commonly shared ideals, to give social validity to existence, to grant
Germans the God-given grace of a superhuman leader in the face of
an unfriendly social and political milieu. As a *Kraftmensch*, Guelfo may
have raged with impunity, but he still did little more than remind Ger-
mans of their own failings.

By contrast, Karl made spectators feel as if they belonged together
as an audience: *Die Räuber's* first auditors responded with intimations
of rebirth, feelings of brotherhood, and expressions of relief. Schiller
dealt with his audience's paucity of social unity by flattering it with its
own strong suit: an inner life so deep that its implications were fright-
ening, a morality so unswerving that it turned society upside-down
so as to demonstrate the divine authority of its inner, moral referent.
In the last analysis, those much-quoted phrases with which Karl rebels
against his ''Kastratenjahrhundert'' do not reflect an attack on society
at all; Karl's rebellion is designed to meet his audience on its own
terms. As a protagonist, he is tailor-made to reinforce, not topple, so-
ciety. Kurt May, one more critic who attempted to evict *Die Räuber* from
the canon of Sturm und Drang, argued that Karl's self-condemnation
in act 5 reflects Schiller's ''poetisches Gericht über den entfesselten,
abstrakten Individualismus der Exzentriker in der Sturm-und-Drang-
Generation, als Absage an das Übermenschentum jenseits von Gut
und Böse.''[28] But remember that Schiller does not clear up Karl's mis-
understanding of his father's rejection until the very end of the play,
when Karl finally learns that his enemy was not ''society'' at all, but
one man, his brother Franz. We overrate Karl's final self-judgment re-
garding the ''beleidigte Gesetze'' and the ''mißhandelte Ordnung'' if
we forget that for four acts Schiller used unlawfulness to flatter, invig-
orate, and unify his audience. This is not a play that leaves audiences
feeling the self-denial of Kantian morality. The end of Karl's career as
robber captain does not, after all, come until the very end of act 5; it
is the violent Karl Moor that fills the first four acts. Thus the claim in
the play's preface that this play deserves a place ''unter den moral-
ischen Büchern'' is entirely accurate, but not because Karl decides in
the last scene to turn himself in to the authorities and accept the con-
sequences of his actions. It is a moral book because the whole play, but
especially the first four acts, made Germans aware of what they inherit
as Germans. In the absence of sufficient unity in the social and political
sphere, Schiller made his first drama succeed by drawing on his au-
dience's religious background. This meant flattering his public, a task

solved by creating a figure who could avert attention from an obvious national disunity while allowing them to feel like a morally sensitive elite.

No dramatist listened as carefully as Schiller to Sturm und Drang's impatient muse. The immediate impression made by *Die Räuber* is one of noble individuality taking its revenge on the broken trust, the underhanded manipulations, of an unsympathetic society. But here it is not society that manipulates, but the author. Schiller, who understood the urgent needs of German audiences, designed a drama to help his countrymen look away from their paucity of national identity and flatter themselves into believing that they were part of a unified and closely knit community. As they fell, sobbing, into each others' arms, *Die Räuber*'s first audiences enjoyed an experience not unlike the communal epiphany created by Lavater for his Zürich congregation. More than any other writer of the tradition, Schiller gave a public that felt limited by the traditions it had inherited license to legitimate its aggressions, challenge God, and be the self-righteous Karl Moor. The play, admired by Wordsworth and Coleridge, Nietzsche and Dostoevsky, owes its stirring effect to that powerful force at the root of so much of Sturm und Drang: an impatience that tempted writers to supply with their texts something that Germany could not yet provide.

7. The Patient Art of J. M. R. Lenz

The work of Jakob Michael Reinhold Lenz is shaped by a recoil in the face of the impatient muse. While the trend in Sturm und Drang is to rush in to compensate Germans for what they have lost to particularism, Lenz will not join the project to build an artificial nation. He fails to develop promising images introduced in the first lines of his poetry, and characters in his plays interrupt the action for no apparent reason: Pätus, in *Der Hofmeister*, throws his landlady's coffeepot out the window as a reaction to a mild insult; Seraphine, in *Die Freunde machen den Philosophen* (1776), inexplicably tears a jewelry box out of Strephon's hands and tosses it into the harbor; and in *Der neue Menoza*, we are thrown off guard first by Herr von Zopf's news that Tandi is married to his sister, then by the equally surprising revelation that he is not. His dramas seem often to be out of control: in act 1, scene 2 of *Die Soldaten*, Marie's conversation with her mother about Stolzius is dropped, only to be picked up again in act 3, scene 9; the thirty-five scenes of *Der Hofmeister* are even more jumbled. Yet there are also clues that Lenz's haphazardness unfolds under a watchful eye. In his most famous essay, *Anmerkungen übers Theater*, paragraphs break off in midsentence with a sobering self-consciousness: "Wollte sagen," stammers the narrator as he fails to pick up his train of thought, "was wollt ich doch sagen?—"[1]

Lenz's expulsion from Weimar on December 2, 1776, helps signal the end of Sturm und Drang. Just why he was asked to leave is unclear, but we do know that he was perceived as a man who could be charming at one moment and tactless the next. We also know that Goethe had a talent for dispatching from his life things that he found unsettling, whether feelings or people. During his second year at court Goethe grew rather moody about certain of his visitors in Weimar: he asked Klinger to leave, then Lenz. The expulsion appears to have had a great impact on Lenz, a former friend, and it was certainly one of the several causes of the mental breakdown that came in 1777. Lenz said he felt "ausgestossen aus dem Himmel"[2]—and indeed he was cast out of that exclusive company of people living and writing in Weimar: Goethe, Wieland, Herder, and later Schiller.

But Lenz had eliminated himself from this company already long before that winter of 1776. In this final chapter I would like to go beyond Lenz's eschewal of the *Kraftmensch*, discussed in chapter 4, to consider why his texts so often abandon the edifices of meaning that surround them, why words and actions so often give up all claim to meaning, and why there seems to be in Lenz a principle higher than creating texts that will help provide the fleeting sense of a unified German culture. Critics have tried to explain Lenz's famous habit of disrupting his own discourse in several different ways, and I would like to begin by considering three of these approaches to the interruptions in Lenz's texts. The first of these is to view Lenz as a specialist in "open form," as opposed to the closed form of classical drama; second, the view that his self-disruption is a result of the class struggle; the third, that gaps in Lenz are there to help audiences in their own self-realization. After considering how each of these contributions adds to our understanding of Lenz, I present my own contribution: that Lenz is a writer compelled to break free of the power of words to which so many writers of Sturm und Drang succumbed in their impatience to write a German nation into existence. In Lenz's sudden exits from his otherwise potentially compelling rhetorical edifices, we see a discarding of facile answers to German nationality. The traffic in Lenz's texts is inexorably outward, away from complacent edifices of meaning and away from the vicarious German national experience longed for by authors and the public alike.

Lenz's self-disruption belongs, first of all, to the history of modern, non-Aristotelian "open form." Closed form refers to drama with a beginning, middle, and an end, a handful of characters possessing a single world-view, and who speak to each other in one style of language, and in a linear plot with a short time-span. Lenz writes dramas with open form. *Der Hofmeister* and *Der neue Menoza*, despite their thematic unity, dispense with an obvious single principle that guides the whole: they are built up out of several strands of action and plots that develop not in linear fashion, but through an associative montage of scenes that seem torn from life. Characters—often with the realistic helplessness and inarticulateness of the modern antihero—display several kinds of speech and world-views, and we find them reacting as much to the impersonal processes of the world at large as to each other.[3] Lenz's drama has a theory to go with it—some might say to go against it—most of which he presents in the eccentric *Anmerkungen übers Theater*, where he reverses Aristotle's primacy of action over character, claiming that in the modern age tragedy is governed by people and comedy by events. "Meiner Meinung nach," he writes, "wäre immer der Hauptgedanke einer Komödie *eine Sache*, einer Tragödie *eine Person*" (1:254). It is a conclusion Lenz arrived at by contrasting the ancient Greek stage with that of the eighteenth century. Classical Greek tragedy, he contends, with its determinism of fated events, grew out of a fear of the gods: "Es war Gottesdienst, die furchtbare Gewalt des Schicksals anzuerkennen, vor seinem blinden Despotismus hinzuzittern. . . . Als Ästhetiker, war diese Furcht das einzige, was dem Trauerspiele der alten den *haut goût*, den Bitterreiz gab, der ihre Leidenschaften allein in Bewegung zu setzen wußte" (1:251). By contrast, in our age fear of God can no longer produce tragedy: our fate is dull and predictable, and when we know the mundane causes of things, our fate is not tragic, but comic. Tragedy is possible in our age only if we can produce heroes "die sich ihre Begebenheiten erschaffen, die selbständig und unveränderlich die ganze große Machine selbst drehen, ohne die Gottheiten in den Wolken anders nötig zu haben, als wenn sie wollen zu Zuschauern, nicht von Bildern, von Marionettenpuppen—von Menschen" (1:236). "Der Held allein," he writes, "ist der Schlüssel zu seinen Schicksalen" (1:254). But quite unlike some of his contemporaries, he never created any dramas or heroes who fit this description—he is involved, as John Osborne argues, in a "renunciation of heroism."[4] William Blake would maintain later in the century that "Character and expression, without which Art is lost can only be expressed by those who feel them."[5] But even though Lenz notices the lack of a sense of character in his society, in his dramas we get "no heroes or heroines, no clear moral message."[6] In his study of Lenz and Büchner, John Guthrie has noted that even Marie of *Die Soldaten* (perhaps the most architectonically structured of all Lenz's plays) diminishes in importance from act to act.[7]

The impressive thing about Lenz is that he knew instinctively that the hero whose autonomy needs no cultural foundation is impossible—a fact he must have learned from living in or near the nonnation of Germany. The *Anmerkungen* begin as the narrator asks us to imagine a gallery of dramatic traditions stretching over the last three thousand years, a theatrical "curiosity cabinet" whose respective cultures allow their drama to flourish in their particular age. As he presents six examples, from ancient drama to that of the eighteenth century, it is striking how far ahead Lenz is of his contemporaries in respect to the issue of characters and the cultures that allow them to be at the center of their drama. Seven years after the publication of the *Anmerkungen* and *Der Hofmeister*, in a famous scene from *Die Räuber*, Schiller's Karl Moor would let a roll call of historical figures from Alexander to Hannibal pass in review, then put down his Plutarch while cursing his own age for being a "schlappes Kastratenjahrhundert."[8] But Lenz goes beyond the rather narrow-minded view that this represents, viewing character as a function of its time and place—thus, it is a list of cultures, not historical figures, that passes in review. Lenz's German culture may simply not be ready to produce a character who could unify the text in which he or she appears. Thus, what he wants is not the traditional protagonist who speaks like every other character in the play, all within an ideal-laden plot custom-made for heroism; Lenz saw too much of this in French Neoclassicism. Instead, he wants characters who create their own situations, adding that he values the painter of caricatures "zehnmal höher als den idealischen" (1:235) because the "Mannigfaltigkeit der Charaktere und Psychologien" (1:244) provides a picture that is truer to nature "als zehn Jahre an einem Ideal der Schönheit zu zirkeln" (1:235). It is on this variety, he maintains, that the genius fastens.

The dramatist who is honest enough to withdraw from unreachable ideals and engage in patient mimesis of the world will have nothing of the Titan in extenuating circumstances, or of any figure whose acts take on significance only because they are framed within a compliant text. This more patient dramatist's protagonists will engage in isolated acts, acts that refuse to resonate heroically, and which therefore come across as comic rather than tragic. Not surprisingly, Lenz's plays, which as a rule he called "Komödien," are worlds away from Goethe's *Götz von Berlichingen*, even though several of *Der Hofmeister*'s first reviewers thought that the play, published anonymously, was the work of Goethe. In *Götz*, fateful portents of the coming revolt—a comet and two fiery swords in the sky—help propel the plot and impart sense, even heroism, to the protagonist's individualism.[9] Drama whose effectiveness depends on a neatly determined world, including *Götz*, is a subspecies of those dramas that have cultures to support them. But Lenz is ready neither to provide such divine help nor to smuggle it in in the form of a self-sure hero. He will not allow a character to be the artificial, godlike compass by which everything else in the play is allowed to orient itself. When Lenz artificially ties together so many loose ends at the end of his plays—in *Hofmeister*, with the Major's discovery of the pond into which Gustchen has just jumped, or with Pätus's lottery win—we, as spectators, are meant to shear away this artificiality and consider what is left: an open-ended world where character is impossible for the same reason that fate no longer exists: there is no culture, no faith, no ritual, no sense of identity to support it.[10]

This, I feel, is the direction that the appeal to open form should take if Lenz is to be fully appreciated. The adversity of German particularism provided a situation that gave German writers what amounted to a head start in developing the art forms of modernity. Treating Germany, as historians have recently suggested, as a backward nation in this period is an error that exaggerates the so-called normalcy of other European nations. For it is easy to forget that even outside Germany, middle-class democracy was still quite undeveloped in the 1770s. David Blackbourn suggests, I think correctly, that if Germany looks different from other places in the eighteenth century it may be only that it was experiencing earlier what the rest of the world would someday experience. Rather than a falling away from normalcy, Germany is a "metaphor of the times," and if it appears backward, it is only because of myths we too easily accept about the supposedly more progressive and civilized history of the rest of Europe: "That it so often appears exceptional probably owes a good deal to the distorting focus of a more acceptable myth—that of a benign and painless 'western civilization.'"[11] Germany has no monopoly on the rhetoric of Schiller and the antirhetoric of Lenz; its unusual circumstances merely allowed it to have slightly earlier and perhaps more jarring experiences of trends that sooner or later would be quite widespread in Western culture.

Class criticism provides another sort of answer to this question of self-disruption, finding in Lenz a chronicle of the contradictory attitudes embraced by the eighteenth-century German bourgeoisie. The middle class, so goes this argument, was more optimistic about its chances in "class society" than was prudent, and out of this contradiction came the rifts, gaps, and blind spots in Lenz. Klaus R. Scherpe, for example, argues that Lenz's texts speak with two voices: on the one hand, an idealistic rhetoric of progress whose optimistic "social imagination" sees the aristocracy and the bourgeoisie as reconcilable; on the other, a more realistic "poetic imagination" that depicts the true status of the Germany of Lenz's day—a world where class differences are irreconcilable.[12] Scherpe is not overly complimentary of Lenz, whom he finds too optimistic and not "concrete" enough; but he also sees that Lenz is enough of a realist to ironize the poverty of pure contemplation, such as in the final scene of *Der Hofmeister*, where Gustchen's illegitimate child is called "one of the advantages of private tutorship." In another typical class interpretation, Heinz Lorenz interprets Lenz's notion of the "Standpunkt" that Lenz says the true poet always takes to mean that Lenz knows that life is always experienced from the point of view of a particular class.[13] "Der wahre Dichter," says Lenz in that famous passage from the *Anmerkungen*, "verbindet nicht in seiner Einbildungskraft, wie es ihm gefällt, was die Herren die schöne Natur zu nennen belieben, was aber mit ihrer Erlaubnis nichts als die verfehlte Natur ist. Er nimmt Standpunkt—und dann *muß er so verbinden*. Man könnte sein Gemälde mit der Sache verwechseln. . . ." (1:230). What class criticism does not seem ever to get a grip on is the willful and provocative nature of these points at which Lenz's texts stop, stutter, and refuse to take advantage of the momentum they have already built up. In an essay on *Anmerkungen übers Theater*, Fritz Martini maintains that many critics of this essay expect to find in it a direct formulation of Lenz's own dramatic practice and are surprised when they do not, concluding that the essay reflects the consciousness and social conditions of his age.[14] He is right on both counts, but one might also go slightly farther and ask where, in this model of writing that jumps from form to society and back again, we are to find Lenz the writer, the man who suddenly halts the flow of his text? Unfortunately, this is a case in which a methodology confronts one of its own blind spots.

The last of the three approaches I want to mention here is one that takes Lenz's gaps as invitations to close them. According to Eva Maria Inbar, Lenz's open form represents the conscious use of a "Kunst der Lücke," an "art of the gap" through which he attempts to activate the imagination of spectators and readers to fill in what is not there.[15] "So aktiviert Lenz die Phantasie des Zuschauers und spart zugleich äußere Ereignisse aus, um psychologische Entwicklungen um so besser ins Licht zu rücken. Durch seine Kunst der Lücke erreicht Lenz in der Szenenverteilung einen ähnlichen Effekt wie im Dialog: Entscheidendes bleibt ungesagt und ungezeigt, kann nur vom Zuschauer erraten werden."[16] Helga S. Madland, in her absorbing study of Lenz's anti-Aristotelianism, finds in Lenz's aposiopesis "an invitation to the reader to think for himself," though her observation comes with a warning against considering Lenz's lacunae an open-ended affair. Generally, the caesura in Lenz, she points out, "occurs after a point has been made, leaving no doubt as to the intention of the complete sentence."[17] Perhaps most flattering to Lenz is Michael Morton, who argues that these gaps amount to a challenge that fosters the "awakening of an active and engaged consciousness in the audience"; with the intention to coax spectators to be co-creators, Lenz wants to help Germans realize themselves.[18] I am convinced that Lenz does imagine he can help others, and this argument also appears to be compatible, as Morton points out, with the altruistic Christianity Lenz espouses in his correspondence and in the early essay "Versuch über das erste Principium der Moral." There, playing on a frequent theme of the Enlightenment found from Addison to Schiller, he recommends helping others develop their own capacities.

Yet we also have to ask ourselves if Lenz was ever in a position to perform such a service for Germans. Certainly anyone familiar with

Lenz's emotional life—from his hopeless and often merely imagined entanglements with women who cared nothing for him, to the self-disparaging tone of his poetry—cannot help but wonder if Lenz was ever in a position to play the role of a powerful and magnanimous figure standing above the problem of German identity and beckoning others to follow. My feeling is that, Lenz's dreams for Germany notwithstanding, these are not gaps that harness what Wolfgang Iser calls "the communicative efficacy of aesthetic experience," not lacunae that can ever be part of a "filling-in process," and not an "inducement to communication." [19] This is not the self-interruption of a Lavater, whose well-rehearsed open-endedness is designed for congregations to complete; these are not gaps meant to be bridged in the next moment by the faith of impatient listeners eager to confirm axiomatic beliefs that, while not demonstrable, were essential to cementing together their lives. Lenz does not provide that "joyous offering" mentioned by Longinus that lets listeners be "filled with delight and pride as if we had ourselves created what we heard." [20] In the Germany of his time he finds it is still impossible, as he writes in the *Anmerkungen*, to "mit einem Blick durch die innerste Natur aller Wesen dringen, mit einer Empfindung alle Wonne, die in der Natur ist, aufnehmen und mit uns vereinigen" (1:228).

This is not to deny that Lenz's life was haunted by the hope that he would someday be able to feel and think and act as a member of a nation. [21] Lenz left Königsberg for Strasbourg in 1771 because he wanted to write as a German and help found a literature for the whole nation. He wrote to Gotter: "Mein Theater ist wie ich Ihnen sage unter freyem Himmel vor der ganzen deutschen Nation, in der mir die untern Stände mit den obern gleich gelten" (*Briefe* 1:104). In Strasbourg, as a member of the "Gesellschaft der deutschen Sprache," he expressed his German chauvinism in essays such as "Über die Bearbeitung der deutschen Sprache im Elsaß, Breisgau und den benachbarten Gegenden," where he called on the solidarity of all Germans in the development of their language and culture, and also warned that the lack of a unifying language has, in the past, resulted in the "Untergang ganzer Familien, Gesellschaften und Nationen" (4:249). But nowhere in Lenz do we see some version of that enthymeme designed to flatter the spectator whose heart, longing for community, is ready to supply the missing term. For it is clear that Lenz was more attuned to the futility of words, not their power: "Alle Redseligkeit," he writes in this same essay, "ist glänzende Armut" (4:243). Typically, the most striking actions in his drama are embedded in a context that refuses to help explain them; his honest mimesis presents life without a space to which it can properly be committed, and what might have been literary momentum can only stutter, stop, and jettison itself. Lenz's dream of a nation is revealed in his texts most often as he flaunts his disappointment with its impossibility, and the freedom he does depict, barred from following through with its impulses, is given no context in which to flourish: thrown objects can end up out of sight in the water (where Seraphine throws the jewelry box) or out of the window (where Pätus throws the coffeepot). Things in Lenz end up in spaces different from those the plot is capable of comprehending.

One of the influences on Lenz was Lawrence Sterne's *Tristram Shandy* (1759–67), a book in which, as Wolfgang Iser points out, interruptions not only convey a realistic sense of spontaneity, but also provide a sense of "freedom from logical constraints."[22] Iser adds that Sterne's gaps present life as action without having to impose a meaning on it: "This dilemma gives a double-edged impetus to the strategy of interruption, in that the interruptions convey the truth of life as a happening, but at the same time prevent it from being captured in any meaningful form."[23] He goes on to say that Sterne's strategy of interruption leads to a break between the hero and the world and, ultimately, to a comic point of view that "defends itself against the narrative process."[24] Now Lenz's characters, too, exhibit a comic critique of the world at large—think, for example, of Robert Hot in *Der Engländer*, or Strephon in *Die Freunde machen den Philosophen*, where, among other things, we are made to laugh at hopeless idealism. Anyone who reads this latter drama must ask themselves how Friedrich Ludwig Schröder could have considered it Lenz's best play. But Lenz's mimetic impulse led him to a new kind of unity. In the *Anmerkungen*, he says that great writing should involve a confusion of the painting with what it depicts—"sein Gemälde mit der Sache verwechseln" (1:230). And if depicting dysfunctional lives leads to a dysfunctional text, then it is precisely a functional narrative that the honest writer must avoid, despite the temptation to write a better Germany into existence. The drama of the *Kraftmensch*, custom-made to create a Germany on the stage before it was part of real life, exemplified business as usual for the dramatist hoping for a powerful effect. As the theory of genius was pressed into service to break the spell of Neoclassicism and pull Germany together (in Young's words) "as if by invisible means," Sturm und Drang—from Lavater through Goethe's *Götz* to Klinger's *Die Zwillinge* to Schiller's *Die Räuber*—harnessed the power of the word to pull Germans together and create a stage that could help build a nation. But when Lenz holds his mirror up to society, he makes sure that we see a system of living and acting and creating that is out of order. Vigorous heroes like Guelfo, Götz, and Karl Moor are out of the question for Lenz, who has Hanns von Engelbrecht announce at the beginning of his fragmentary play *Die Kleinen* (1775–76): "Das sei mein Zweck, die unberühmten Tugenden zu studieren, die jedermann mit Füßen tritt. Lebt wohl, große Männer, Genies, Ideale! euren hohen Flug mach ich nicht mehr mit; man versengt sich Schwingen und Einbildungskraft, glaubt sich einen Gott und ist ein Tor" (3:315).

Lenz knew that such theater pleased for the moment while leading nowhere, thus, like many twentieth-century dramatists, he was ambivalent about the theater in general and its aims. His general skepticism about the drama has been pointed out by Hans M. Wolff, who in 1939 discussed the debate in act 1, scene 4 of *Die Soldaten* that pits Haudy and Mary against Eisenhardt on the topic of whether the theater is advantageous or disadvantageous to society. Wolff writes: "It is interesting to see that such an enthusiastic lover of the theater as Lenz considers it necessary at all to raise the question of whether a theater is desirable or not, without reaching an unconditional affirmative answer."[25] Lenz's ambivalence about the theater arises from a fact taken for granted by Lavater, but which the author of *Die Soldaten* rejects: the fact that you can create your own version of the truth if you can supply the right language. As Hans Blumenberg notes, all rhetoric "substitutes verbal accomplishments for physical ones."[26] By and large, writers of the 1770s want definitive, powerful answers, but Lenz will not allow his own readers to come under the sway of characters and their verbiage: he insists on inhabiting the calm at the eye of the storm—a place where precisely those human weaknesses that make it possible for a text to be powerful are analyzed critically. Norman R. Diffey has pointed out how disturbed Lenz was not only by mankind's "infinite capacity for self-love,"[27] but by how that capacity underlies even our apparently virtuous feelings: "Vielleicht liegt die Ursache," writes Lenz in *Zerbin oder die neuere Philosophie* (1776), "in der Natur der menschlichen Seele und ihrer Entschliessungen, die, wenn sie entstehen, immer auf den Baum der Eigenliebe gepropft werden, und erst durch die Zeit und Anwendung der Umstände ihre Uneigennützigkeit erhalten" (5:81). Suspicious (as Kant would be) even of our moments of moral feeling, Lenz refuses to allow the impatient muse to lead him toward a view of life based primarily on rhetoric; as a result, his work constantly involves an attempt to *exit*, not enter, edifices of meaning.

Understandably, the consensus is that the most remarkable feature of Lenz's work is his sensitivity to language. In a 1958 article, Walter Höllerer produced a classic study of the different spheres of language analyzed in Lenz: in *Die Soldaten* we follow Marie through several—

the business language of her father, the aristocratic language of Desportes, the language of sentimentality, and the language of genius. Lenz is the one writer of Sturm und Drang truly aware that language is not a neutral medium, and what Bakhtin said of Dostoevsky is at least partly true for Lenz: that his texts are "populated—overpopulated—with the intentions of others."[28] But the main point I want to make in this final chapter is concerned not with Lenz's recognition of the intricate linguistic crisscrossing of our everyday speech, but with his refusal to give any one language a rhetorical advantage, even that of the author. This refusal also applies to the figurative language of poetry. "A happy symbol," wrote Emerson, "is a sort of evidence that your thought is just. . . . There is no more welcome gift to men than a new symbol. That satiates, transports, converts them."[29] But Lenz refuses to wield the power of the symbol. If the hero also comes under this ban, it is because a character in a literary work is also a symbolic expression. "Character," as W. K. Wimsatt has observed, "is one type of concrete universal . . . a new conception for which there is no other expression."[30] Lenz will not "use God" even when it amounts to making a poet's use of the invisible world of metaphors. Just as he distrusts the compelling character (despite his comments on tragedy), he distrusts the symbolic world in general.

The subtlest, yet most powerful way that German particularism translates into self-disruption in Lenz is by way of his recoil in the face of the most widespread compensatory mechanism for German disunity: religion. During his childhood in Livonia, in what is now Estonia, Lenz read the poetry of Klopstock, wrote poetry himself, and was encouraged by the historian and judge Friedrich Conrad Gadebusch, the religious poet Oldekop, and Dorpat school superintendent Martin Hehn. Still, his biographers agree that he never came under the personal influence of anyone who had a powerful and decisive impact on his writing—no one, that is, except his father, Christian David Lenz (1720–98). C. D. Lenz was an overbearing man who all but demanded that his son become a clergyman like himself and settle down into middle-class family life. Educated as a Pietist clergyman in Halle, C. D. Lenz traveled to Livonia to accept a position as a private tutor, quickly obtained a parish, and rose eventually to the position of general superintendent of Livonia. Lenz's fear of being locked into someone else's rhetoric may stem primarily from his father, whose religion reflected not only Pietism's self-righteous quest to build a kingdom within, but also the apocalyptic resonances of the baroque. "An meiner Wiege," Lenz once said (using the same formulation his father used in a tirade against the residents of Wenden two decades before) "stand das schreckliche Gericht Gottes."[31] This man who presided over the young writer's confirmation was an energetic and gifted speaker who apparently could bring a congregation to tears.[32] And to his son, he appeared beyond reproach: "Ich habe einen Vater," he wrote in an April 1776 letter, "der Pietist ist, er ist der treflichste Mann unter der Sonne."[33]

At first, Lenz honored his father's wish that he study theology and enrolled at the University of Königsberg, but he left after about a year to travel to Strasbourg. Although he refused to be outwardly critical of his father, his fear of well-crafted rhetoric may have derived in great part from that relationship. In essays of the late 1920s, Otto Petersen and Max Marcuse use the elder Lenz's 1741 diary to show how profound the influence was from father to son.[34] Interestingly, what these diaries reflect is a faith that is barely sustaining itself, and a tendency to recriminate himself for his lack of religious feeling and excessive pride. It is clear, especially in the poetry, that the son inherited these tendencies; yet he went even farther, submitting them to self-ironic criticism. The headaches that C. D. Lenz welcomed because they helped him empathize with Christ's suffering (he felt they gave him the depth of religious feeling that he lacked) are raised to a new level in the son and satirized in such places as *Der Hofmeister*, where Pastor Wenzeslaus praises Läuffer for emasculating himself so as to be a better Christian, and smokes to help obliterate his sex drive.[35] In *Die Soldaten*, Gräfin la Roche's heartless eviction of Marie, in act 4, scene 3, is probably best understood in the light of Lenz's awareness of the ultimately grotesque nature of all excessive single-mindedness: the Gräfin was trying to rehabilitate Marie morally, but she abandoned the project merely because Marie secretly spoke with a man.

But the subspecies of fanaticism about which Lenz worries most is that favorite child of the age: the imagination. And for this reason, we are to read the lines the Gräfin speaks at the end of the same act quite critically. She asks, rhetorically, as she second-guesses her decision to evict Marie: "Was behält das Leben für Reiz übrig, wenn unsere Imagination nicht welchen hineinträgt . . ." (3:81). That Lenz gives this statement to the Gräfin, a woman who has just made a mistake stemming from the obsessive way she pursues her avocation as political liberal, links the dangers of the imagination to the dangers inherent in all obsession. Lenz, as we know from works in every genre he employed, felt his own susceptibility to the sway of his imagination; he knew that he had to fight his own tendency to let the imaginary obliterate the real: "Gieb mir mehr wirkliche Schmerzen," he wrote to Lavater in May 1776, "damit mich die imaginairen nicht unterkriegen."[36]

Very likely the impulse that governs Lenz's textual stutter is very much like the attitude toward the imagination expressed by Herr von Biederling in act 3, scene 1 of *Menoza*, when he speaks to Graf Camäleon: "Es ist, wie so ein glänzender Nebel, ein Firniß, den wir über alle Dinge streichen, die uns in Weg kommen, und wodurch wir sie reizend und angenehm machen" (2:286).

It is from the suffocating world of obsession to his own free practical action that Lenz needs urgently to escape: "Platz zu handeln: Guter Gott Platz zu handeln und wenn es ein Chaos wäre das du geschaffen, wüste und leer, aber Freiheit wohnte nur da und wir könnten dir nachahmend drüber brüten, bis was herauskäme—Seligkeit! Seligkeit! Göttergefühl das!"[37] What does Lenz mean by "Platz zu Handeln"? Something like a space to act is already in place in Lenz's early poetry, such as "Die Landplagen," where the world made sense because all its details fit into God's plan: the natural disasters it chronicles result from mankind's sin, and we all have our appropriate space in which to live. In his youth, Lenz seemed resigned to and even happy with this moral "space" described in "Landplagen." But things changed quite radically in a very short time, as Lenz left home and found himself satirizing the suffocating world of his father's homiletics. He would not reject it as Werther did, by trading one side of his German inheritance (the specifics of his traditions) for another (the world of Klopstock's eternals, a kind of writing he fell back on only after his 1777 mental collapse). Neither would he build texts to persuade Germans that they had something they did not. Lenz was not ready to give his characters what they needed to delight audiences with some temporary resonance and momentum; instead, he would throw all momentum away, as if it had not been honestly won. In Lavater, the gaps pointed inward, toward the text; in Lenz, they point outward to thin air. He deliberately constructs his most engaging dramas, and the *Anmerkungen*, with a loosening, disengaging rhetoric that makes them canvases over which our eye is invited to wander freely, without coming under the tyranny of a god—or of a writer trying to invent a ritual that gives us an artificial space in which to act. Lenz will not create worlds that cloy to characters. In the *Götz* essay, where he speaks of his need for space to act, the deterministic power of society comes across as a power chiefly rhetorical: "Ha, er muß in was Besserm stecken, der Reiz des Lebens: denn ein Ball anderer zu sein, ist ein trauriger, niederdrückender Gedanke, eine ewige Sklaverei, eine nur künstlichere, eine vernünftige, aber eben um dessentwillen desto elendere Tierschaft" (4:223). It is not surprising that Brecht was attracted to this man. Lenz's work is a forum for the intellect that constantly keeps itself open to truth that resides outside of the obsessive behavior common to rhetoric and to every flattering ritual, including those initiated from behind the pulpit. With his eye for detail and his repulsion in the face of smothering rhetoric, he flew in the face of Germany's impatient project to write a Germany into existence as soon as possible, and by whatever method was needed.

This flight, as I have already suggested, is probably at the root of his difficulty as a poet. Even Gruppe, who hardly ever found fault with Lenz, notes that Lenz's talent as a poet simply did not keep pace with his dramatic talent.[38] While Goethe's poetry, under the influence of Herder, moved quickly from the ornamental metaphor of the mid-eighteenth century to the functional metaphor of Romanticism, Lenz never completed this transition. His lyric voice, lacking a middle ground where it could slow down and employ metaphors of nature, seems either to drift abruptly into banality or to fall back upon a lame and powerless version of baroque antithetics. Already present in the Petrarchan self-critique of the 1766 "Versöhnungstod Jesu Christi," this sensibility finds its clearest expression in his 1775 poem "Der verlorene Augenblick, die verlorene Seligkeit," a poem of fifty-six lines written with Goethe's sister Cornelia Schlosser in mind. It bears the subtitle: "Eine Predigt über den Text: die Mahlzeit war bereitet, aber die Gäste waren ihrer nicht wert," and its first strophe introduces a theme very frequent in Lenz's poetry—unworthiness of heaven.

> Von nun an die Sonne in Trauer,
> Von nun an Finster der Tag,
> Des Himmels Thore verschlossen!
> Wer ist, der wieder eröffnen,
> Mir wieder entschliessen sie mag?
> Hier ausgesperrt, verloren,
> Sitzt der Verworfne und weint
> Und kennt in seeliger Schöpfung,
> Gehässig nichts als sich selber,
> Ach, ausser sich selbst keinen Feind.
>
> (1:114)

Then there follows a conceit in which the image of Cornelia appears floating on the clouds, surrounded by roses:

> Auf gingen die Tore.
> Ich sah die Erscheinung.
> Und war's kein Traum?
> Und war's so fremd mir?—

But the chance to enter is lost:

> In dem einzigen Augenblick,
> Große Götter! was hielt mich zurück?
> Kommt er nicht wieder,
> Ach, er ist hin, der Augenblick
> Und der Tod mein einziges Glück!—

(1:115)

Here and elsewhere in Lenz's poetry we find gates—to heaven, to love, to life—that he will not allow himself to enter. "Eduard Allwills einziges geistliches Lied" (1775), speaks of "Funken . . . von Freuden" that never grow to become the "Flamme des Lebens" (1:185–87). In "Freundin aus der Wolke" (1772?), it is Friederike Brion who speaks from a cloud. Lenz is a writer whose attitude toward the imagination is quite different from those optimistic theorists of genius who helped found the Romantic movement, for it is singularly ambivalent about what is imagined and desired: in his texts he feels constantly held back from entry into gates leading to what he wants, and from giving into what he calls "the flame of life." Forget Addison's eloquent defense of "The Pleasures of the Imagination" and the praise Edward Young showers on writers who lead us on "bold excursions of the human mind."[39] Lenz's poetry is under the control of a mind that puts such bold excursions in check.

Yet he also says in his review of *Götz von Berlichingen* that our goal as human beings should be to build freedom around us—"Freiheit um uns her schaffen," and that "unsere Seele ist nicht zum Stillsitzen, sondern zum Gehen, Arbeiten, Handeln geschaffen." How do we reconcile the urge for freedom in Lenz with his equally strong impulse to check himself? A clue to this seeming contradiction is found in a piece he wrote shortly after arriving in Strasbourg, "Supplement zur Abhandlung vom Baum des Erkenntnisses Gutes und Bösen." Its subject is God's first command to human beings in the Garden of Eden: the warning against eating the apple. Lenz's contemporaries were already finding ways to exercise otherwise forbidden urges through the literary casuistry of the *Kraftmensch*, which allowed for the instant—and blameless—gratification of authors, characters, and sometimes audiences. But Lenz's solution to the urge to act with autonomy is entirely different: he tells us in the "Supplement" that the crime of Adam and Eve, committed in that first "space to act," was not a sin, but only a crime of impatience: "War sie also eine Sünde?—Das sei ferne! Nur ihre zu *ungeduldige* Befriedigung war es" (4:70, Lenz's italics). The will that led them to do what God had prohibited, he says, is itself a gift of God, one necessary for our happiness; our will and God's laws are, he says, like centrifugal and centripetal forces that work together to guarantee "*Freiheit im Handeln*" (4:71). The language of sophists and moralists may attempt to sway us with the urgent antithetics of heaven and hell—and "uns gern zu *nichts* machen wollten um uns gut zu machen" (4:72)—but real freedom means honoring and promoting "freie Handlung . . . so weit du reichen magst, auch bei andern dies Lebensfeuer wieder anzuzünden, das unser Prometheus vom Himmel brachte" (4:74). We are not to extirpate our desire, but only patiently to defer it. Impatience, on the other hand, betrays superficiality and artifice: "Daher dürfen die Boshaften oder die Faulen keine Empfindung durchempfinden, sie trauen nicht, die *Dauer* ist ihnen eine zu fürchterliche Probe und sie schwimmen lieber über der Oberfläche von hundert flüchtigen erkünstelten Empfindungen wie Kartenmänner fort, als daß sie sich in eine wahre untertauchen sollten" (4:76).

Patience is at the heart of Lenz's plan for himself and for Germany. At the end of his "Selbstrezension des Neuen Menoza" (1775), he estimates that his German public needs to be carefully prepared for tragedy by writers who can write comedy and tragedy at the same time: "Daher müssen unsere deutschen Komödienschreiber komisch und tragisch zugleich schreiben, weil das Volk, für das sie schreiben, oder doch wenigstens schreiben sollten, ein solcher Mischmasch von Kultur und Rohigkeit, Sittigkeit und Wildheit ist. So erschafft der komische Dichter dem tragischen sein Publikum" (2:334). Whether Lenz's own work is capable of serving such a preparatory function realistically is doubtful. But it represents groundwork that Lenz feels compelled to do, even if the only liberating rhetorical force his texts can offer is an ability to interrupt themselves. He does not pretend to find that "Platz zu handeln" that he covets; instead, he engages in what he conceives as a prerequisite for its discovery. "Dazu gehört aber Zeit," he wrote, "und viel Experimente" (*Briefe* 1:115). In the grip of a deep-rooted compulsion to undercut ritualistic shortcuts to a national culture, Lenz avoids misrepresenting Germany even at the cost of creating texts that stutter, undercut themselves, and grind to a halt.

Conclusion

There is more than explosive frustration in those rolling eyes of Sturm und Drang; there is communal grace for a people whose national reach exceeds its grasp. More often than not, studies of Sturm und Drang open with a chapter on Herder and Goethe that presents their work—Herder's adulation of the *Volk*, Goethe's *Götz von Berlichingen*—as the impetus for the entire tradition. In beginning with Lavater, I hope I have not given the impression that I see him as just such a prime mover, for I do not think that the tradition unfolds from the work of just one or two authors. However, I do think that Sturm und Drang's infatuation with Lavater tells us something about what these writers wanted and what they were willing to do to get it. Anxious for experiences they imagined only a national community could bring, they were tempted to simulate with language what they could not have in reality.

The vast rhetorical talent of Goethe's Werther, whose *Empfindsamkeit* is complex and ambiguous, offers one enactment of this project. More graphic is the open-textured *Urfaust*, which, although a mere draft, displays the gulf between particularist Germany and the Germany Goethe can imagine by showing that Faust and Margarete cannot even cohabit the same drama. In Klinger, the drama of the *Kraftmensch* strives to make violent individualism resound with shared principles until, like an exclamation point, the reception of Schiller's *Die Räuber* confirms that, after a decade, authors finally found the heightened sense of national identity they sought—even if what they found was not the autonomy they imagined they wanted, but a species of group behavior. In contrast to Schiller, Lenz is a writer who will not allow violence to create invigorating feelings of community: here, every anti-social act leads away from a sense of communal power, and the continual self-disruption of his texts is a rhetorical tactic quite the opposite of that practiced by his more optimistic contemporaries.

My argument that Lenz's more patient approach to Germany puts him a step ahead of the rest may suggest at times that there is something wrong with the artifice employed by the others. But moralizing can only cloud the issue. Sturm und Drang is a tradition rich enough to encompass widely different reactions to the desire to have a German nation as soon as possible. Every cultural tradition seeks and finds its own form, and the creative tension of Sturm und Drang is in its impatience to invent a Germany that did not yet exist.

Notes

Chapter 1

1. See Hettner, *Literaturgeschichte*, 3:437. An increasing number of critics consider the concept "Preromanticism" misleading. See Paul van Tieghem's *Le Préromantisme* (especially 1:37, 146–51). For reactions to the view that Sturm und Drang belongs to the early history of Romanticism, see Schröder, "Die Präromantiktheorie—eine Etappe in der Geschichte der Literaturwissenschaft?" See also Sauder, "Empfindsamkeit und Frühromantik," and Vietta, "Frühromantik und Aufklärung." However, Marshall Brown, in *Preromanticism*, makes a strong case for recognizing a distinct tradition of Preromanticism in English literature.

2. Schmidt, *Lenz und Klinger*, 3. See also Kindermann, *J. M. R. Lenz und die Deutsche Romantik*.

3. Keckeis, *Dramaturgische Probleme im Sturm und Drang*, 20–21.

4. Korff, *Geist der Goethezeit*, 1:278.

5. Lukács, *Faust und Faustus*, 180.

6. Braemer, *Goethes Prometheus und die Grundpositionen des Sturm und Drang*, for example, 40–69. See also Krauß, *Studien zur deutschen und französischen Aufklärung*, which suggests ways in which both Sturm und Drang and Weimar Classicism continue the *Aufklärung*. Rasch's essay "Der junge Goethe und die Aufklärung" does the same for Goethe, especially with reference to *Faust*. In Rausch's view, foremost among these continuities is the emphasis on individuality. See also Stellmacher, "Grundfragen der Shakespeare-Rezeption in der Frühphase des Sturm und Drang," which, extending Lukács's studies of Realism to Sturm und Drang's Shakespeare reception, is quite good on Herder. See also Stolpe's *Die Auffassung des jungen Herder vom Mittelalter*, especially 229–33 and 100–102.

7. "Karl Moor's Charisma in Its Historical Context," read at the Schiller Symposium in New York and published as "Karl Moor's Charisma" in *Friedrich von Schiller and the Drama of Human Existence*, 57–62. An expanded version appeared in the 1986 *Goethe Yearbook* as "'Fremde Menschen fielen einander schluchzend in die Arme': *Die Räuber* and the Communal Response." Chapter 6 of this study is an expanded and reworked version of that article.

8. Ordinarily, the charismatic figure involves a rather old-fashioned, idealistic notion of character—if a figure were truly individualistic, it is difficult to see how he or she could be charismatic. But as I argue in chapters 2 and 6, Sturm und Drang makes use of charisma precisely because it allows audiences to flee from an individualism it pretends to promote. In his essay "The Charismatic Hero: Goethe, Schiller, and the Tragedy of Character,"

Lamport concludes (more categorically than I do, but I think still correctly) that "The tragedy of character turns out to be a tragedy of charisma" (p. 66). Still, in his 1990 *German Classical Drama: Theatre, Humanity and Nation*, he writes that there is, in *Die Räuber*, "a neglect of the public dimension" (p. 37), an issue to which chapter 6 may be seen as a response. On the issue of character, see also Mason, "Schönheit, Ausdruck und Charakter im ästhetischen Denken des 18. Jahrhunderts."

9. On the eighteenth-century German writer and his lack of a developed public, see especially Bennett, *Modern Drama and German Classicism*, 15–21, 60–63; Reed, "Theatre, Enlightenment, and Nation: A German Problem"; McInnes, "The Sturm und Drang and the Development of Social Drama"; and Sokel, *The Writer in Extremis*, 7–23. My article, "The Dream of Identity: Lenz and the Problem of *Standpunkt*," also deals with this issue. For a fascinating primary text that deals with this phenomenon, see Möser, *Über die deutsche Sprache und Litteratur.*

10. Lenz, *Briefe*, 1:203. Further citations to the two-volume set of Lenz's correspondence will be in parentheses.

11. Klinger, *Briefbuch*, 394.

12. Klinger, *Jugendwerke*, 2:269.

13. The idea of the concept of *Genie* as compensation—"ein instinktiv gebildetes Gegengewicht" for insufficiencies—probably has its best formulation in Keckeis, *Dramaturgische Probleme im Sturm und Drang*, 14. Schmidt, *Geschichte des Genie-Gedankens* notes the origin of a new rhetoric in the Sturm und Drang, one that provides the illusion of the natural and spontaneous (1:59). Blumenberg, quite appropriately, writes that rhetoric always responds to "a specific difficulty of mankind." Blumenberg, "An Anthropological Approach," 432. He argues that rhetoric "creates institutions where evident truths are lacking" (p. 435). "Action compensates for the 'indeterminateness' of the creature man, and rhetoric is the effort to produce the accords that have to take the place of the 'substantial' base of regulatory processes in order to make action possible" (p. 433). See also Holborn, "German Idealism in the Light of Social History," and Dockhorn, *Macht und Wirkung der Rhetorik*, 1:46–96. On eighteenth-century German melancholy, see Lepenies, *Melancholie und Gesellschaft*, and Mattenklott, *Melancholie in der Dramatik des Sturm und Drang.*

14. Young, *Conjectures*, 16.

15. Ibid.

16. Herder, *Sämtliche Werke*, 1:227.

17. Goethe, *Werke*, Weimarer Ausgabe (WA), 1:29:146. Unless otherwise noted, citations to Goethe throughout the book refer to this edition.

18. Gerstenberg, *Briefe über Merkwürdigkeiten der Litteratur*, 222.

19. The *Volk* as conceived by these writers is just that: an illusion, and many of the figures I deal with in this book were aware of this. An unusual study that stresses the invention of national communities through the imaginative power of languages and literatures is Anderson's *Imagined Communi-*

ties. Anderson, who deals only briefly with Germany, focuses on Southeast Asia. On inherent problems involved in having a community, see also Sandel's interesting book *Liberalism and the Limits of Justice.* When I use the term "community" in the following chapters, I use it in a way quite similar to Sandel's "constitutive" conception of community, that is, community as describing "not just what [people] *have* as fellow citizens but also what they *are,* not a relationship they choose (as in a voluntary association) but an attachment they discover, not merely an attribute but a constituent of their identity" (p. 150).

20. Herder, *Sämtliche Werke,* 3:137.

21. Klinger, *Briefbuch,* 394. For Goethe's ideas on Gothic art and Herder's appreciation of Shakespeare, see Herder et al., *Von deutscher Art und Kunst,* 53–80, 96–109.

22. Glaser, "Überlegungen," 128.

23. As will soon become clear, I use the word "mimesis" in the Aristotelian sense of the representation of nature, not in the sense René Girard uses the word in his various discussions of idolatry, where he speaks of mimetic (or triangular or metaphysical) desire. See, for example, *Violence and the Sacred,* 145.

24. "Nichts hat der Sturm und Drang höher gehalten als die Sprache." Keckeis, *Dramaturgische Probleme im Sturm und Drang,* 130. Blackall's brief essay "The Language of Sturm und Drang" is the most interesting essay so far on Sturm und Drang language; he argues that it combines two contrasting styles—a "low," broken, inarticulate style derived from the *Volkslied* and sixteenth-century Germany, and a "high," expansive, articulate style with its roots in Klopstock. See chapter 5. Kieffer's *The Storm and Stress of Language* focuses on another subject: language as a theme of Sturm und Drang. It is, however, the most complete study of Sturm und Drang's awareness of how embedded our lives are in language—how we are manipulated by it and how we use it to manipulate others. See also de Man, *The Rhetoric of Romanticism,* 2–8. On Lenz's language in Sturm und Drang, see also Pfütze, "Die Sprache in J. M. R. Lenzens Dramen," and Höllerer, "Lenz: *Die Soldaten.*"

25. On the idea of incompleteness in German history and on the status of Germany in the eighteenth century, see especially Blackbourn and Eley, *The Peculiarities of German History;* Sheehan, "What is German History?"; and Schieder, "Grundfragen."

26. Blackall, *Emergence,* 337–38.

27. Siegfried Melchinger's *Dramaturgie des Sturms und Drangs* and Korff's *Geist der Goethezeit* are typical examples of this approach.

28. Korff, *Geist der Goethezeit,* 1:278.

Chapter 2

1. Goethe, *Dichtung und Wahrheit,* WA, 3:28:265. Goethe spends more time discussing Lavater in *Dichtung und Wahrheit* than any other figure of his

Sturm und Drang days. Weigelt also notes, incidentally, in his recent book on Lavater, that it was through his personality that Lavater had his greatest influence. *Johann Kaspar Lavater*, 119.

2. "Autobiographie" (1779), Nachlaß von Johann Kaspar Lavater. Handschriftenabteilung der Zentralbibliothek Zürich, MS. 1–2, pp. 20–21; also quoted in Farner, *Lavaters Jugend*, 30–31. Henceforth, endnote citations to manuscripts from the Lavater Nachlaß will be cited as they appear in the Katalog der Handschriften der Zentralbibliothek Zürich as "Lav. MS" followed by the manuscript and, where appropriate, page or section numbers (some manuscripts are numbered by section rather than by page). In the case of quotations from Lavater's 1779 autobiography, I also cite Farner's 1939 edition of that text, as above. I would advise against using Geßner's 1802 edition of this text, as Janentzky does; not only does it contain errors of orthography, Geßner also deletes several passages that I quote in this chapter, perhaps to help preserve his father-in-law's reputation.

3. Lav. MS. 1–2, p. 18; Farner, *Lavaters Jugend*, 28.

4. Lavater, *Aussichten in die Ewigkeit*, 2:lxxi. Subsequent references to this text will be cited in parentheses in the text by volume and page number. Schnorf spends about thirty pages on Lavater in his *Sturm und Drang in der Schweiz* (pp. 120–59), but his treatment deals almost exclusively with Lavater's sympathetic reaction to Lenz, Herder, and Goethe. Schnorf notes as he begins his treatment of Lavater: "Nirgends im deutschen Sprachgebiet konnten die Stürmer und Dränger zu Beginn der 70er Jahre so viele verwandte Tendenzen auf kleinem Raum beisammen in hoher Blüte treffen wie in der zeitgenössischen Schweiz" (pp. 120–21).

5. Schiller, *Sämtliche Werke*, 1:561.

6. Lavater, "Abhandlung von der unausdenklichen Theilbarkeit des Raums und der Zeit," Lav. MS. 55a. The twenty-fourth book of *Aussichten* appears to be another version of this essay.

7. Pestalozzi, "Lavaters Utopie," 298.

8. To H. Heß, September 14, 1759. Quoted in Janentzky, *J. C. Lavaters Sturm und Drang*, 16.

9. See, for instance, *Poesien* and *Schweizerlieder*. The poems of the *Schweizerlieder*, which he wrote on the suggestion of Martin von Planta and were later set to music by Heinrich Egli, are full of evocations of "Bruderschaft" and conceived as patriotic. Most deal with famous battles, and one is about Wilhelm Tell. The "Lied für Schweizermädchen" contrasts industrious Swiss women with Parisian women, who "Mögen nur auf Moden sinnen" (p. 142). See Schnorf, *Sturm und Drang in der Schweiz*.

10. As Alice Kuzniar has pointed out, "Lavater's breed of physiognomy does not have a syntax." Kuzniar, "Signs of the Future: Reading (in) Lavater's *Aussichten*," 14. She suggests that Lavater's appeal to Goethe, Herder, and Hamann can be found in his semiotics—in the nature of signs and how they point to the future in his work. On Lavater's semiotics, see also Gray, "Transcendence" and Abbott, "The Semiotics of Young Werther."

11. Lavater, *Geheimes Tagebuch,* 1:4.

12. Ibid., 1:78.

13. Ibid., 1:25.

14. "Magnetismus und Christenthum," Lav. MS. 48.3a, sections 7 and 8.

15. Janentzky, J. C. *Lavaters Sturm und Drang,* 46.

16. Lavater, "Autobiographie," Lav. MS. 1–2, pp. 20–21; Farner, *Lavaters Jugend,* 30–31.

17. Lavater, "Autobiographie," Lav. MS. 1–2, p. 19; Farner, *Lavaters Jugend,* 29.

18. Bennett, *Modern Drama and German Classicism,* 3.

19. Aristotle calls enthymeme the main instrument of oratorical persuasion, and he defines it as a syllogism that skips swiftly over a vital premise, relying on a truth already accepted by an audience. See book 2, paragraphs 22–26, of *The Rhetoric of Aristotle,* ed. Cooper. See also book 2, chapters 27–28, of *The Prior Analytics,* 191–395. On Lavater's language, see Radwan, *Die Sprache Lavaters im Spiegel der Geistesgeschichte.*

20. "Tagebuch Aufzeichnungen aus dem Mai 1761," Lav. MS. 4, May 11, 1761.

21. Meister, *Ueber die Schwärmerei.* 1:45–46. The worst attacks on Lavater come in the 1786–89 editions of the *Berlinische Monatsschrift* and in the anonymous *Archiv für Narrheit und Schwärmerei,* which calls him a charlatan, a performer of hocus-pocus (p. 9), and a "Schwärmer der ersten Klasse" (p. 14).

22. Meister, *Ueber die Schwärmerei,* 1:45.

23. To Goethe, September 1, 1773. Funck, *Die Anfänge von Goethe's Freundschaft mit Lavater,* 30.

24. The *Volkslieder* Herder admires employ images, not abstractions, and their immediacy brings a quality Herder often describes with the words *Wurf* and *Sprung,* for example, "so viel Würfe, so viel Sprünge," and "Sprünge und kühne Würfe." "Über Oßian und die Lieder alter Völker," in Herder et al., *Von deutscher Art und Kunst,* 1–50 (here, pp. 33–34).

25. Lavater, *Geheimes Tagebuch,* 1:100.

26. Lavater, "Autobiographie," Lav. MS. 1–2, p. 39. Farner, *Lavaters Jugend,* 49.

27. Lavater, *Geheimes Tagebuch,* 1:155.

28. Quoted by Janentzky, J. C. *Lavaters Sturm und Drang,* 19.

29. Herder wrote this to his fiancée in January 1773, after reading the first two volumes of *Aussichten.*

30. This is one of Wilhelm von Humboldt's recollections in a short sketch of Lavater. Humboldt, *Werke,* 5:27.

31. Lavater, "Autobiographie," Lav. MS. 1–2, p. 18. Farner, *Lavaters Jugend,* 28.

32. Haym, *Herder,* 1:537.

33. Lavater, "Autobiographie," Lav. MS. 1–2, p. 4. Farner, *Lavaters Jugend,* 50.

34. Lavater, *Geheimes Tagebuch*, 1:99.

35. Ibid., 129.

36. Shaftesbury, "A Letter Concerning Enthusiasm," in Shaftesbury, *Soliloquy*, 1:5–39 (here, p. 36). Shaftesbury, incidentally, seems as interested in character as in art.

37. Meister, *Ueber die Schwärmerei*, 1:27.

38. Ibid., 28.

39. Goethe's harsh review of volume 3 of the *Aussichten* can be found in *Der junge Goethe*, ed. Fischer-Lamberg, 3:90–93. Goethe found the third volume of the *Aussichten* to be inferior to the first two. Among his objections: Lavater's purported audience of "Denkende und Gelehrte" seems to neglect the domain of feelings; and Lavater preserves class distinctions in the hereafter. In *Dichtung und Wahrheit* Goethe tried to play down his contributions to the *Physiognomische Fragmente* (he said he only contributed to the sections on animal skulls), but as Eduard von der Hellen has shown in *Goethes Anteil an Lavaters Physiognomischen Fragmenten*, his contributions were much greater than he admitted. It is evident from correspondence that Goethe and Lavater were exchanging opinions on portraits as late as October 4, 1782; see Hirzel, *Briefe von Goethe an Lavater*, 149–55. A letter to Lavater of January 8, 1777, contains an ironic poem by Goethe called "Lied des Phisiognomischen Zeichners," which ends with the strophe:

> Wirst alle deine Kräfte mir
> In meinem Sinn erheitern,
> Und dieses enge Daseyn hier
> Zur Ewigkeit erweitern.

(Hirzel, Briefe, 29–30)

40. "Goethes Werther (mir ganz unschädlich) halt ich fürs beste lehrreichste Buch, das Deutschland für mich hervorgebracht hat." Lav. MS. 553. Lavater makes this statement while answering Branconi's request for a list of his favorite books, which also include the New Testament, *Ossian*, the works of Goethe and Haller, the first book of Moses, the first chapter of Daniel, and the story of Elias and Elisa. See also Atkins, "J. C. Lavater and Goethe."

41. Lavater, *Aussichten*, 1:289, 308–9.

42. Weber, *Wirtschaft und Gesellschaft*, 1:40.

43. Schiffer, *Charisma*, 19.

44. Ibid., 21.

45. Ibid., 50.

46. Ibid., 50.

47. Ibid., 66–67. Weiskel, whose Freudian treatment of the sublime has a number of features in common with Schiffer's theory of charisma, points out that a crucial affective element of the Kantian sublime is its invitation to "conspiratorial self-aggrandizement." *The Romantic Sublime*, 76.

48. Longinus, *On Great Writing*, 6, 47–48.

49. Ibid., 10.

50. Ibid., 50. "In the theatre, as in life," Edward Young wrote, in an observation that could apply as well to Lavater's congregations, "delusion is the charm"; *Conjectures*, 50. And one of the deluding elements is flattery. "The reason that there is such a general outcry among us against flatterers," wrote Addison, "is that there are so few very good ones"; *Tattler*, 352.

51. R. M. Werner refers to this phrase in his review of Oscar Erdmann's book *Über F. M. Klingers dramatische Dichtungen*, 293. The question of the tradition's name is taken up by several critics, most recently by Bernd Horlitz in his article "Zur Bedeutung der Formel 'Sturm und Drang.'"

52. Schiller, *Sämtliche Werke*, 1:554.

Chapter 3

1. My interest in this chapter is primarily in the original version of *Die Leiden des jungen Werthers*, which was published in 1774, then reprinted almost unchanged in 1775 (Goethe added the warning: "Sei ein Mann, und folge mir nicht"). As a rule, the text I cite is the 1774–75 version, not the later 1787 version that contains numerous changes and additions by Goethe, who by that time had been at the court of Weimar for twelve years. The 1787 version is the one usually cited by scholars and the version that is always translated into English. But this is a book about the Sturm und Drang, and as I argue later on in the chapter, the 1774 version must be considered the *Werther* of Sturm und Drang. The 1787 version is cited only when that part of the text does not exist in the 1774 version. So that readers know which version I am using, I cite page numbers within my text with an "A" or a "B," following the convention of the Akademie-Verlag edition (1954), which provides both the 1774 (designated "A") and 1778 ("B") editions.

2. Another inheritance issue is added in the 1787 version, where we learn on September 4, 1772 that the brother of the Peasant Boy's employer does not want his sister to remarry for fear of a diluted inheritance (95B). See Saine, "The Two Versions of Goethe's *Werther*."

3. Of course, there are many opinions as to what is the dominant metaphor of this book. Max Diez, for example, has argued that the dominant images in *Werther* are all common metaphors of Romanticism: sickness, pain, and death. Diez, "The Principle of the Dominant Metaphor in Goethe's *Werther*," 830; yet as I suggest here, an equally prevalent metaphor is inheritance, here the literal inheritance of estates.

4. It is not always an escape from Germany. Aspermonte tells Julius in Leisewitz's *Julius von Tarent* that they will escape to Germany: "So sei Deutschland die Freistatt der Liebe"; Klinger, *Jugendwerke*, 2:1571. That *Werther* was an international success does not seem to me to contradict the argument that it was a response to a specifically German situation.

5. Generally speaking, such matters as this "stormy element" that Goethe criticizes in himself belong to the *Schwärmerei* and enthusiasm for which the age is known, and *Schwärmerei* is usually an accusation in the eighteenth

century—an accusation, more often than not, of mindless and irrational fanaticism. Still, as early as 1707, such emotions are defended by Shaftesbury. See especially "A Letter Concerning Enthusiasm," in Shaftesbury, *Soliloquy*, 1:5–39. Incidentally, another theme of *Werther*, ill humor, is cited by Shaftesbury in this same essay as a cause of atheism (p. 17). Lavater devoted an entire book to ill humor and suicide: *Predigten über das Buch Jonas*, which deals mainly with Jonah's cranky reaction to God's decision to forgive the citizens of Nineveh. This book is the source both of Werther's comments on Herr Schmidt's ill humor and Albert's observations on suicide. For Lavater, suicide is the result of "a failure of sweet hope" (*Predigten*, 2:189–90). I have always thought Thorlby's "From What Did Goethe Save Himself in *Werther*?" to be one of the best essays ever written on this novel.

6. In Jacobi's *Eduard Allwills Briefsammlung*, Luzie calls Allwill a sophist and, with irony, "an extraordinary human being" for being able to combine unbound sensuality and a propensity for stoicism, the coldest courage and the firmest fidelity. Jacobi, *Briefsammlung*, 202.

7. See Bruford, *Germany in the Eighteenth Century*, 260–69. On this topic see also Lange, *The Classical Age of German Literature*.

8. Van den Heuvel, *Beamtenschaft und Territorialstaat*, 208.

9. See ibid., 205–6.

10. Still, even with the help of middle-class bureaucrats, the Reichskammergericht was horribly inefficient: by 1767, when completing about sixty cases per year, it was approximately twenty thousand cases behind, and when Napoleon came through Wetzlar shortly after the turn of the century, his lieutenants found unopened and unbegun cases dating as far back as 1690. See Gloël, *Der Wetzlarer Goethe*, 10–12, Demeter, "Das Reichskammergericht in Wetzlar zu Goethes Zeit," and Mignon, *Goethe in Wetzlar*.

11. Goethe, *Werke*, WA, 1:9:544–45.

12. See Gloël, *Der Wetzlarer Goethe*, 18–22.

13. *Allgemeine Deutsche Biographie*, 13:784.

14. Herbst, *Goethe in Wetzlar*, 62.

15. Ibid., 65.

16. Ibid., 68.

17. Shaftesbury, "Advice to an Author," in *Soliloquy*, 1:102–234. (here, p. 136).

18. Young, *Conjectures*, 28, 38.

19. Rousseau, *Confessions*, 17.

20. In a letter to Kant, July 27, 1759, quoted in Blackall, *Emergence*, 426. See also Hamann's *Sokratische Denkwürdigkeiten* (1759), where he upholds the truths of faith and paradox over those of reason. On the bankruptcy of "wit," see also Lessing's *Hamburgische Dramaturgie*, part 32, where he asserts that a "witziger Kopf" will never write a tragedy that evokes Aristotelian pity and fear. See also Alasdair MacIntyre on the propensity of the eighteenth-century Enlightenment to strip away tradition in order to guarantee the rights of the individual, a process that makes morality available in a new way. MacIntyre, *After Virtue*, 110, 155, 205.

21. Vico, *The New Science*, 424.
22. Rousseau, *Confessions*, 191–92.
23. Hegel, *Phänomenologie des Geistes*, 391–400.
24. Blackall, *Goethe and the Novel*, 40.
25. Ibid., 21.
26. In a famous conversation in Erfurt on October 2, 1808, Napoleon criticized *Werther* for mixing two themes he thought did not belong together in the same work: "eine Vermischung der Motive der gekränkten Ehrgeizes mit denen der leidenschaftlichen Liebe. Das ist nicht naturgemäß und schwächt bei dem Leser die Vorstellungen von dem übermäßigen Einfluß, den die Liebe auf Werther gehabt. Warum haben Sie das getan?" Goethe, *Werke* (Hamburger Ausgabe), 6:532–33. The theme of failed ambition goes back to Kestner's letter to Goethe about Jerusalem of October 30, 1772, written eight weeks after Goethe left Wetzlar, in which Kestner writes that Jerusalem despaired because "Zutritt in den großen Gesellschaften [war] auf eine unangenehme Art versagt worden." Goethe, *Werke* (Hamburger Ausgabe), 6:518. Goethe seems to have agreed with Napoleon, or at least to an extent, and he compared Napoleon's comment to that of a knowledgeable tailor who, in a presumably threadless sleeve, suddenly finds the fine, hidden thread. Goethe, *Werke* (Hamburger Ausgabe), 6:532. Many twentieth-century critics have followed suit: "Man könnte daher sagen: die Liebeshandlung im Werther steht ebenso geschlossen da wie die Gretchenepisode im Faust. Hier wie dort bildet sie aber nur eine Etappe im Lebensproblem des Helden." Borchert, *Der Roman der Goethezeit*, 32.
27. See, for example, Alewyn, " 'Klopstock!,' " 358–60. See also McCarthy, "The Art of Reading and the Goals of the German Enlightenment."
28. Schiller, "Selbstrezension der *Räuber*," *Sämtliche Werke*, 1:634.
29. Blackall, *Emergence*, 338.
30. Ibid., 413.
31. Ibid., 274.
32. Haller, "Unvollkommenes Gedicht über die Ewigkeit," in *Haller und Salis-Seewis*, ed. Frey, 109–13 (here, p. 110).
33. Klopstock, "Dem Allgegenwärtigen," in *Klopstocks Werke*, ed. Hamel, 3:98–104 (here, pp. 99–100).
34. Graham, "*Die Leiden des jungen Werther*: A Requiem for Inwardness," 126, 136.
35. To cite just one example, Robert Hot's love for the princess in *Der Engländer*. This aspect of Lenz, particularly with reference to his poetry, is treated in chapter 7. It is interesting that Beaumarchais's *The Marriage of Figaro* (1775) turns such hyperbolic love into a comedy at the same time that German literature is treating it as a grave matter.
36. Bruford, *Germany in the Eighteenth Century*, 267.
37. Bosl, *Die Grundlagen der modernen Gesellschaft im Mittelalter*, 4:227–28.
38. Borst, "Das Rittertum im Hochmittelalter: Idee und Wirklichkeit," 228.

39. Humboldt, *Werke*, 2:235–36.

40. Schöffler, *"Die Leiden des jungen Werther*: Ihr geistesgeschichtlicher Hintergrund,"* 181.

41. See Blackall, *Goethe and the Novel*, 39, for a discussion of the wide-ranging qualities some critics have seen in Werther.

42. During the meeting with Albert at the hearing for the Peasant Boy, a section added in 1787, Werther's refusal to abide by the law is stretched to its limits. Albert quietly sides with the judge, but Werther mounts a vigorous defense of the boy. One has to wonder where Werther gets the self-confidence to defend the boy even after the murder confession, and it is Werther's inability to share a framework of morality with others that brands him as an outcast. Incidentally, one of the few critics to suggest an arrogance in Werther (although I do not believe she uses the word) is Louise Z. Smith, who notes that Werther, from the first page on, "resolves not to let the suffering of others bother him." Smith, "Sensibility and Epistolary Form in *Héloïse* and *Werther*," 370.

43. Nolan, "Goethes *Die Leiden des jungen Werthers*: Absicht und Methode," 213–15. For another view, see Warrick, "Lotte's Sexuality and her Responsibility for Werther's Death."

44. Mann, "Goethe's Werther," 652.

45. Troeltsch, *Gesammelte Schriften*, 1:440.

46. Ibid., 1:550.

47. Weber, *Wirtschaft und Gesellschaft*, 2:727.

48. "Für den Asketen bewährt sich die Gewißheit des Heils stets im rationalen, nach Sinn, Mittel und Zweck eindeutigen Handeln, nach Prinzipien und Regeln. Für den Mystiker, der im realen Besitz des zuständlich erfaßten Heilsgutes ist, kann die Konsequenz dieses Zustandes gerade umgekehrt der Anomismus sein: das Gefühl, welches sich ja nicht an dem Tun und dessen art, sondern in einem gefühlten Zustand und dessen Qualität manifestiert, an keine Regel des Handelns mehr gebunden zu sein, vielmehr in allem und jedem, was man auch tue, des Heils gewiß zu bleiben." Ibid., 1:333.

49. Lenz, "Über Götz von Berlichingen," in *Gesammelte Schriften*, ed. Blei, 4:223.

50. Schiller, *Sämtliche Werke*, 1:503.

51. Feuerlicht, "Werther's Suicide: Instinct, Reasons, and Defense," 477.

52. Capitalism, Weber argued, made society more calculable than ever before, and less constrained by traditions, feelings, and loyalty. Thus he called it the most rational form of organization. "Der moderne kapitalistische Betrieb ruht innerlich vor allem auf der Kalkulation. Er braucht für seine Existenz eine Justiz und Verwaltung, deren Funktionieren wenigstens im Prinzip ebenso an festen generellen Normen rational kalkuliert werden kann, wie man die voraussichtliche Leistung einer Maschine kalkuliert," *Wirtschaft und Gesellschaft*, 2:834. The work of Jürgen Habermas and many others is based in great part on Weber's idea that the rationality of capital-

ism is the element that dissolves traditional society. A useful book on this development is Schluchter, *The Rise of Western Rationalism*.

53. Scherpe, *Werther und Wertherwirkung*, 58, for example.

Chapter 4

1. Shelley, *Complete Poetical Works*, 205. For the Romantics, writes Peter L. Thorslev, the Prometheus myth "tends in its Romantic development toward a vision of a *naturalistic* universe colored by a *humanist* faith" and toward "the belief that the heart or the soul of man is so constituted that . . . he will most of the time choose the good"; the Romantic Prometheus stands for the value of "mercy, sympathy, and kindness toward one's fellow men." Thorslev, *The Byronic Hero*, 117. This generalization includes Byron's Prometheus, whose "Godlike crime was to be kind." Byron, *The Complete Poetical Works*, 4:32.

2. Shelley, *Complete Poetical Works*, 214.

3. Schiller, *Sämtliche Werke*, 1:554.

4. Originally titled *Prometheus. Dramatisches Fragment*, Goethe's fragmentary two-act drama was found in 1818 among the papers of J. M. R. Lenz, who apparently made a copy of it when he was in Weimar. Both here and in the 1785 Pindaric ode, Goethe's Prometheus is a son of Zeus and thus technically not a Titan, though of course as a rebel against authority he is a Titan in the common sense of the term. Interpretations of Goethe's treatments of Prometheus fall roughly into three schools: the "aesthetic" view, which holds that Goethe "recognizes in the fate of Prometheus the fate of the artist" (Walzel, *Das Prometheus-Symbol von Shaftesbury zu Goethe*, 57); the view that Prometheus engages in "metaphysical rebellion"—that is, not against specific restrictions but, rather, "against the idea of human subordination in general" (Korff, *Geist der Goethezeit*, 1:278); and class interpretations, according to which Goethe's drama fragment and the ode depict the struggle between the German bourgeoisie and feudal absolutism. Class studies range all the way from Edith Braemer's picture of an optimistic Goethe whose Prometheus, representing "the development of the consciousness of the people" (*Goethes Prometheus und die Grundpositionen des Sturm und Drang*, 364), provokes the middle class to seize its socioeconomic destiny, to Andreas Huyssen's view that the 1773 play remained a fragment precisely because Goethe was too pessimistic about the chances of the middle class to believe in "Bürger Prometheus" (Huyssen, *Drama des Sturm und Drang*, 60).

5. Shaftesbury, *Soliloquy*, 1:136.

6. Grimm, *Deutsches Wörterbuch*, 5:1952. Other terms for the figure include *Kraftgeist, Kraftmann, Kraftfrau*, and *großer Kerl*. The trend in class criticism has been to use the term *Selbsthelfer*, a word Goethe used occasionally to refer to *Götz von Berlichingen* (e.g., Goethe, *Werke*, WA, 1:27:321) and *Selbsthelferfigur*. Siegrist also uses this terminology. Huyssen argues that terms like *Kraftkerl* gloss over the class struggle and its complexities (Huyssen,

Drama des Sturm und Drang, 82). But it may be that *Selbsthelfer* and *Selbsthelferfigur*, with their entrepreneurial overtones, contain the even greater danger of applying a single point of view exclusively.

7. Korff, *Geist der Goethezeit*, 1:225, 229. Artaud believes that twentieth-century theater will never find itself until the spectator's "taste for crime, his erotic obsessions, his savagery, his chimeras, his utopian sense of life and matter, even his cannibalism, pour out." *The Theater and Its Double*, 92. While Artaud's demand that audiences be plunged back into ritual, incantation, and violence had a seminal influence on the French avant-garde theater, my argument here is, of course, that violent and ritualistic theater is in great part abused and misdirected in Sturm und Drang's idealistic attempt to realize Germany as a literary experience.

8. Schmidt, "The Language of Confinement," 184.

9. Goethe, *Werke*, WA, 1:39:196.

10. Ibid., 28:225.

11. Klinger, *Briefbuch*, 388.

12. May, "Fr. Max. Klingers Sturm und Drang," 407.

13. Hering, *Friedrich Maximilian Klinger: Der Weltmann als Dichter*, 34, 36.

14. Guthke, "F. M. Klingers *Zwillinge*: Höhepunkt und Krise des Sturm und Drang," 706.

15. Ibid., 712. Goethe, *Werke*, WA, 1:28:254.

16. Zenke, "Das Drama des Sturm und Drang," 122.

17. On Sturm und Drang's internal self-critique, see also Walzel, *Das Prometheus-Symbol von Shaftesbury zu Goethe*, 107; Huyssen, *Drama des Sturm und Drang*, 79, 192; Gray, "The Ambivalence of Revolt in Klinger's *Zwillinge*"; Schmidt, "The Language of Confinement"; and Harris, who raises the issue in the context of Klinger's four versions of *Die Zwillinge* in "Vier Stücke in einem." See also Wolff, *Goethes Weg zur Humanität*, 117–72.

18. Jennings, " 'Vergessen von aller Welt': Literatur, Politik und Identität in Klingers Dramen des Sturm und Drang," 500.

19. Herder, *Sämtliche Werke*, 1:349.

20. Ibid., 4:227.

21. Ibid., 5:584.

22. Ibid., 502.

23. Ibid., 563.

24. Ibid., 601, 605.

25. Wolf, "Die Genielehre des jungen Herder," 430. Wolf provides the most thorough treatment of Herder's rather sudden rejection of extreme subjectivism. Walzel also deals with the topic (*Das Prometheus-Symbol von Shaftesbury zu Goethe*, 106–7).

26. Herder, *Sämtliche Werke*, 8:296, 216, 216, 296.

27. Ibid., 295.

28. Ibid., 296, 260.

29. Carnois, *The Coherence of Kant's Doctrine of Freedom*, 45. See also Allison, "Practical and Transcendental Freedom in the *Critique of Pure Reason*."

30. Kant, *Kritik der reinen Vernunft*, in *Gesammelte Schriften*, Akademie-Ausgabe, 3:464 (in the original manuscript, B 561/A 533).

31. Smith, *A Commentary to Kant's* Critique of Pure Reason, 57.

32. Kant, *Kritik der reinen Vernunft*, 3:634 (B 831/A 803).

33. Ibid., 465 (B 562/A 534).

34. Kant's views on Sturm und Drang's general sensibility can be found in paragraph 47 of the *Kritik der Urteilskraft*, in his correspondence with Hamann and Herder, and in the interesting section on genius in the *Reflexionen zur Anthropologie* (15:406–44), where he writes that while Rousseau was "ein achtungswürdiger Schwärmer," Lavater "schwärmt in dem er Ideen ganz über den Kreis der Erfahrungserkenntnis ausdehnt" (15:406–7).

35. Schmidt, "The Language of Confinement," 184.

36. Ryder, "Toward a Revaluation of Goethe's *Götz*," 61.

37. Goethe, *Werke*, WA, 1:8:124.

38. Ibid., 116.

39. Ibid., 28:142.

40. Ibid., 8:116.

41. Ibid., 138, 142.

42. Ibid., 119.

43. Ibid., 1:160.

44. Ibid., 8:159.

45. Ibid., 169.

46. Despite being written quite rapidly, Goethe's 1773 play is only apparently disorganized. In her "Submerged Symmetry and Surface Chaos," Teraoka argues that this drama's apparent impulsiveness, immediacy, and "exhuberant individuality and boundless freedom" are in fact undergirded by strict compositional principles (pp. 33, 13).

47. Klinger, *Jugendwerke*, 1:243–44.

48. Ibid., 275.

49. Ibid., 236.

50. Ibid., 244.

51. Ibid., 240.

52. Harris, in the introduction to Klinger, *Werke: Historisch-kritische Gesamtausgabe*, vol. 2., forthcoming 1994.

53. Jones, *Revolution and Romanticism*, 234.

54. Melchinger, *Dramaturgie des Sturms und Drangs*, 26.

55. In 1880 Otto Brahm categorized several kinds of repetition employed in Sturm und Drang and other late eighteenth-century drama and surmised that *Stürmer und Dränger* used the technique in much the same way as Shakespeare, Klopstock, and Lessing did (*Ritterdrama*, 204–27). But Kurt May argued in 1930 that repetition in Klinger expressed "the inner intensification of the impulse to expand" (May, "Beitrag," 268), and Gerhard Kaiser, in the 1973 essay "Friedrich Maximilian Klingers Schauspiel *Sturm und Drang*," maintained: "Die Wortwiederholungen bezeichnen hier nicht Wendungen des Gedankens, sondern ein unersättliches Auskosten der Wörter

auf ihren Gefühlsgehalt hin, ohne daß die Sprache gedanklich auch nur einen Schritt weiterrückte" (pp. 21–22). Kaiser argued that, unlike Klopstock, who used repetition to communicate feelings, writers of Sturm und Drang used it to express "the *being-by-itself* [*Für-sich-sein*] of the individual engrossed in its experience" (p. 23). It is also worth remembering Oskar Walzel's argument in his essay "Leitmotive in Dichtungen," in which he calls repetition simply a necessity of all art.

56. Wild, in Klinger's *Sturm und Drang*, in *Jugendwerke*, 2:319.

57. Goethe, *Werke*, WA, 4:2:7.

58. Nietzsche, *Die Geburt der Tragödie*, 59. Compare Girard's notion of myth as "part of the process by which man conceals from himself the human origin of his own violence by attributing it to the gods." *Violence and the Sacred*, 161.

59. Schiller, *Sämtliche Werke*, 1:483.

60. Ibid., 597.

61. Nicole Loraux, whose approach in *Tragic Ways of Killing a Woman* should someday be applied to Sturm und Drang, might say that Amalia's virginity qualifies her for the typically female death she suffers at Karl's hands: virgin blood flows so that warriors can prosper. Karl helps repay his debt to society by killing Amalia, his possession, and the death saves Karl's honor and purifies his evil. Loraux shows how Greek tragedy was clever enough to make an engaging communal ritual out of women's deaths while still banning women to the sidelines of culture.

62. Lenz, *Gesammelte Schriften*, ed. Blei, 1:403.

63. Ibid., 3:46.

64. Ibid., 74.

65. Ibid., 2:331. As a religious man, Lenz obviously puts great value on what he calls "die unmittelbare Einwirkung der Gottheit" (Lenz, *Briefe*, 1:53), but he apparently sees divine grace as a prerogative of God, not a matter of literary casuistry. For another approach to the problem of responsibility in Lenz, see Herbert Haffner, who argues that for Lenz, the individual can never reach his or her potential until society can learn to emulate the altruism of Christ. *Lenz: Der Hofmeister. Die Soldaten*, 17–34. "So haben alle Figuren, die anfangs egoistische Züge aufweisen, am Schluß Reue und Buße im Sinne des Altruismus zu leisten" (p. 30). In general, there is a much less pronounced turn toward conservatism in Lenz. One example is his warning in his 1776 essay "Etwas über die Veränderung der Sprache," in which he backpedals slightly on the license he gave dramatists in the *Anmerkungen* to change scenes at will; here, two years later, he warns of "breaking the scenic illusion."

66. Goethe, *Werke*, WA, 1:2:77.

Chapter 5

1. Goethe's interest in the Faust theme, according to a June 1, 1831 letter to Zelter, began in 1768–69. In a March 17, 1832 letter to Wilhelm von Hum-

boldt he claimed that the Faust theme occupied his mind for more than sixty years. Nollendorfs estimates that Goethe conceived the *Urfaust* sometime between his residence in Strasbourg and Wetzlar and wrote it during his second stay in Frankfurt, thus around 1771–72 (Nollendorfs, *Streit*, 291). See also Castle, "Plan und Einheit in der ersten Konzeption des Goetheschen *Faust*"; Krogmann, *Goethes* Urfaust; and Petsch, "Neue Beiträge," "Zum Urfaust," and "Zur Chronologie des Faust."

2. Goethe, *Werke*, Hamburger Ausgabe, 3:421. The sources are Heinrich Christian Boie's diary of October 15, 1774, and Karl Ludwig von Knebel's correspondence with Friedrich Justin Bertuch, December 23, 1774. Knebel saw Goethe on December 11. Johann Georg Zimmerman was writing to Reich in January 1776. Goethe also read the draft to Friedrich Jacobi and Klopstock in 1775 and discussed the plot with Heinrich Leopold Wagner. See also Nollendorfs, *Streit*, 19–20.

3. On September 17, 1775. Goethe, *Werke*, Hamburger Ausgabe, 3:421.

4. Nollendorfs, *Streit*, 295. See also Binder, "Die Einheit der Faustgestalt im Urfaust," and Schneider, *Urfaust? Eine Studie.*

5. Schmidt, *Goethes Faust in Ursprünglicher Gestalt.* The edition I use in this chapter is based on Schmidt's manuscript, which was published in 1888. Parenthetical citations in the text are to the *Urfaust* in the parallel edition by Ernst Grumach: Goethe, *Urfaust, Faust: Ein Fragment, Faust: Der Tragödie erster Theil.*

6. This last section, while it shows up in *Faust I* partly altered and enlarged, contains a long discussion of the student's room and board that is not preserved in *Faust I*. See Robertson, "The Oldest Scenes in Goethe's *Faust.*"

7. *Faust: Ein Fragment* appeared in the 1790 edition of *Goethes Schriften*. This premature publication of *Faust* seems to have occurred because of a commitment to the publisher, not Goethe's desire to make his unfinished drama public.

8. Butler, *Ritual Magic*, 3.

9. Baron, *Faustus: Geschichte, Sage, Dichtung*, 111.

10. There are other similarities between Wagner's Evchen and Goethe's Margarete. Evchen tells Gröningseck: "Gnade für mich? Gröningseck! wo denken Sie hin?—soll ich zehntausend Tode sterben—lieber heut als morgen." Wagner, *Die Kindermörderin*, 1519. "Ja, ja! Ich—Ich! ich bin die Muttermörderin" (p. 1513). She laughs as well and sings like Ophelia (pp. 1515–16). Also, compare Bianka of Leisewitz's *Julius von Tarent*, who, as she goes mad in the cloister, exclaims: "Heut, heut ist endlich der Tag meiner Verbindung!" (p. 1585). On Goethe's broad view of Christian grace, see also Henkel, "The 'Salvation' of Faust."

11. Beutler, *Der Frankfurter Faust.* Child murder is a crime that fits the time frame of both the historical Faust and the eighteenth century: in the sixteenth century infanticide became a serious crime in Europe and began to fall clearly outside the power of a king to pardon. Natalie Zemon Davis re-

ports finding no letters of remission for infanticide in sixteenth-century France (Davis, *Fiction in the Archives,* 86). It may be that what attracted Goethe to the themes of black magic and child murder was precisely their unpardonable nature; Goethe wants a tragedy that will not admit of extenuating circumstances. What interests Goethe in the 1770s is the free act entirely apart from any institution's—or any text's—ability to pardon it. The motives of child murder include shame, as well as possible religious sanctions, public flogging, and even expulsion from the city (Weber, "Kindesmord," 78). While in Wagner's *Die Kindermörderin,* we see (especially in act 6) the way the community turns the unwed mother into a devil, in the *Urfaust* (and *Faust I*) it is only suggested.

12. See Fairley, *Six Essays,* 48–50, and Politzer, "Margarete," 49. See also Elschenbroich, "Anfänge einer Theorie der Ballade," and Richter, "*Urfaust* oder *Ururfaust.*"

13. Hans M. Wolff suggests that what the Gretchen tragedy gains from being connected to the scholar's tragedy is to make Faust something *more* than a Weislingen, to give some credence and sympathy to his position as the true *Genie* (Wolff, *Goethes Weg,* 154–55). See also Fairley, *Six Essays* on Margarete and Friederike (p. 62).

14. The German *Knüttelvers* employed by Hans Sachs is made up generally of iambic lines of four stressed syllables each, between which stands an irregular number of unstressed syllables. Its innocence and naturalness relate closely in tone to the puppet theater, and Morris, *Goethe-Studien,* 1:3, suggests that Goethe may have been attracted to it precisely for its capacity to awaken the child in us. Another way to describe the styles Goethe uses would be to use Gottsched's vocabulary in his *Ausführiche Redekunst* (1736): *natürlich* (the succinct and unartificial), *sinnreich* (artificial, with ideas connecting clauses), and *beweglich* (the language of emotions); on this see Blackall, *Emergence,* 503–25.

15. Santoli, "Per la critica dell' *Urfaust,*" 35. Translation by Eleanor T. Williams.

16. Fairley, *A Study of Goethe,* 18.

17. Wolff, *Goethes Weg,* 146–47.

18. Knebel's December 23, 1774, letter to Bertuch refers to the fact that Goethe had his Faust play scattered about his room in Frankfurt, and in 1832 August Wilhelm Schlegel reports that Zimmermann, too, found the early *Faust* to be an amalgamation of scraps. It was out of such reports, especially the recollection of Schlegel, that Roethe built his "scrap theory" of the play. Nollendorfs, *Streit,* 19–24, 79–98 takes issue with Roethe.

19. Goethe, *Werke,* WA, 3:32:288.

20. Nollendorfs, *Streit,* 189.

21. Ibid., 291; see also 129–30.

22. Schütze, *Illusions,* 63. Schütze: "The *Urfaust* was not originally intended to be a preliminary work . . . but a complete drama" (p. 63) . . . the one supremely great tragic drama of modern German literature" (p. 65). See

also Krogmann, *Goethes* Urfaust, 109, and Nollendorfs, *Streit*, 102. Fairley argues that the Gretchen tragedy was written for its own sake and that it was by good luck, not good management, that it became part of *Faust* (*Six Essays*, 44).

23. Blackall, "Language," 275.

24. Herder, *Sämtliche Werke*, 2:160. Quoted in Blackall, "Language," 281.

25. Politzer, "Margarete," 49–64. Ernst Beutler argues that Goethe wrote "Der König von Thule" while boating in the summer of 1774 with Basedow, Schmoll, and Lavater. Beutler, "Thule," 307, 312–13. See also Michelsen, "Gretchen am Spinnrad."

26. Goethe and Schiller, *Briefwechsel*, 1:404.

27. Haym, *Herder*, 1:473. See also Reinhold Grimm's interesting observations on the dignified rhetoric of lowly heroes. Grimm, "Vom hohen Stil der Niedrigkeit."

28. Herder, *Sämtliche Werke*, 5:218, 14:485. See also Koepke, "Das Wort *Volk* im Sprachgebrauch Johann Gottfried Herders," 212.

29. Lugowski, "Der junge Herder und das Volkslied," 275.

30. Browning, "Structure of the *Urfaust*," 488.

31. Politzer, "Margarete," 52.

32. Browning, "Structure of the *Urfaust*," 488.

33. Goethe writes to Schiller on June 22, 1797: "So habe ich mich entschlossen, an meinen Faust zu gehen und ihn, wo nicht zu vollenden, doch wenigstens um ein gutes Teil weiter zu bringen, indem ich das, was gedrukt ist, wieder auflöse und mit dem, was schon fertig oder erfunden ist, in große Massen disponiere und so die Ausführung des Plans, der eigentlich nur eine Idee ist, näher vorbereite" (*Briefwechsel*, 1:404). Then he goes on to tell Schiller that it was their discussions of the ballad that had led him to this decision. Schiller answers the next day, saying that he finds his decision to return to *Faust* surprising, then continues: "So viel bemerke ich hier nur, daß der Faust, das Stück nämlich, bei aller seiner dichterischen Individualität, die Foderung an eine symbolische Bedeutsamkeit nicht ganz von sich weisen kann, wie auch wahrscheinlich Ihre eigene Idee ist. Die Duplizität der menschlichen Natur und das verunglückte Bestreben, das Göttliche und das Physische im Menschen zu vereinigen, verliert man nicht aus den Augen, und weil die Fabel ins Grelle und Formlose geht und gehen muß, so will man nicht bei dem Gegenstand stille stehen, sondern von ihm zu Ideen geleitet werden. Kurz, die Anforderungen an den Faust sind zugleich philosophisch und poetisch . . ." (1:405–6).

34. Ong, *Orality and Literacy*, 152, 101.

35. Said, *The World, the Text, and the Critic*, 17–20.

36. Korff argues that treatments of Faust express the spirit of Sturm und Drang most deeply because Faust grasps the rebellion of the subject against the objective law metaphysically and not merely socially (Korff, *Geist der Goethezeit*, 1:279). The new idea in Goethe's *Faust*, he writes, is that the path to God runs through the world (p. 280) and his unprecedented success in

letting the devil lead him to God (p. 280). In the opposite camp are Marxist critics Lukács and Doke, who have both written on the *Urfaust* and see it as predominantly a social tragedy. For Lukács, it expresses the main theme of the German Enlightenment by opposing the moral nihilism of the nobility (i.e., Faust, whom Margarete and the students in Auerbach's Keller take at first to be an aristocrat) to the healthy moral feeling of the bourgeoisie (Lukács, *Faust und Faustus*, 180). Doke, who is not interested in the origins of *Faust* and claims that he wants instead to limit himself to a few motifs (Doke, "Faustdichtungen," 36), generally follows Lukács, though he comes to the conclusion that the *Urfaust* is a tragedy of "das Recht der freien Liebe" (p. 42).

37. Fairley, *Six Essays*, 68–71.
38. Ibid., 72, 69.
39. Ibid., 74.
40. Ibid,. 76–77.
41. Nollendorfs, *Streit*, 197–216. On the question of whether Goethe always meant to lead his Faust to Christian salvation, see Metz, "War schon im *Urfaust* die 'Rettung' des Helden vom Dichter beabsichtet?"
42. Gervinus, *Geschichte der deutschen Dichtung*, 5:195. See also Brown, *Faust: The German Tragedy*, on *Faust* as world theater.

Chapter 6

1. Korff, *Geist der Goethezeit*, 1:266.
2. Pascal, "The 'Sturm und Drang' Movement," 138.
3. Wacker, *Schillers* Räuber *und der Sturm und Drang*, and Wacker, *Sturm und Drang*. McInnes, in his absorbing book *Ein ungeheures Theater*, 117–126, also suggests that Schiller's *Die Räuber* is not part of Sturm und Drang. In an argument based on the tradition's involvement in socially committed realism, he maintains that Schiller's topic is, instead, moral regeneration (p. 118). In chapter 1 I suggested that Sturm und Drang had a rather well defined canon, but in the case of one or two texts there has been some controversy. Henri Peyre considers *Die Räuber* the beginning of the tradition (*What Is Romanticism?* 30), while Ludwig W. Kahn (*Social Ideals in German Literature*, 15) argues that even *Werther* does not belong to the tradition.
4. Buchwald, *Der junge Schiller*, 352.
5. Quoted in Braun, *Schiller und Goethe*, 410. See also Liewerscheidt, *Die Dramen des jungen Schiller*, 146.
6. See Magill and Willoughby, in "Introduction" to Schiller, *Die Räuber. Ein Schauspiel*, xxviii; Braun, *Schiller und Goethe*; Linder-Beroud, "Theater," 151–54.
7. Quoted in Braun, *Schiller und Goethe*, 50–51.
8. Rosanow points this out. *Jakob M. R. Lenz*, 321.
9. Quoted in Ibel, *Schiller: Die Räuber*, 6.

10. Schiller, *Sämtliche Werke*, 1:484. Subsequent references to this edition will be within parentheses in the text.

11. Kindermann, *Theatergeschichte Europas*, 4:560.

12. Lavater, *Aussichten*, 2:191.

13. Lav. MS. 1, p. 30; Farner, *Lavaters Jugend*, 39.

14. Shaftesbury, *Soliloquy*, 2:318, 1:218.

15. Boileau-Despréaux, *Selected Criticism*, 24.

16. For a discussion of what social psychologists call "ingroup dynamics," see, for example, Gusfield, *Community: A Critical Response*, 26–38. A related parallel between "healing" projects in Lavater and Schiller's play can be traced by way of actual references to medicine. The motto printed under the title of the second edition of *Die Räuber* is from Hippocrates and recommends that iron can heal what medicine cannot, and that fire can heal what iron cannot: "Quae medicamenta non sanant, *ferrum* sanat, quae ferrum non sanat, *ignis* sanat." Lavater, too, occasionally has medicine in mind in his pseudoscientific treatises, for example, when he writes of the powers of animal magnetism. Magnetism, he writes in the unpublished manuscript "Magnetismus und Christenthum" (1785), is a healing power residing in mankind, and human beings, he says, can be their own physicians (Lav. MS. 48.3, section 18). In the following year, in a manuscript titled "Meine jezigen Gedanken über den sogenannten animalischen Magnetismus," he reformulates his idea that we all have powers similar to those of Christ: "So giebt nach meiner auf mehrere Erfahrungen gegrundeten Überzeugung— gewisse Situationen, Berührungen, Bewegungen, Willensregungen wodurch gewisse gesunde Personen bei gewissen weniger gesunden *Effekte* hervorbringen, die so wohl *medizinisch* als *psychologisch betrachtet*, sehr sonderbar sind—die ich aber, durchaus *nicht* für *wunder*—sondern für sehr natürlich halte" (Lav. MS. 49.4, section 17).

17. Korff, *Geist der Goethezeit*, 1:273.

18. Wiese, *Schiller*, 145, 136–38.

19. May, *Schiller*, 23–24.

20. Müller, *Der Herzog und das Genie*, 148–52, 167–69.

21. Blackall, *Emergence*, 343.

22. Müller, *Der Herzog und das Genie*, 151.

23. Uhland, *Geschichte der hohen Karlsschule in Stuttgart*, 130.

24. Müller-Seidel, "Georg Friedrich Gaus," 82–97. On the "Himmel und Hölle" theme, see Joachim Müller, *Von Schiller bis Heine*, 116–132. In Wagner's *Die Kindermörderin*, Frau Marthan recommends to the fallen Evchen Humbrecht that she read a (fictitious) book entitled *Der Himmels- und Höllenweg* (Wagner, *Die Kindermörderin*, 1510). On Schiller's religious training, see also Müller-Seidel, "Gaus," 104. See Michelsen, *Der Bruch mit der Vater-Welt*, and Timm, *Ketzer und Dichter*, especially the chapter "Der Ketzergedanke und die individuelle Seele," 48–58. For Schiffer, the psychologist mentioned in connection with Lavater in chapter 2, the charismatic leader must also awaken the aggressive fantasies of the Oedipus complex: "Through both the

hoaxter and the charismatic leader, we can express our contempt and our derogation for traditional fathers" (Schiffer, *Charisma*, 51). Karl, with his "gestörte Vaterordnung" (Wiese, *Schiller*, 145) fits Schiffer's charismatic mold in this respect as well.

25. See Schiller, *Sämtliche Werke*, 1:486, 624.
26. Müller, *Der Herzog und das Genie*, 169–70.
27. Wiese, *Schiller*, 168.
28. May, *Schiller*, 28.

Chapter 7

1. Lenz, *Gesammelte Schriften*, ed. Blei, 1:230. Blei's 1909 edition is still the most complete. Parenthetical references in the text refer to this edition. See Rüdiger Scholz, "Gesamtausgabe," on the problem of citing primary sources in Lenz scholarship.
2. Lenz, *Briefe*, 2:56.
3. See Klotz, *Geschlossene und offene Form im Drama*, on open form in Lenz. Noting that open-formed plays need unity of one kind or another, Klotz argues that "complimentary strands" hold such dramas together—for example, a public strand and a private strand. Inbar, *Shakespeare*, shows that the scenes of *Die Soldaten* are unified in many different ways, noting for example that the first three scenes of act 1 are unifed through letter writing. See also Guthrie, *Lenz and Büchner*, in which he argues that the theory of complimentary strands does not explain Lenz's forms (pp. 58–59). Guthrie contends that the play is simply not very unified aesthetically (p. 71). On Lenz's tendency to end scenes just at their moment of suspense, see Pütz, *Die Zeit im Drama*, 57–60, and Inbar, *Shakespeare*, 224–5. Guthke calls Lenz the first German writer of tragicomedy, saying that Lenz creates "comic characters in tragic situations" (Guthke, "Ein neuer Formtypus," 55). Schwarz contends that this statement could just as easily be reversed, and that Lenz simply sees the modern age as in need of serious writing that contains both the elements of tragedy and comedy (Schwarz, *Dasein und Realität*, 96, 99). Erich Schmidt realized already in 1878 that Lenz's attempt at a mixed genre was not entirely new to German writers, stemming in fact from ideas stretching back at least to Gellert (*Lenz und Klinger*, 26). See also René Girard (the Sturm und Drang scholar, not the author of *Violence and the Sacred*), "Die Umwertung des Tragischen" and *J. M. R. Lenz*.
4. See Osborne, *J. M. R. Lenz: The Renunciation of Heroism*.
5. Blake, "Public Address," 569.
6. Blunden, "Jakob Michael Reinhold Lenz," 212. For Lenz's criticism of the traditional idea of moral perfection, see his essay "Meinungen eines Laien," where he opposes restless striving to "wunderschöne Ideale" (*Gesammelte Schriften*, ed. Blei, 4:160).
7. Guthrie, *Lenz and Büchner*, 81.
8. Schiller, *Sämtliche Werke*, 1:503.

9. See chapter 4's discussion of *Götz von Berlichingen*. Although Lenz's most famous example of a culture that believes in determinism is Greek antiquity, his early religious poetry, under the influence of his father's conservative Pietism, suggests that he simply grew up seeing God's retributive hand in history. It is obvious from his long poem "Die Landplagen" (1768), which explains the plagues, drought, and conflagrations suffered by his fellow Livonians as the will of God, that Lenz (under the influence of an unorthodox Protestantism clearly laced with the apocalyptic tones of the Counter-Reformation), saw rather heavy-handed omens still at work in his own age. As I argue in what follows, this sensibility is part of the sense of determinism against which, just a few years later, he will rebel.

10. Hans H. Hiebel discusses the open-endedness of Lenz's texts as an aspect of their suggestive and polysemous quality in his essay "Das 'offene' Kunstwerk als Signum der Moderne." See *J. M. R. Lenz als Alternative?*, ed. Wurst, 179–97. Hiebel makes use of Umberto Eco's *The Open Work*.

11. Blackbourn, "The Discreet Charm of the Bourgeoisie: Reappraising German History in the Nineteenth Century," in Blackbourn and Eley, *The Peculiarities of German History*, 159–286 (here, p. 292).

12. This is Scherpe's argument in "Projektemacherei." The poverty of contemplation (as opposed to acting, sensing, and feeling) and the notion that all our psychic activities are united, is a theme that runs through Sturm und Drang. Herder, in the 1774 version of "Vom Erkennen und Empfinden der menschlichen Seele," calls our life of the senses, and all our actions, a necessary part of the process of cognition (*Sämtliche Werke*, 8:425). Wild, in act 2, scene 1 of *Sturm und Drang*, realizes that he is miserable living eternally in a world of thought, and Lenz, in the *Anmerkungen*, says that he cannot respect dramatists who embrace an ideal of beauty that does not exist (*Gesammelte Schriften*, ed. Blei, 1:235). On this issue see also Glaser, "Heteroklisie—der Fall Lenz."

13. Lorenz, "Programmschrift," 125. On the other hand, I think that Lenz did want to be a political "fox" who could contribute a few innovative ideas to society. Some, like Blunden, think that the Colonel's proposal in the last scene of *Die Soldaten* for an official military brothel should be taken ironically ("Jakob Michael Reinhold Lenz," 223–24); others, like Rosanov and Guthrie, argue that he took the plan quite seriously; after all, he followed up *Die Soldaten* with an essay recommending much the same thing. Eibl, "Realismus," argues that the last scenes of this play, *Der Hofmeister*, and *Der neue Menoza* are codas whose artificiality is an attempt by Lenz to show that the neat ending is no longer viable. See also Inbar, *Shakespeare*, 229.

14. Martini, "Anmerkungen," 163. Friedrich, *Die Anmerkungen*, 47–57, argues that, despite its appearance of randomness, the *Anmerkungen* are made up of four originally separate parts that Lenz composed between 1771 and 1774.

15. Inbar, *Shakespeare*, 225.

16. Ibid.

17. Madland, *Non-Aristotelian Drama*, 120, 119. She is, as far as I know, the first critic to address the gaps in Lenz at length as a serious matter of rhetoric. See also her article "Gesture as Evidence of Language Skepticism." Carl Pfütze, in his long 1890 article on Lenz's language, does deal in passing with Lenzian aposiopesis (p. 166), but Madland carries out the implications of Lenz's gaps much further (pp. 117–22).

18. Morton, "Exemplary Poetics," 145.

19. Iser, *The Act of Reading*, 165–66.

20. Longinus, *On Great Writing*, 10.

21. This is the general argument of my "The Dream of Identity." See also David Hill's essay on Lenz's view of community as a place where mutual respect is possible (in a world where we too often find ourselves manipulating one another), "Stolz und Demut, Illusion und Mitleid bei Lenz," in *J. M. R. Lenz als Alternative?*, ed. Wurst, 64–91.

22. Iser, *Tristram Shandy*, 61–62.

23. Ibid., 69.

24. Ibid., 80.

25. Wolff, "The Controversy over the Theater in Lenz's *Die Soldaten*," 164.

26. Blumenberg, "An Anthropological Approach," 438. Again, Artaud is relevant, especially his concept of theater as a sort of gratuitous plague (the word "plague" comes from St. Augustine's diatribe against the theater) that does not harm the body.

27. Diffey, "Lenz, Rousseau, and the Problem of Striving," 176.

28. Bakhtin, *Problems of Dostoevsky's Poetics*, 294. Interestingly, Kindermann, writing of Lenz in 1925, uses a vocabulary for which Bakhtin will soon become famous, referring to Lenz as a "centrifugal" and Goethe as a "centripetal" writer. Kindermann, *J. M. R. Lenz und die deutsche Romantik*, 197. See also the late Henry J. Schmidt's fine essay on Lenz in *How Dramas End*, "The Impossibility of Ending: J. M. R. Lenz," 63–89.

29. Emerson, "Letters and Social Aims," 18–19.

30. Wimsatt, *The Verbal Icon*, 79.

31. "Bekenntnisse einer armen Seele," quoted in Falck, *J. M. R. Lenz in Livland*, 5.

32. Freye, "Knabenjahre," 175.

33. Lenz, *Briefe*, 1:235. Schöne's study of the literary sons of German pastors, *Säkularisation als sprachbildende Kraft*, as useful as it is, does not examine the father-son relationship as closely as it might.

34. Petersen and Marcuse's articles both have the title, "Lenz, Vater und Sohn."

35. On the similarites between J. M. R. Lenz and his father, see also Ottomar Rudolf's essay "Lenz: Vater und Sohn: Zwischen patriarchalem Pietismus und pädagogischem Eros," in *J. M. R. Lenz als Alternative?*, ed. Wurst, 29–45.

36. Lenz, *Briefe* 1:262.

37. *Gesammelte Schriften*, ed. Blei, 4:224. Lenz's metaphor of "space to act"

prefigures, in both its vehicle and tenor, the "square yard of space" metaphor used by Dostoevsky in *Crime and Punishment* (1866): "Where is it I've read that someone condemned to death says or thinks, an hour before his death, that if he had to live on some high rock, on such a narrow ledge that he'd only room to stand, and the ocean, everlasting darkness, everlasting solitude, everlasting tempest around him, if he had to remain standing on a square yard of space all his life, a thousand years, eternity, it were better to live so than to die at once! Only to live, to live and live! Life, whatever it may be! . . . How true it is! Good God, how true!" (p. 20). In both texts, that of Lenz and that of Dostoevsky, a small and even uncomfortable—but free—space becomes a metaphor for a particular posture of mind in which one does not continually see oneself obliged to have to measure oneself against someone else's standard, but where one can live. Whether it is the "space to act" or the "square yard of space," it is a limited but life-giving realm that does not yet exist. Still, in Lenz, "space to act" is different: Dostoevsky was coming from his nihilism of the 1840s back to the conservative Christian tradition of his upbringing, back to traditions. Lenz is moving in the opposite direction. Readers who have seen my essay "Selbstunterbrechungen in den Werken von J. M. R. Lenz" will note that my views on this metaphor in Lenz have changed slightly since then. In *J. M. R. Lenz als Alternative?*, ed. Wurst, 46–63. See also Pope, "The Concept of Action in the Work of J. M. R. Lenz," a dissertation whose publication is long overdue.

   38. Gruppe, *Reinhold Lenz*, 301.

   39. Young, *Conjectures*, 38. In regard to patience in Lenz, it is also worth noting that Lenz says in a letter to Salzmann that while he values God's promise of immediate salvation—"die unmittelbare Wirkung der Gottheit" (*Briefe*, 1:53)—he says he also likes its mystery. This instant salvation, he says, is God's prerogative.

Works Cited

Abbott, Scott. "The Semiotics of Young Werther." *Goethe Yearbook* 6 (1992): 41–65.

Addison, Joseph. *The Tattler*. Edited by Richard Steele. Philadelphia: Woodward, 1835.

Alewyn, Richard. " 'Klopstock!' " *Euphorion* 73 (1979): 357–64.

Allgemeine Deutsche Biographie. 56 vols. Leipzig: Duncker und Humblodt, 1875–1912.

Allison, Henry E. "Practical and Transcendental Freedom in the *Critique of Pure Reason*." *Kant-Studien* 73 (1982): 271–90.

Anderson, Benedict. *Imagined Communities: Reflections on the Origin and Spread of Nationalism*. New York: Verso, 1991.

Archiv für Narrheit und Schwärmerei, Im neunten Dezennio des aufgeklärten Jahrhunderts. Erstes hoffentlich letztes Stük. Germanien, 1788.

Aristotle. *The Prior Analytics*. In *The Works of Aristotle*, edited and translated by Thomas Taylor, 191–395. London: Wilks, 1812.

———. *The Rhetoric of Aristotle*, edited and translated by Lane Cooper. Englewood Cliffs, N.J.: Prentice-Hall, 1960.

Artaud, Antonin. *The Theater and its Double*. Translated by Mary Caroline Richards. New York: Grove, 1958.

Atkins, Stuart Pratt. "J. C. Lavater and Goethe: Problems of Psychology and Theology in *Die Leiden des jungen Werthers*." *PMLA* 63 (1948): 520–76.

Bakhtin, Mikhail M. *Problems of Dostoevsky's Poetics*, translated by Caryl Emerson. Minneapolis: University of Minnesota Press, 1984.

Baron, Frank. *Faustus: Geschichte, Sage, Dichtung*. Munich: Winkler, 1982.

Bennett, Benjamin. *Modern Drama and German Classicism*. Ithaca: Cornell University Press, 1979.

Beutler, Ernst. *Der Frankfurter Faust*. Frankfurt: Jahrbuch des freien Deutschen Hochstifts, 1940.

———. " 'Der König in Thule' und die Dichtungen von der Lorelei." In Beutler, *Essays um Goethe*, 2:307–28. Wiesbaden: Dieterich, 1947.

Binder, Wolfgang. "Die Einheit der Faustgestalt im Urfaust." *Wirkendes Wort* 1 (1983): 4–18.

Blackall, Eric A. *The Emergence of German as a Literary Language*. Cambridge: Cambridge University Press, 1959.

———. *Goethe and the Novel*. Ithaca: Cornell University Press, 1976.

———. "The Language of Sturm und Drang." In *Stil- und Formprobleme in der Literatur*, edited by Paul Böckmann, 272–83. Heidelberg: Winter, 1959.

Blackbourn, David, and Geoff Eley. *The Peculiarities of German History: Bourgeois Society and Politics in Nineteenth-Century Germany*. Oxford: Oxford University Press, 1984.

Blake, William. "Public Address." In *The Complete Poetry and Prose of William Blake*, edited by David V. Erdman, 571–82. Berkeley: University of California Press, 1982.

Blumenberg, Hans. "An Anthropological Approach to the Contemporary Significance of Rhetoric." Translated by Robert M. Wallace. In *After Philosophy: End or Transformation?*, edited by Kenneth Baynes, James Bohman, and Thomas McCarthy, 429–458. Cambridge: MIT Press, 1988.

Blunden, Allen G. "Jakob Michael Reinhold Lenz." In *German Men of Letters*, edited by Alex Natan, 6:209–40. London: Wolff, 1972.

Boileau-Despréaux, Nicolas. *Selected Criticism*, edited by Ernest Dilworth. Indianapolis: Bobbs-Merrill, 1965.

Borchert, Hans Heinrich. *Der Roman der Goethezeit*. Urach: Port, 1949.

Borst, Arno. "Das Rittertum im Hochmittelalter: Idee und Wirklichkeit." *Saeculum* 10 (1959): 213–31.

Bosl, Karl. *Die Grundlagen der modernen Gesellschaft im Mittelalter*. 4 vols. Stuttgart: Hiersemann, 1972.

Braemer, Edith. *Goethes Prometheus und die Grundpositionen des Sturm und Drang*. Weimar: Arion, 1959.

Brahm, Otto. *Das deutsche Ritterdrama des achtzehnten Jahrhunderts*. Strassburg: Trübner, 1880.

Braun, Julius W., ed. *Schiller und Goethe im Urtheile ihrer Zeitgenossen*. Leipzig: Schlicke, 1882.

Brown, Jane K. *Goethe's Faust: The German Tragedy*. Ithaca: Cornell University Press, 1986.

Brown, Marshall. *Preromanticism*. Stanford: Stanford University Press, 1991.

Browning, R. M. "On the Structure of the *Urfaust*." *PMLA* 68 (1953): 458–95.

Bruford, Walter. *Germany in the Eighteenth Century: The Social Background of the Literary Revival*. Cambridge: Cambridge University Press, 1935.

Buchwald, Reinhard. *Der junge Schiller*. Vol. 1 of *Schiller*. Leipzig: Insel, 1937.

Burke, Edmund. *A Philosophical Enquiry into the Origins of Our Ideas of the Sublime and Beautiful*. Edited by J. T. Boulton. Notre Dame: University of Notre Dame Press, 1968.

Butler, E. M. *Ritual Magic*. Cambridge: Cambridge University Press, 1949.

Byron, George. *The Complete Poetical Works*. Edited by Jerome J. McGann. 5 vols. Oxford: Clarendon, 1980–86.

Carnois, Bernard. *The Coherence of Kant's Doctrine of Freedom*. Translated by David Booth. Chicago: University of Chicago Press, 1987.

Castle, Eduard. "Plan und Einheit in der ersten Konzeption des Goetheschen *Faust*." *Jahrbuch des Wiener Goethe-Vereins* 25 (1911): 64–72.

Coleridge, Samuel. *Collected Works*. Edited by Lewis Patton and Peter Mann. 16 vols. London: Routledge, 1971–84.

Davis, Natalie Zemon. *Fiction in the Archives: Pardon Tales and Their Tellers in Sixteenth-Century France*. Stanford: Stanford University Press, 1987.

De Man, Paul. *The Rhetoric of Romanticism*. New York: Columbia University Press, 1984.

Demeter, Karl. "Das Reichskammergericht in Wetzlar zu Goethes Zeit." *Goethe-Kalendar* 33 (1940): 41–68.

Diez, Max. "The Principle of the Dominant Metaphor in Goethe's *Werther.*" *PMLA* 51 (1936): 821–41, 985–1006.

Diffey, Norman R. "Lenz, Rousseau, and the Problem of Striving." *Seminar* 10 (1974): 165–80.

Dockhorn, Klaus. *Macht und Wirkung der Rhetorik: Vier Aufsätze zur Ideengeschichte der Vormoderne.* 2 vols. Bad Homburg: Gehlen, 1968.

Doke, Tadamichi. "Faustdichtungen des Sturm und Drang." *Goethe-Jahrbuch* 32 (1970): 29–49.

Dostoevsky, Feodor Michaelovich. *Crime and Punishment.* Translated by Constance Garnett. New York: Bantam, 1981.

Eco, Umberto. *The Open Work.* Translated by Anna Cancogni. Cambridge: Harvard University Press, 1989.

Eibl, Karl. " 'Realismus als Widerlegung von Literatur: Dargestellt am Beispiel von Lenz' *Hofmeister.*" *Poetica* 6 (1974): 456–67.

Elschenbroich, Adalbert. "Anfänge einer Theorie der Ballade im Sturm und Drang." *Jahrbuch des freien deutschen Hochstifts* (1982): 1–56.

Emerson, Ralph Waldo. *Letters and Social Aims.* Boston: Houghton, Mifflin, 1885.

Fairley, Barker. *Goethe's Faust: Six Essays.* Oxford: Clarendon, 1953.

———. *A Study of Goethe.* Oxford: Clarendon, 1947.

Falck, P. T. J. M. R. *Lenz in Livland.* Winterthur: Westfehling, 1878.

Farner, Oskar. *Lavaters Jugend von ihm selbst erzählt.* Zürich: Zwingli, 1939.

Feuerlicht, Ignace. "Werther's Suicide: Instinct, Reasons and Defense." *German Quarterly* 51 (1978): 476–92.

Frey, A., ed. *Haller und Salis-Seewis, Auswahl.* Deutsche National-Litteratur, edited by Joseph Kürschner, vol. 41, part 2. Berlin: Spemann, 1884.

Freye, Karl. "Jakob Michael Reinhold Lenzens Knabenjahre." *Zeitschrift für Geschichte der Erziehung und des Unterrichts* 7 (1917): 174–93.

Friedrich, Theodor. *Die "Anmerkungen übers Theaters" des Dichters Jakob Michael Reinhold Lenz.* Leipzig: Voigtländer, 1908.

Funck, Heinrich. *Die Anfänge von Goethe's Freundschaft mit Lavater in Briefen von Lavater an Goethe.* Munich: Allgemeine Zeitung, 1898.

Gerstenberg, Heinrich Wilhelm. *Briefe über Merkwürdigkeiten der Litteratur.* Edited by A. von Weilen. Heilbronn: Henninger, 1888–90.

Gervinus, Georg Gottfried. *Geschichte der deutschen Dichtung.* 4th ed. Leipzig: Engelmann, 1853.

Geßner, Georg. *Johann Kaspar Lavaters Lebensbeschreibung.* Winterthur: Steiner, 1802.

Girard, René. *J. M. R. Lenz: Genèse d'une dramaturgie du tragi-comique.* Paris: Klincksiek, 1968.

———. "Die Umwertung des Tragischen in Lenzens Dramaturgie." In *Dialog: Literatur und Literaturwissenschaft im Zeichen deutsch-französischer Begegnung. Festgabe für Josef Kunz,* edited by Rainer Schönhaar, 127–38. Berlin: Erich Schmidt, 1973.

Girard, René. *Violence and the Sacred*. Translated by Yvonne Freccero. Baltimore: Johns Hopkins University Press, 1977.

Glaser, Horst Albert. "Heteroklisie—der Fall Lenz." In *Gestaltungsgeschichte und Gesellschaftsgeschichte*, edited by Helmut Kreuzer, 132–51. Stuttgart: Metzler, 1969.

———. "Überlegungen eines Herausgebers. Zu methodologischen Problemen neuerer Literaturgeschichtsschreibung." *Comparatistica Annuario Italiano* (1991): 127–37.

Gloël, Heinrich. *Der Wetzlarer Goethe*. Wetzlar: Heimatverlag, 1932.

Goethe, Johann Wolfgang von. *Der junge Goethe*. Edited by Hanna Fischer-Lamberg. 6 vols. Berlin: de Gruyter, 1963–73.

———. *Die Leiden des jungen Werthers*. Berlin: Akademie-Verlag, 1954.

———. *Werke*. Weimarer Ausgabe. 143 vols. in 4 pts. Weimar: Böhlau, 1887–1918.

———. *Werke*. Edited by Erich Trunz. Hamburger Ausgabe. 14 vols. Hamburg: Wegner, 1948–64.

———. *Urfaust, Faust: Ein Fragment, Faust. Der Tragödie erster Theil*. (Paralleldruck). Edited by Ernst Grumach and Inge Jensen. Berlin: Akademie, 1958.

Goethe, Johann Wolfgang von, and Friedrich Schiller. *Briefwechsel*. Edited by Richard Müller-Freienfels. 2 vols. Berlin: Wegweiser, 1924.

Gottsched, Johann Christoph. *Ausführiche Redekunst*. Leipzig: Breitkopf, 1739.

Graham, Ilse. "*Die Leiden des jungen Werther*: A Requiem for Inwardness." In Graham, *Goethe and Lessing: The Wellsprings of Creation*, 115–36. New York: Barnes and Noble, 1973.

Gray, Richard. "The Ambivalence of Revolt in Klinger's *Zwillinge*: An Apologia for Political Inconsequence?" *Colloquia Germanica* 19 (1986): 203–27.

———. "The Transcendence of the Body in the Transparency of Its En-Signment: Johann Kaspar Lavater's Physiognomical 'Surface Hermeneutics' and the Ideological (Con-)Text of Bourgeois Modernism." *Lessing Yearbook* 23 (1991): 127–48.

Grimm, Jakob, and Wilhelm Grimm. *Deutsches Wörterbuch*. 16 vols. Leipzig: Hirzel, 1854–1960.

Grimm, Reinhold. "Vom hohen Stil der Niedrigkeit: Ausdrucksmittel des nichtheroischen Tragödienhelden." *MLN* 104 (1989): 636–95.

Gruppe, O. F. *Reinhold Lenz, Leben und Werke. Mit Ergänzungen der Tieckschen Ausgabe*. Berlin: Charisius, 1861.

Gusfield, Joseph R. *Community: A Critical Response*. New York: Harper, 1975.

Guthke, Karl S. "F. M. Klingers *Zwillinge*: Höhepunkt und Krise des Sturm und Drang." *German Quarterly* 43 (1970): 703–14. Reprinted in *Die Zwillinge* by F. M. Klinger, 67–79. Stuttgart: Reclam, 1972. Reprinted in *Literarisches Leben im achtzehnten Jahrhundert in Deutschland und in der Schweiz*, by Karl S. Guthke, 282–89. Berne: Francke, 1975.

———. "Lenzens 'Hofmeister' und 'Soldaten.' Ein neuer Formtypus in der Geschichte des deutschen Dramas." *Wirkendes Wort* 9 (1959): 274–86.

Guthrie, John. *Lenz and Büchner: Studies in Dramatic Form.* New York: Lang, 1984.

Haffner, Herbert. *Lenz: Der Hofmeister. Die Soldaten.* Munich: Oldenbourg, 1979.

Hamann, J. G. *Sämtliche Werke. Historisch-kritische Ausgabe.* Edited by Josef Nadler. 6 vols. Vienna: Herder, 1949–57.

Harris, Edward P. "Vier Stücke in einem. Die Entstehungsgeschichte von F. M. Klingers *Die Zwillinge.*" *Zeitschrift für deutsche Philologie* 101 (1982): 481–95.

Haym, Rudolf. *Herder.* 2 vols. Berlin: Aufbau, 1954.

Hegel, Georg Wilhelm Friedrich. *Phänomenologie des Geistes.* Frankfurt: Suhrkamp, 1973.

Henkel, Arthur. "The 'Salvation' of Faust—by Goethe." In *Faust through Four Centuries: Retrospect and Analysis. Vierhundert Jahre Faust: Rückblick und Analyse,* edited by Peter Boerner and Sidney Johnson, 91–98. Tübingen: Niemeyer, 1989.

Herbst, Wilhelm. *Goethe in Wetzlar. 1772. Vier Monate aus des Dichters Jugendleben.* Gotha: Perthes, 1881.

Herder, Johann Gottfried. *Sämtliche Werke.* Edited by Bernhard Ludwig Suphan. 33 volumes. Berlin: Weidmann, 1877–1913.

Herder, Johann Gottfried, Johann Wolfgang von Goethe, Paolo Frisi, and Justus Möser. *Von deutscher Art und Kunst: Einige fliegende Blätter.* Hamburg: Bode, 1773. Reprint. Nendeln: Kraus, 1968.

Hering, Christoph. *Friedrich Maximilian Klinger. Der Weltmann als Dichter.* Berlin: de Gruyter, 1966.

Hettner, Hermann. *Literaturgeschichte des achtzehnten Jahrhunderts.* 6 vols. 3rd edition. Braunschweig: Vieweg, 1856–70.

Hirzel, Heinrich, ed. *Briefe von Goethe an Lavater aus den Jahren 1774 bis 1783.* Leipzig: Weidman, 1833.

Holborn, Hajo. "German Idealism in the Light of Social History." In *Germany and Europe: Historical Essays,* 1–32. Garden City, N.Y.: Doubleday, 1970.

Höllerer, Walter. "Lenz: Die Soldaten." In *Das deutsche Drama vom Barock bis zur Gegenwart,* edited by Benno von Wiese, 1:127–46. Düsseldorf: Bagel, 1962.

Horlitz, Bernd. "Zur Bedeutung der Formel 'Sturm und Drang.'" *Archiv für das Studium der neueren Sprachen und Literaturen* 271 (1980): 93–95.

Humboldt, Wilhelm von. *Werke.* 5 vols. Stuttgart: Cotta, 1960.

Huyssen, Andreas. *Drama des Sturm und Drang.* Munich: Winkler, 1980.

Ibel, Rudolf. *Schiller: Die Räuber.* Frankfurt: Diesterweg.

Inbar, Eva Maria. *Shakespeare in Deutschland: Der Fall Lenz.* Tübingen: Niemeyer, 1982.

Iser, Wolfgang. *The Act of Reading: A Theory of Aesthetic Response.* Baltimore: Johns Hopkins University Press, 1978.

———. *Tristram Shandy.* Translated by David Henry Wilson. Cambridge: Cambridge University Press, 1988.

Jacobi, Friedrich Heinrich. *Eduard Allwills Briefsammlung.* Leipzig: Fleischer, 1826.

Janentzky, Christian. *J. C. Lavaters Sturm und Drang im Zusammenhang seines religiösen Bewusstseins.* Halle: Niemeyer, 1916.

Jennings, Michael W. " 'Vergessen von aller Welt': Literatur, Politik und Identität in Klingers Dramen des Sturm und Drang." *Zeitschrift für deutsche Philologie* 104 (1985): 494–506.

Jones, Howard Mumford. *Revolution and Romanticism.* Cambridge: Harvard University Press, 1974.

Kahn, Ludwig W. *Social Ideals in German Literature, 1770–1830.* New York: Columbia University Press, 1938.

Kaiser, Gerhard. "Friedrich Maximilian Klingers Schauspiel *Sturm und Drang.* Zur Typologie des Sturm-und-Drang Dramas." In *Untersuchungen zur Literatur als Geschichte. Festschrift für Benno von Wiese,* edited by V. J. Günther et al., 15–35. Berlin: Schmidt, 1973.

Kant, Immanuel. *Gesammelte Schriften.* Akademie-Ausgabe. 29 vols. Berlin: Reimer, 1902–83.

Keckeis, Gustav. *Dramaturgische Probleme im Sturm und Drang.* Berne: Francke, 1907.

Kieffer, Bruce. *The Storm and Stress of Language: Linguistic Catastrophe in the Early Works of Goethe, Lenz, Klinger, and Schiller.* University Park: Pennsylvania State University Press, 1986.

Kindermann, Heinz. *J. M. R. Lenz und die Deutsche Romantik.* Vienna and Leipzig: Braumüller, 1925.

———. *Theatergeschichte Europas.* 4 vols. Salzburg: Müller, 1961.

Klinger, Friedrich Maximilian. *Briefbuch.* Vol. 3 of *Friedrich Maximilian Klinger: Sein Leben und Werk,* edited by Max Rieger. Darmstadt: Bergsträsser, 1896.

———. *Friedrich Maximilian Klingers dramatische Jugendwerke.* Edited by Hans Berendt and Kurt Wolff. 3 vols. Leipzig: Rowohlt, 1912.

———. *Werke. Historisch-kritische Gesamtausgabe.* Edited by Georg Bangen, Sander Gilman, Edward P. Harris, and Ulrich Profitlich. 24 vols. Tübingen: Niemeyer, 1978–.

Klopstock, Friedrich Gottlieb. *Klopstocks Werke.* Edited by R. Hamel. Deutsche National-Litteratur, edited by Joseph Kürschner, vols. 45–48. Berlin: Spemann, 1884.

Klotz, Volker. *Geschlossene und offene Form im Drama.* Munich: Hanser, 1962.

Koepke, Wulf. "Das Wort 'Volk' im Sprachgebrauch Johann Gottfried Herders." *Lessing Yearbook* 19 (1987): 207–19.

Korff, Hermann August. *Geist der Goethezeit. Versuch einer ideellen Entwicklung der klassisch-romantischen Literaturgeschichte.* 5 vols. Leipzig: Koehler, 1955–57.

Krauß, Werner. *Studien zur deutschen und französischen Aufklärung.* Berlin: Rütten, 1963.

Krogmann, Willy. *Goethes Urfaust.* Berlin, 1933. Reprint. Nendeln: Kraus, 1967.

Kuzniar, Alice A. "Signs of the Future: Reading (in) Lavater's *Aussichten*." *Seminar* 22 (1986): 1–19.

Lamport. F. J. "The Charismatic Hero: Goethe, Schiller, and the Tragedy of Character." *Publications of the English Goethe Society* 59 (1987–88): 62–83.

———. *German Classical Drama: Theatre, Humanity and Nation.* Cambridge: Cambridge University Press, 1990.

Lange, Victor. *The Classical Age of German Literature, 1740–1815.* London: Holmes & Meier, 1982.

Lavater, Johann Caspar. *Aussichten in die Ewigkeit, in Briefen an Herrn Joh. Georg Zimmermann.* 2nd ed. Vols. 1–2. Zürich: Geßner, 1770.

———. *Aussichten in die Ewigkeit, in Briefen an Herrn Joh. Georg Zimmermann.* Vol. 3. Zürich: Geßner, 1773.

———. *Geheimes Tagebuch von einem Beobachter seiner Selbst.* 2 vols. Leipzig: Weidmann, 1771–73.

———. *Nachlaß.* Handschriftenabteilung der Zentralbibliothek Zürich.

———. *Physiognomische Fragmente zur Beförderung der Menschenkenntnis und Menschenliebe.* 3 vols. Leipzig: Weidmann, 1775–78.

———. *Poesien von Johann Caspar Lavater.* 2 vols. Leipzig: Weidman, 1781.

———. *Predigten über das Buch Jonas.* 2 vols. Winterthur: Steiner, 1773.

———. *Schweizerlieder. Von einem Mitgliede der helvetischen Gesellschaft zu Schinznach.* Berne: Walthard, 1767. (Signed only with the initial "L" at the end of the introduction.)

Leidner, Alan C. "The Dream of Identity: Lenz and the Problem of *Standpunkt*." *German Quarterly* 59 (1986): 387–400.

———. "A Titan in Extenuating Circumstances: Sturm und Drang and the *Kraftmensch*." *PMLA* 104 (1989): 178–89.

———. " 'Fremde Menschen fielen einander schluchzend in die Arme': *Die Räuber* and the Communal Response." *Goethe Yearbook* 3 (1986): 57–71.

———. "Karl Moor's Charisma." In *Friedrich von Schiller and the Drama of Human Existence*, edited by Alexej Ugrinsky, 57–61. New York: Greenwood Press, 1987.

Leisewitz, Johann Anton. *Julius von Tarent. Ein Trauerspiel.* In *Sturm und Drang. Dichtungen und Theoretische Texte*, edited by Heinz Nicolai, 2:1537–93. Munich: Winkler, 1971.

Lenz, J. M. R. *Briefe.* Edited by Karl Freye and Wolfgang Stammler. 2 vols. Berne: Lang, 1969.

———. *Gesammelte Schriften.* Edited by Franz Blei. 5 vols. Munich: Müller, 1909.

Lepenies, Wolf. *Melancholie und Gesellschaft.* Frankfurt: Suhrkamp, 1969.

Lessing, Gotthold Ephraim. *Hamburgische Dramaturgie.* Edited by Kurt Wölfel. Frankfurt: Insel, 1986.

Liewerscheidt, Dieter. *Die Dramen des jungen Schiller.* Munich: Oldenbourg, 1982.

Linder-Beroud, Waltraud. " 'Das Theater glich einem Irrenhause.' 200 Jahre Rezeptionsgeschichte der 'Räuber' und des 'Räuberliedes.' " *Jahrbuch für Volksliedforschung* 27–28 (1982–83): 148–61.

Longinus. *On Great Writing (On the Sublime)*. Translated by G. M. A. Grube. New York: Bobbs-Merrill, 1957.

Loraux, Nicole. *Tragic Ways of Killing a Woman*. Translated by Anthony Forster. Cambridge: Harvard University Press, 1987.

Lorenz, Heinz. "Die 'Anmerkungen übers Theater' als Programmschrift des Dramatikers Lenz." *Wissenschaftliche Zeitschrift der Ernst-Moritz-Arndt-Universität Greifswald* 19 (1970): 121–38.

Lugowski, Clemens. "Der junge Herder und das Volkslied." *Zeitschrift für Deutsche Bildung* 14 (1938): 265–77.

Lukács, Georg. *Faust und Faustus*. Reinbek: Rowohlt, 1967.

Madland, Helga Stipa. "Gesture as Evidence of Language Skepticism in Lenz's *Der Hofmeister* and *Die Soldaten*." *German Quarterly* 57 (1984): 546–57.

———. *Non-Aristotelian Drama in Eighteenth-Century Germany and its Modernity: J. M. R. Lenz*. Berne: Lang, 1982.

Mann, Thomas. "Goethe's 'Werther.'" In *Gesammelte Werke in zwölf Bänden*, edited by Rudolf Hirsch, 9:640–55. Oldenburg: Fischer, 1960.

Marcuse, Max. "Lenz, Vater und Sohn." *Zeitschrift für Sexualwissenschaft* 14 (1928): 395–97.

Martini, Fritz. "Die Einheit der Konzeption in J. M. R. Lenz' 'Anmerkungen übers Theater.'" *Jahrbuch der deutschen Schiller-Gesellschaft* 14 (1970): 159–82.

Mason, Eudo. "Schönheit, Ausdruck und Charakter im ästhetischen Denken des 18. Jahrhunderts." In *Geschichte, Deutung, Kritik: Literaturwissenschaftliche Beiträge dargebracht zum 65. Geburtstag Werner Kohlschmidts*, edited by Maria Bindschedler, 91–108. Berne: Francke, 1969.

Mattenklott, Gert. *Melancholie in der Dramatik des Sturm und Drang*. Stuttgart: Metzler, 1968.

May, Kurt. "Beitrag zur Phänomenologie des Dramas im Sturm und Drang." *Germanisch-romanische Monatsschrift* 18 (1930): 260–68.

———. "Fr. Max. Klingers Sturm und Drang." *Deutsche Vierteljahrsschrift für Literatur und Geisteswissenschaft* 11 (1933): 398–407.

———. *Schiller*. Göttingen: Vanderhoeck & Ruprecht, 1948.

McCarthy, John A. "The Art of Reading and the Goals of the German Enlightenment." *Lessing Yearbook* 16 (1984): 79–94.

McInnes, Edward. "The Sturm und Drang and the Development of Social Drama." *Deutsche Vierteljahrsschrift* 46 (1972): 61–68.

———. *Ein ungeheures Theater: The Drama of the Sturm und Drang*. Berne: Lang, 1987.

MacIntyre, Alasdair. *After Virtue*. Notre Dame: University of Notre Dame Press, 1981.

Meister, Leonhard. *Ueber die Schwärmerei. Eine Vorlesung*. 2 vols. Berne: Typographische Gesellschaft, 1775–77.

Melchinger, Siegfried. *Dramaturgie des Sturms und Drangs*. Gotha: Klotz, 1929.

Metz, Adolf. "War schon im *Urfaust* die 'Rettung' des Helden vom Dichter beabsichtet?" *Jahrbuch der deutschen Goethe-Gesellschaft* 7 (1920): 45–95.

Michelsen, Peter. *Der Bruch mit der Vater-Welt. Studien zu Schillers Räuber.* Heidelberg: Winter, 1979.

———. "Gretchen am Spinnrad: Zur Szene 'Gretchens Stube' in Goethes *Faust I."* In *Texte, Motive und Gestalten der Goethezeit. Festschrift für Hans Reiss,* edited by John L. Hibberd and H. B. Nisbet, 81–93. Tübingen: Niemeyer, 1989.

Mignon, Heinrich. *Goethe in Wetzlar. Kleine Chronik aus dem Sommer 1772.* Wetzlar: Pegasus, 1972.

Morris, Max. *Goethe-Studien.* 2 vols. Berlin: Skopnik, 1902.

Morton, Michael. "Exemplary Poetics: The Rhetoric of Lenz's *Anmerkungen übers Theater* and *Pandaemonium Germanicum."* *Lessing Yearbook* 20 (1988): 121–51.

Möser, Justus. *Über die deutsche Sprache und Literatur.* Osnabrück: Schmidt, 1781. Reprint. Nendeln: Kraus, 1968.

Müller, Ernst. *Der Herzog und das Genie. Friedrich Schillers Jugendjahre.* Stuttgart: Kohlhammer, 1955.

———. *Der Junge Schiller.* Tübingen: Wunderlich, 1947.

Müller, Friedrich. *Golo und Genoveva.* In *Stürmer und Dränger,* edited by A. Sauer, 1–159. Deutsche National-Litteratur, edited by Joseph Kürschner, 81. Berlin: Spemann, 1883.

Müller, Joachim. *Von Schiller bis Heine.* Halle: Niemeyer, 1972.

Müller-Seidel, Walter. "Georg Friedrich Gaus. Zur religiösen Situation des jungen Schiller." *Deutsche Vierteljahrsschrift* 26 (1952): 76–99.

Nietzsche, Friedrich Wilhelm. *Die Geburt der Tragödie.* In *Werke.* edited by Karl Schlechta, 1:7–134. Munich: Hanser, 1954.

Nolan, Erika. "Goethes *Die Leiden des jungen Werther.* Absicht und Methode." *Jahrbuch der deutschen Schiller-Gesellschaft* 28 (1984): 191–222.

Nollendorfs, Valters. *Der Streit um den Urfaust.* The Hague: Mouton, 1967.

Ong, Walter J. *Orality and Literacy.* London: Methuen, 1982.

Osborne, John. *J. M. R. Lenz: The Renunciation of Heroism.* Göttingen: Vandenhoeck & Ruprecht, 1975.

Pascal, Roy. *The German Sturm und Drang.* New York: Philosophical Library, 1953.

———. "The 'Sturm und Drang' Movement." *MLR* 47 (1952): 129–51.

Pestalozzi, Karl. "Lavaters Utopie." In *Literaturwissenschaft und Geschichtsphilosophie: Festschrift für Wilhelm Emrich,* edited by Helmut Arntzen, Bernd Balzer, Karl Pestalozzi, and Rainer Wagner, 283–301. Berlin: de Gruyter, 1975.

Petersen, Otto von. "Lenz, Vater und Sohn." In *Dankesgabe für Albert Leitzmann,* edited by Fritz Braun and Kurt Stegmann von Pritzwald, 91–103. Jena: Frommann, 1927.

Petsch, Robert. "Neue Beiträge zur Erklärung des 'Urfaust.'" *Germanisch-Römische Monatsschrift* 10 (1922): 138–50, 203–13.

————. "Zum Urfaust." *Chronik des Wiener Goethe-Vereins* 27 (1913): 39–40.

————. "Zur Chronologie des Faust." *Euphorion* 27 (1926): 207–22.

Peyre, Henri. *What Is Romanticism?* Translated by Roda Roberts. University: University of Alabama Press, 1977.

Pfütze, Carl. "Die Sprache in J. M. R. Lenzens Dramen." *Archiv für das Studium der neueren Sprachen und Literaturen* 8 (1890): 129–202.

Politzer, Heinz. "Margarete im *Urfaust.*" *Monatshefte* 49 (1957): 49–64.

Pope, Timothy. "The Concept of Action in the Work of J. M. R. Lenz." Ph.D. diss., University of British Columbia, 1980.

Pütz, Peter. *Die Zeit im Drama.* Göttingen: Vandenhoeck & Ruprecht, 1970.

Radwan, Kamal. *Die Sprache Lavaters im Spiegel der Geistesgeschichte.* Göppingen: Kümmerle, 1972.

Rasch, Wolfdietrich. "Der junge Goethe und die Aufklärung." In *Literatur und Geistesgeschichte: Festgabe für Heinz Otto Burger,* edited by R. Grimm and C. Wiedemann, 127–39. Berlin: Schmidt, 1968.

Reed, T. J. "Theatre, Enlightenment, and Nation: A German Problem." In Reed, *The Classical Centre: Goethe and Weimar, 1775-1832,* 47–68. London: Helm, 1980.

Richter, Werner. "*Urfaust* oder *Ururfaust.*" *Monatshefte* 42 (1950): 166–77.

Robertson, John G. "The Oldest Scenes in Goethe's *Faust.*" *MLN* 15 (1900): 270–79.

Roethe, Gustav. *Goethe.* Berlin: Ebering, 1932.

Rosanow, M. N. *Jakob M. R. Lenz: Der Dichter der Sturm- und Drangperiode. Sein Leben und seine Werke.* Translated by C. von Gütschow. Leipzig: Schulze, 1909.

Rousseau, Jean-Jacques. *The Confessions.* Translated by J. M. Cohen. Middlesex: Penguin, 1979.

Ryder, Frank G. "Toward a Revaluation of Goethe's *Götz*: The Protagonist." *PMLA* 77 (1962): 58–70.

Said, Edward W. *The World, the Text, and the Critic.* Cambridge: Harvard University Press, 1983.

Saine, Thomas P. "The Two Versions of Goethe's *Werther.*" *JEGP* 80 (1981): 54–77.

Sandel, Michael J. *Liberalism and the Limits of Justice.* Cambridge: Cambridge University Press, 1982.

Santoli, Vittorio. "Per la critica dell' *Urfaust.*" *Rivista di letterature moderne* 1–2 (1950–51): 31–36.

Sauder, Gerhard. "Empfindsamkeit und Frühromantik." In *Die literarische Frühromantik,* edited by Silvio Vietta, 85–111. Göttingen: Vandenhoeck & Ruprecht, 1983.

Scherpe, Klaus R. "Dichterische Erkenntnis und 'Projektemacherei': Widersprüche im Werk von J. M. R. Lenz." *Goethe Jahrbuch* 94 (1977): 206–35. Reprinted in *Poesie der Demokratie: Literarische Widersprüche zur deutschen Wirklichkeit vom 18. zum 20. Jahrhundert,* by Klaus R. Scherpe, 12–42. Cologne: Pahl-Rugenstein, 1980.

————. *Werther und Wertherwirkung. Zum Syndrom bürgerlicher Gesellschafts-ordnung im 18. Jahrhundert.* Bad Homburg: Gehlen, 1970.

Schieder, Theodor. "Grundfragen der neueren deutschen Geschichte." *Historische Zeitschrift* 192 (1961): 1–16.

Schiffer, Irvine. *Charisma: A Psychoanalytic Look at Mass Society.* Toronto: University of Toronto Press, 1973.

Schiller, Friedrich. *Die Räuber: Ein Schauspiel.* Edited by C. P. Magill and L. A. Willoughby. Oxford: Blackwell, 1974.

————. *Sämtliche Werke.* Edited by G. Fricke and H. G. Göpfert. 6 vols. Munich: Hanser, 1967.

Schluchter, Wolfgang. *The Rise of Western Rationalism. Max Weber's Developmental History.* Berkeley: University of California Press, 1981.

Schmidt, Erich. *Goethes Faust in ursprünglicher Gestalt.* Weimar: Böhlau, 1888.

————. *Lenz und Klinger: Zwei Dichter der Geniezeit.* Berlin: Wiedmann, 1878.

Schmidt, Henry J. *How Dramas End: Essays on the German Sturm und Drang, Büchner, Hauptmann, and Fleisser.* Ann Arbor: University of Michigan Press, 1992.

————. "The Language of Confinement: Gerstenberg's *Ugolino* and Klinger's *Sturm und Drang.*" *Lessing Yearbook* 11 (1979): 165–97.

Schmidt, Jochen. *Die Geschichte des Genie-Gedankens in der deutschen Literatur, Philosophie, und Politik: 1750–1945.* 2 vols. Darmstadt: Wissenschaftliche Buchgesellschaft, 1988.

Schneider, Hermann. *Urfaust? Eine Studie.* Tübingen: Laupp, 1949.

Schnorf, Hans. *Sturm und Drang in der Schweiz.* Zürich: Schultheß, 1914.

Schöffler, Herbert. "*Die Leiden des jungen Werther:* Ihr geistesgeschichtlicher Hintergrund." In *Deutscher Geist im 18. Jahrhundert. Essays zur Geistes- und Religionsgeschichte,* by Herbert Schöffler, 155–81. Göttingen: Vandenhoeck & Ruprecht, 1967.

Scholz, Rüdiger. "Eine längst fällige historisch-kritische Gesamtausgabe: Jakob Michael Reinhold Lenz." *Jahrbuch der deutschen Schillergesellschaft* 34 (1990): 195–229.

Schöne, Albrecht. *Säkularisation als sprachbildende Kraft: Studien zur Dichtung deutscher Pfarrersöhne.* Göttingen: Vandenhoeck & Ruprecht, 1958.

Schröder, Winfried. "Die Präromantiktheorie—eine Etappe in der Geschichte der Literaturwissenschaft?" *Weimarer Beiträge* 12, nos. 5–6 (1966): 723–64.

Schütze, Martin. *Academic Illusions in the Field of Letters and the Arts.* Chicago: University of Chicago Press, 1933.

Schwarz, Hans Günther. *Dasein und Realität: Theorie und Praxis des Realismus bei J. M. R. Lenz.* Bonn: Bouvier, 1985.

Shaftesbury, Anthony Ashley Cooper, Earl of. *Soliloquy: or, Advice to an Author* and *Characteristics of Men, Manners, Opinions, Times.* Edited by John M. Robertson. 2 vols. Reprint of 1710 edition. Gloucester: Smith, 1963.

Sheehan, James J. "What is German History? Reflections on the Role of the *Nation* in German History and Historiography." *The Journal of Modern History* 53 (1981): 1–23.

Shelley, Percy Bysshe. *Complete Poetical Works*. Edited by Thomas Hutchinson. London: Cambridge University Press, 1968.

Siegrist, Christoph. "Aufklärung und Sturm und Drang: Gegeneinander oder Nebeneinander?" In *Sturm und Drang: Ein literaturwissenschaftliches Studienbuch*, edited by Walter Hinck, 1–13. Kronberg: Athenäum, 1978.

Smith, Louise Z. "Sensibility and Epistolary Form in *Héloïse* and *Werther*." *Susquehanna Centennial Review* 17 (1977): 361-76.

Smith, Norman Kemp. *A Commentary to Kant's* Critique of Pure Reason. New York: Humanities Press, 1962.

Sokel, Walter H. *The Writer in Extremis: Expressionism in Twentieth-Century German Literature*. Stanford: Stanford University Press, 1959.

Stellmacher, Wolfgang. "Grundfragen der Shakespeare-Rezeption in der Frühphase des Sturm und Drang." *Weimarer Beiträge* 10 (1964): 323–45.

Stolpe, Heinz. *Die Auffassung des jungen Herder vom Mittelalter: Ein Beitrag zur Geschichte der Aufklärung*. Weimar: Arion, 1955.

Teraoka, Arlene Akiko. "Submerged Symmetry and Surface Chaos: The Structure of Goethe's *Götz von Berlichingen*." *Goethe Yearbook* 2 (1984): 13–41.

Thorlby, Anthony. "From What Did Goethe Save Himself in *Werther*?" In *Versuche zu Goethe: Festschrift für Erich Heller*, edited by Volker Dürr and Géza von Molnar, 150–166. Heidelberg: Stiehm, 1976.

Thorslev, Peter L. *The Byronic Hero: Types and Prototypes*. Minneapolis: University of Minnesota Press, 1962.

Timm, Eitel. *Ketzer und Dichter: Lessing, Goethe, Thomas Mann und die Postmoderne in der Tradition des Häresiegedankens*. Heidelberg: Winter, 1989.

Troeltsch, Ernst. *Gesammelte Schriften*. 4 vols. Vol. 4 edited by Hans Baron. Tübingen: Mohr, 1912–25.

Uhland, Robert. *Geschichte der hohen Karlsschule in Stuttgart*. Stuttgart: Kohlhammer, 1953.

Van den Heuvel, Christine. *Beamtenschaft und Territorialstaat: Behördenentwicklung und Sozialstruktur der Beamtenschaft im Hochstift Osnabrück, 1550–1800*. Osnabrück: Wenner, 1984.

Van Tieghem, Paul. *Le Préromantisme: Études d'histoire littéraire européenne*. 3 vols. Paris: Sfelt, 1947.

Vico, Giambattista. *The New Science*. Translated by Thomas Goddard Bergin and Max Harold Fisch. Ithaca: Cornell University Press, 1968.

Vietta, Silvio. "Frühromantik und Aufklärung." In *Die literarische Frühromantik*, edited by Silvio Vietta, 7–84. Göttingen: Vandenhoeck & Ruprecht, 1983.

Von der Hellen, Eduard. *Goethes Anteil an Lavaters Physiognomischen Fragmenten*. Frankfurt: Literarische Anstalt, 1888.

Wacker, Manfred. *Schillers Räuber und der Sturm und Drang: Stilkritische und typologische Überprüfung eines Epochenbegriffs*. Göppingen: Kümmerle, 1973.

———, ed. *Sturm und Drang*. Wege der Forschung, vol. 559. Darmstadt: Wissenschaftliche Buchgesellschaft, 1985.

Wagner, Heinrich Leopold. *Die Kindermörderin. Ein Trauerspiel.* In *Sturm und Drang. Dichtungen und Theoretische Texte,* edited by Heinz Nicolai. 2:1454–1520. Munich: Winkler, 1971.

Walzel, Oskar. "Leitmotive in Dichtungen." In *Das Wortkunstwerk,* by Oskar Walzel, 152–81. Leipzig: Quelle & Meyer, 1926.

———. *Das Prometheus-Symbol von Shaftesbury zu Goethe.* 2nd ed. Darmstadt: Wissenschaftliche Buchgesellschaft, 1932.

Warrick, E. Kathleen. "Lotte's Sexuality and Her Responsibility for Werther's Death." *Essays in Literature* 5 (1978): 129–35.

Weber, Heinz-Dieter. "Kindesmord als tragische Handlung." *Der Deutschunterricht.* 28, no .2 (1976): 75–97.

Weber, Max. *Wirtschaft und Gesellschaft: Grundriss der Verstehenden Soziologie.* Edited by Johannes Winckelmann. 2 vols. Tübingen: Mohr, 1956.

Weigelt, Horst. *Johann Kaspar Lavater: Leben, Werk und Wirkung.* Göttingen: Vandenhoeck & Ruprecht, 1991.

Weiskel, Thomas. *The Romantic Sublime. Studies in the Structure and Psychology of Transcendence.* Baltimore: Johns Hopkins University Press, 1976.

Werner, R. M. Review of *Über F. M. Klingers dramatische Dichtungen,* by Oscar Erdmann. *Zeitschrift für die österreichischen Gymnasien* 30, no. 4 (1879): 276–98.

Wiese, Benno von. *Friedrich Schiller.* Stuttgart: Metzler, 1959.

Wimsatt, W. K. *The Verbal Icon. Studies in the Meaning of Poetry.* Lexington: University Press of Kentucky, 1989.

Wolf, Herman. "Die Genielehre des jungen Herder." *Deutsche Vierteljahrsschrift für Literatur und Geisteswissenschaft* 3 (1925): 401–30.

Wolff, Hans M. "The Controversy over the Theater in Lenz's *Die Soldaten.*" *Germanic Review* 14, no. 3 (1939): 159–64.

———. *Goethes Weg zur Humanität.* Berne: Francke, 1951.

Wurst, Karin A., ed. *J. M. R. Lenz als Alternative? Positionsanalysen zum 200. Todestag.* Cologne: Böhlau, 1992.

Young, Edward. *Conjectures on Original Composition. In a Letter to the Author of Sir Charles Grandison.* Dublin: Wilson, 1759. Reprint. New York: Garland, 1970.

Zenke, Jürgen. "Das Drama des Sturm und Drang." In *Handbuch des deutschen Dramas,* edited by Walter Hinck, 120–32. Düsseldorf: Bagel, 1980.

Zimmermann, Johann Georg. *Betrachtungen über die Einsamkeit.* Zürich: Heidegger, 1756.

———. *Über die Einsamkeit.* 4 vols. Leipzig: Weidmann, 1784–85.

———. *Vom Nationalstolze.* Zürich: Heidegger, 1758.

Index

CPSIA information can be obtained
at www.ICGtesting.com
Printed in the USA
LVHW031033250323
742408LV00012B/338